HANDBOOK OF WORK AND ORGANIZATIONAL PSYCHOLOGY

Volume 2: Work Psychology

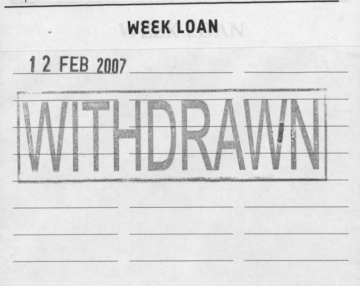

HANDBOOK OF WORK AND ORGANIZATIONAL PSYCHOLOGY

(Second Edition)

Volume 2: Work Psychology

Edited by

Pieter J.D. Drenth

Vrije Universiteit,
Amsterdam,
The Netherlands

Henk Thierry

Tilburg University,
The Netherlands

Charles J. de Wolff

Catholic University,
Nijmegen,
The Netherlands

Psychology Press

a member of the Taylor & Francis group

Psychology Press Ltd
27 Church Road
Hove
East Sussex, BN3 2FA, UK

British Library Cataloguing in Publication Data
A catalogue record for this title is available from the British Library

Volume 2
ISBN 0–86377–522–5 (Hbk)

Cover illustration by Clive Goodyer
Cover design by Rachael Adams
Typeset by Mendip Communications Ltd, Frome, Somerset
Printed and bound in the United Kingdom by Redwood Books Ltd, Trowbridge, Wilts, UK

Contents

Contributors to Volume 2

Jacques T. Allegro, Universiteit Leiden, Faculteit Sociale Wetenschappen, Wassenaarseweg 52, 2333 AK Leiden, The Netherlands.

Johannes Gerrit Boerlijst, Rupperink 4, 7491 GR Delden, The Netherlands.

Bram P. Buunk, Universiteit Groningen, Faculteit Psychologische, Pedagogische, Sociologische Wetenschappen, Grote Kruisstraat 2/1, 9712 TS Groningen, The Netherlands.

Pieter J.D. Drenth, Vrije Universiteit, Faculteit Psychologie en Pedagogiek, Van der Boechorststraat 1, 1081 BT Amsterdam, The Netherlands.

Arne Evers, Universiteit van Amsterdam, Faculteit Psychologie, Roetersstraat 15, 1018 WB Amsterdam, The Netherlands.

Henk van der Flier, Vrije Universiteit, Faculteit Psychologie en Pedagogiek, Van der Boechorststraat 1, 1081 BT Amsterdam, The Netherlands.

David Fryer, Department of Psychology, University of Stirling, Stirling FK94 4LA, UK.

Beate van der Heijden, Universiteit Twente, Faculteit Technologie en Management, Postbus 217, 7500 AE Enschede, The Netherlands.

Patrick T.W. Hudson, Universiteit Leiden, Faculteit Sociale Wetenschappen, Wassenaarseweg 52, Postbus 9555, 2300 RB Leiden, The Netherlands.

Ben Jansen, ATOS, Beleidsadries en-onderzoek BV, Gelderland plein 75d, 1082 LV Amsterdam, The Netherlands.

Jan de Jonge, Katholieke Universiteit Nijmegen, Faculteit Sociale Wetenschappen, Postbus 9104, 6500 HE Nijmegen, The Netherlands.

Theo F. Meijman, Universiteit Groningen, Faculteit Psychologische, Pedagogische, Sociologische Wetenschappen, Grote Kruisstraat 2/1, 9712 TS Groningen, The Netherlands.

Gijsbertus Mulder, Universiteit Groningen, Faculteit Psychologische, Pedagogische, Sociologische Wetenschappen, Grote Kruisstraat 2/1, 9712 TS Groningen, The Netherlands.

Joep M.A. Munnichs, Katholieke Universiteit Nijmegen, Montessorilaan 3, 6525 HR Nijmegen, The Netherlands.

Theo Poiesz, Katholieke Universiteit Brabant, Faculteit Sociale Wetenschappen, Warandalaan 2, 5037 AB Tilburg, The Netherlands.

Andries F. Sanders, Vrije Universiteit, Faculteit Psychologie en Pedagogiek, Van der Boechorststraat 1, 1081 BT Amsterdam, The Netherlands.

Henk Thierry, Katholieke Universiteit Brabant, Faculteit Sociale Wetenschappen, Postbus 90153, 5000 LE Tilburg, The Netherlands.

Theo J. Veerman, ASTRI, Sationsweg 26, 2312 AV Leiden, The Netherlands.

Willem A. Wagenaar, Universiteit Leiden, Faculteit Sociale Wetenschappen, Wassenaarseweg 52, 2333 AK Leiden, The Netherlands.

Charles J. de Wolff, Gomarius Messtraat 19, Alverna, 6603 CS Wychen, The Netherlands.

Jan F. Ybema, Vrije Universiteit, Faculteit Psychologie en Pedagogiek, Van der Boechorststraat 1, 1081 BT Amsterdam, The Netherlands.

Harry L.G. Zanders, Katholieke Universiteit Brabant, Faculteit Sociale Wetenschappen, Postbus 90153, 5000 LE Tilburg, The Netherlands.

1

Introduction

Pieter J.D. Drenth

As was indicated in the general introduction given in Volume 1 each of the following three volumes has its own accent. The emphasis of this first volume is on the micro-world of the worker and his or her task. It comprises the many chapters from the classical tradition of work psychology, including human factors psychology or, as it is sometimes called, ergonomics. The history of "work psychology" goes back about a hundred years. In fact, it was the main area of research of the first pioneers in applied industrial psychology, such as Münsterberg, Viteles, Weimar, Lahy and others. Numerous studies have been carried out since the early beginning, and each year hundreds of articles and books have contributed to a substantial body of knowledge and a well established tradition in this particular area.

This is not to say that no new issues have emerged and that no new studies are or can be undertaken. As an example the more recent interest in welfare, health and safety in work organizations can be mentioned. New and stricter laws and regulations on health and safety conditions at the workplace have stimulated work and organization psychologists in many countries to (re)study their causes and conditions, to provide training and to develop measurement devices in the field of occupational health and welfare. Subjects like safety, occupational stress, workload and sickness absence, therefore, are given a predominant place in this volume. Likewise, specific attention will be given to problems in work organizations and the labour market which have received a lot of attention of the work psychologists lately and which will continue to do so in the near future. One can think of issues related to work and aging, the problems of ethnic diversity and the consequences of the loss of work and unemployment.

Meijman and Mulder open this volume with a chapter on psychological aspects of workload. In their contribution they develop a conceptual outline of the psychological study of workload in which two traditions are combined; the study of mental load and the study of physical load. In the former the emphasis is on the effects of the nature and level of information load on task performance, and the latter focuses on the effects of energetical and biomechanical processes on task performance and health.

In the third chapter Sanders illustrates how ergonomics distinguishes itself from work and organizational psychology in general, in having different roots (psychonomics, work physiology and engineering as opposed to psychometrics, personality and social psychology) on the one hand, but that it is an indispensable chapter in work and organizational psychology on the other.

Too often human factors are disregarded in the design of machines, tools and work systems, which causes (sometimes serious) errors and accidents. Further integration of the ergonomic tradition in work psychology will certainly lead to an enrichment of this domain of psychology.

In a chapter on industrial safety Wagenaar shows that this is not simply determined by the use of safe equipment, and is not merely the corollary of low accident statistics. Whilst accidents usually occur on the shop floor, this is not the only level at which they must be prevented. Safety is the consequence of a good safety policy, and practicably effective measures to this end should be initiated at the management level. Information about the effectiveness of such measures is only gained on the shop floor, however, where indications of latent faults become discernible. Safety is therefore the responsibility of every employee in the organization.

During recent decades an increasing desire, or even need, for far-reaching changes in the arrangement of working hours has arisen. This concerns not so much shorter hours—the source of much social conflict in the past—but rather different timetabling and greater flexibility. The question concerns not so much the employee's health (the traditional argument), but rather his or her need for free time and a changing work ethos. Thierry and Jansen provide an overview of the various different working arrangements, such as flexible hours, intensive working weeks, part-time work and temporary contracts, as well as different types of shift work. Both actual arrangements and the results of research into their effects are considered.

Allegro and Veerman provide an approach to sickness absence and long-term inability to work from a social-scientific perspective. In this respect, avoidable absenteeism—in which there is no direct and unambiguous question of unfitness for work—is of especial interest.

Although abseenteeism itself is easy to measure, it is a complex phenomenon which encompasses many factors at different levels: the narrow (personal circumstances), the intermediate (workplace circumstances and social factors) and the broad (legislation and social protection). Authors offer an explanatory framework of thinking, which also has practical relevance in terms of a possible preventive, threshold-raising and curative policy.

Buunk, De Jonge, Ybema and De Wolff highlight a long-recognized problem: the negative effects of the work situation upon health. Only during the past few decades has the term "health" been expanded to encompass mental health, and the influence of the psychosocial aspects of the working environment begun to be considered. The principal idea in this respect is stress. Given how central work is in many people's lives, the circumstances of and events at their work have the potential to create strongly negative emotions. The perspective offered in this chapter is sociopsychological, emphasizing the social factors involved in the development and processing of negative emotions which may arise from stress at work.

In the next three chapters three specific groups of employees are described who have deserved greater attention from psychologists recently. The first of these is the older worker, which is given attention in a contribution by Boerlijst, Munnichs and Van der Heijden. Older employees are a vulnerable group where prejudice associates with falling productivity, inflexibility and health problems. Using the literature and their own research, the authors discuss whether these and other widely held opinions about older workers are justified, whether any other—positive—qualities counteract them, and in what ways the mobility and employment of older employees can be encouraged. In this respect, the importance of social support from leaders and colleagues is pointed out. The need for more longitudinal career research is also underlined.

In the next chapter Fryer provides an analysis of the psychological consequences of a phenomenon which has unfortunately become much more common in recent years: unemployment. The literature on this subject specifies a large number of physical and psychological complaints, including anxiety, depression, passivity, isolation, and a loss of self-esteem and hope, as well as various health problems. The author considers the extent to which empirical findings support these supposed consequences. His critical analysis shows that unemployment is indeed the cause of many of the psychological changes cited, although there are great differences between individuals as regards their experiences of and the consequences of unemployment.

Evers and Van der Flier discuss the position of a third specific group in work organizations: foreign workers, often including large numbers of refugees, immigrants and ethnic minorities. The position of this category on the labour market in most Western countries is quite unfavourable: high unemployment, low level of education and training, high turnover, and specific cultural and attitudinal traditions that hinder an easy and smooth integration in the local work culture. Authors give a comprehensive overview of the various problems related to the proper assessment of the capacities and skills of these "allochthonous" workers, and try to indicate ways to achieve an optimal balance between economic efficacy and a fair treatment of this vulnerable category of personnel.

The last two chapters in this volume deal with two domains that are somewhat distinct from, but at the same time conceptually closely linked to work psychology. The first deals with human economic behaviour. Poiesz convincingly shows that economic psychology is to be distinguished from economics. Both focus upon economic phenomena; however, the psychologist does so considering individual behaviour as their determi-nant, whereas the economist considers an "aggregated" level: economic phenomena and processes on a large scale. In this contribution, it is shown that—with their different perspectives—organizational and economic psychologists are clearly complementary.

In Chapter 12 Zanders pays attention to a movement that is strongly based on work psychological insights, namely the attempt to describe and to evaluate large and complex systems, such as modern companies, in terms of social and human indicators. Traditionally these descriptions and evaluations were made using economic models. During the 1960s and 1970s, however, a demand arose for more than simple economic information. This was the beginning of the development of social indicator systems. A variety of models and parameters, built upon insights from social work psychology, were developed. Zanders provides an overview of the nature and evaluative possibilities of such systems, and the way they have been applied in social policy making.

Together the 12 chapters in this volume try to present a comprehensive overview of the relevant issues and achievements in the domain of work psychology; a domain with a long and established tradition, but in which also novel and new-sprung issues are raised and are being studied.

2

Psychological Aspects of Workload

Theo F. Meijman and Gijsbertus Mulder

1 INTRODUCTION

Working activities are always productive in more than one respect. Concrete or imaginary objects are converted into a product as a result of working activities and in performing the activities people are altered. The outcome may be positive, i.e. the task has been completed successfully and people have developed their skills or have found satisfaction through working activities. However, the outcome of work may also fail to meet the standards specified in the work assignment or a person's state may take a turn for the worse in performing the task. Positive outcomes are not likely to be associated with the term "load", although meeting task demands is always taxing and requires effort, for demands are made on the abilities and on the willingness to dedicate these abilities to the task. Thus, exposure to task demands does not necessarily have to be conceived of as a predominantly negative process, although it usually is. The term workload tends to be associated with decrements in performance or willingness to perform, or with the risk of impair-

ment of the well-being and health of the task operator. We will adhere to this convention.

The study of mental load focuses traditionally on decrements in performance due to changes in the nature and level of the information load of a specific task (Gopher & Donchin, 1986). In the study of physical load the emphasis is much more on the energetical and biomechanical processes in task performance, and their effects on health and well-being (Rohmert, 1983). In this chapter we shall present an outline of a conceptual framework of the work psychological study of workload that includes both aspects. Thereto a scheme is being developed which will be called the "effort-recovery" model. It is rooted in the classical frame of thought of exercise physiology and elaborates its prevailing concepts on the basis of insights from work psychology and occupational medicine.

2 THE CLASSICAL MODEL

2.1 Load and capacity

The classical frame of thought for the study of workload stems from exercise physiology. In The

Netherlands it is referred to as the "load-capacity" model (Burger, 1959; Bonjer, 1965; Ettema, 1973). In this model, load refers to a threatening disruption of the balance of certain physiological systems due to task performance or environmental influences. According to Ettema (1967) this threat will induce physiological responses which can be viewed as compensation mechanisms. He gives the example of a raised energy output needed to shift a heavy object. To be able to meet this demand, a raised energy uptake and transport are needed to keep the energy in the body at the required level. One of the physiological responses that does just that is an accelerated heart rate, as it enables the organism through compensation to maintain the threatened energy balance.

The load-capacity model distinguishes several concepts that in a modified or unmodified form are of interest to the work psychological study of workload. It concerns the concepts' external load or objective task demands, functional load and effort, capacity, and maximum capacity. External load comprises all external factors that stem from the task contents, task organization and work conditions, and give rise to responses of the organism. The effort expended by the organism to maintain the balance disturbed by a concrete external factor can be inferred from the responses of the physiological systems that are affected by that factor and play a role in the compensation mechanisms. These responses are referred to as functional load. They provide information on the exercise or effort that is needed to perform the task. Their nature and intensity depend on the person's capacity, which can be expressed as the percentage of maximum capacity. The latter is understood to mean (Zielhuis, 1967; Ettema, 1973) the maximum external load which, with a given work form, an individual is able to cope with or can endure during a certain period of time, which is still followed by full recovery. As both entities, i.e. external load and maximum capacity, are expressed in the same units, the percentage of maximum capacity can be represented by a ratio. As long as the percentage is more than zero the person is expending effort, which will show in changes in the relevant functional load parameters. With a percentage below one, the person remains within the limits of his own competence

and no negative effects need to occur. For then the external load does not exceed the maximum capacity. However, if the percentage exceeds the value one, a situation of overload will arise with the risk of negative effects. A similar situation may arise, if a certain exercise or level of effort has to be maintained for longer than an acceptable period of time. Thus, negative effects depend on the relationship between the external load and maximum capacity, and on the time during which the effort is exerted. Less well-trained people are, also depending on their age, unable or unwilling to cycle at 70% of their maximum capacity on a bicycle ergometer for much more than 15 minutes (Astrand & Rodahl, 1986). Van der Sluis and Dirken (1970) calculated that, in the energetical model, a percentage of maximum capacity of about 33% during an 8.5 hour working day is acceptable to industrial workers.

In the sixties Kalsbeek (1967) and Ettema (1967) applied this conceptual framework, which was originally constructed for energetical load, to the study of mental load. The latter focuses primarily on the demands made on the human information processing system. External load should be expressed in units relevant to this specific form of load, such as the number of signals per time unit that has to be reacted to, or the number of decisions needed to arrive at the proper solution for a certain task in relation to the available time. Functional load could be inferred from the changes in the functional systems that in one way or another are related to the mental processes of interest. On the basis of such indicators statements could be made about the mental effort needed to perform a particular information processing task. In their study Kalsbeek and Ettema used a classical indicator, i.e. the variability of the heart rhythm. Since the end of the last century this entity has played a role in the psychophysiological study of mental processes (Meijman et al., 1989). In the eighties Mulder (G. Mulder, 1980) and Mulder (L. Mulder, 1988) refined this measure and developed it into a standard indicator in the study of mental effort.

2.2   Elaborations of the classical model

The classical "load-capacity" conceptual framework has been criticized and supplemented at various points from the perspective of occupational medicine as well as work psychology. Meijman and O'Hanlon (1983), Kuiper (1985), Kompier (1988) and Van Dijk et al. (1990) commented on the classical conceptual framework and proposed changes for various parts. The objections mainly pertain to the static character of the model and its too little relevance to the practice of occupational medicine. We will discuss a number of these objections, because they are relevant to the work psychological conceptual framework for the study of workload that will be developed below.

2.2.1 The controversial concept of maximum capacity

The strength of the classical model is its quantitative character. However, in practice this is also its weakness. This can best be illustrated by a discussion of the concept of maximum capacity. Maximum capacity is a normative concept which in the classical model is operationalized in a specific way, i.e. the maximum external load which is still followed by complete recovery. Thus strictly defined, maximum capacity can be calculated on the conditions that the external load can be determined quantitatively and the quantified relationship is known between the functional load indicator studied and the load process of interest. In addition, the situations of maximum effort and complete recovery must be identifiable. This ideal is approximated in the energetical model, because it allows the load process to be measured directly by means of changes in the oxygen uptake. In practice the load process can be measured indirectly by means of changes in the heart rate, provided that its relationship is known with the individual's oxygen uptake in a standardized test for the determination of the maximum capacity, e.g. a test on the bicycle ergometer. If the latter proves impossible, more or less insurmountable difficulties will arise as a consequence of which we have to make use of all kinds of indirect parameters. For all other forms of load, including biomechanical load and information load, it has as yet not been possible to determine, even by approximation, the maximum capacity of an individual in consistency with the definition from the classical load-capacity model. In practice the

concept of maximum capacity has therefore mainly a heuristic value.

2.2.2 A static model

In the classical model the individual is regarded as a physiologically actively responding organism. In all other respects the individual appears to be a rather passive receiver and an easy target of external factors, irrespective of his work style, motives and attitudes. Thus, the classical model falls short of an illusion, viz. that the maximum capacity in a strict sense is in fact determinable. The classical model did recognize this. Kalsbeek & Ettema (1964) remarked that apart from the level of external load, the functional load is determined by numerous other factors with the willingness to actually expend the required effort being of major importance. According to Ettema (1967), it is not the maximum capacity but the willingness to spend capacity or the "Leistungsbereitschaft" (Graf, 1954; Lehmann, 1962) which is commonly determined. The energetical model allows for a reasonably adequate determination of whether someone has done his utmost by means of the measured oxygen uptake in relation to the observed heart rate. But then again, this is more or less the only model that allows such determination.

2.2.3 Work potential, work procedure and decision latitude

In an attempt to meet the above-mentioned problems, Meijman and O'Hanlon (1983) introduced the concept of work potential, therewith recognizing the fact that outside the energetical model the concept of maximum capacity has very little formal meaning. Its use had, therefore, better be restricted to this model. In addition, a concept like work potential does do better justice to the dynamic facets of the interaction between the working human and the demands work makes on him. The question is not so much whether someone is able to cope with certain demands, but rather whether someone is able to expend the effort at any given moment to meet these demands and with what intensity someone is willing to do so. Work potential seems here the more appropriate term.

In the interaction between person and demands

the adopted work procedure is important as it determines what abilities are deployed and the way in which this is done (Sperandio, 1972; Hacker, 1973; Bainbridge, 1974). It in turn determines the character of the load and its ensuing effects. That is to say, the adopted work procedure is a necessary link between the demands that are made and the abilities the working person has to mobilize at any moment to meet the demands. In the classical load-capacity model this was hardly taken into account. By now, partly because of work psychological considerations (Hacker, 1978), the load-capacity model has been adapted as to this aspect in the work physiology literature (Rohmert, 1983, 1984).

Endorsement of the importance of the work procedure raises the question as to what extent the task assignment and the work situation allow the operator to regulate the job demands and to adjust the work procedure when he/she considers this necessary. As said above, the classical model hardly takes such varieties into account, although in practice they are the rule rather than the exception. Hence, the study of workload in real task situations requires information on this matter (Van Dijk et al., 1990). In particular the study of work stress has pointed to the importance of decision latitude in work situations. Its effective use is not only important to the quality and level of the performance to be made (Fisher, 1986; Frese, 1987), it is also an essential link in the etiology of health and well-being problems ensuing from workload (Karasek & Theorell, 1990; Johnson & Johansson, 1991).

2.2.4   *The relevance to health*
In its original form the classical conceptual framework failed to work out the role of workload in the etiology of health and well-being problems. Kompier (1988) and Meijman (1988), among others, elaborated it into a cumulative process model of workload-related health outcomes. The core idea of this model is that the momentaneous compensation responses (functional load phenomena) can develop into negative load effects under the influence of continued exposure to work demands and insufficient recovery. Such load effects show initially as detriments to well-being and perceived health and in the long run even as manifest losses of function, health impairment or illness.

3   THE EFFORT-RECOVERY MODEL

The conceptual framework presented in this section gives an elaboration of the load-capacity model in which the above-mentioned comments are incorporated.

The work psychological study of workload is based on the premise that people will always try to interfere actively in their work situation and environment when confronted with certain demands. To avoid passive exposure, they always adopt a certain work procedure. What procedure will be adopted, depends on: (1) the character and the level of the demands, (2) the decision latitude the situation allows, (3) the level of knowledge and skills, and the willingness to meet the demands and to exercise control, and (4) the current psychophysiological state of the task operator. At a mental level the work procedure is controlled by a plan of action or strategy. Such a strategy may differ for the same work assignment, not only between persons but also within a person from situation to situation (Matern, 1984; Hacker, 1986). Figure 2.1 presents a scheme which summarizes these various aspects and which may serve as a conceptual framework for the work psychological study of workload. The scheme is an elaboration of a framework that was presented earlier (Meijman, 1988, 1989).

The scheme distinguishes three determinants: (1) the actual level of the task demands and the environmental factors, summarized in the scheme under the term "work demands", (2) the actual mobilization of work abilities and effort, summarized in the scheme under the term "work potential", and (3) decision latitude. Together these three factors determine the work procedure, which in turn results in two kinds of outcome: the product and the short-term physiological and psychological reactions. The product is the tangible result of work activities. It is always evaluated in some way or another by standards and regulations that are implicitly or explicitly included in the original work assignment. As has been argued in the discussion of the classical load-capacity model (see section 2.1), the short-term physiological and psychological reactions can be seen as adaptive

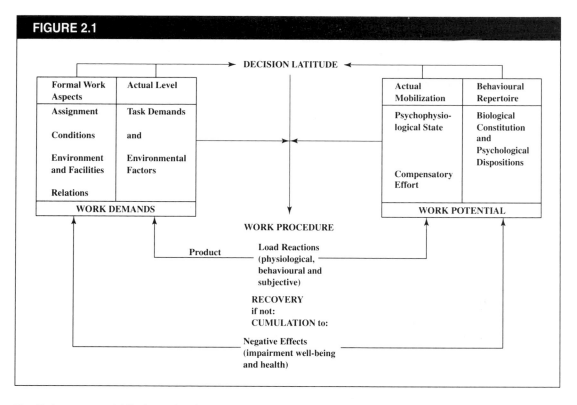

The effort-recovery model (further explanation see text).

responses. In the practice of the study of workload, the short-term reactions include all the responses at a physiological, behavioural and subjective level that can be related to the load process. These reactions are in principle reversible. When the exposure to load ceases, the respective psycho-biological systems will stabilize again at a specific baseline level within a certain period of time. This process is called recovery. In the practice of load research, the baseline level is assessed by means of measurements in a situation in which no special demands are made on the operator. It is then assumed that the operator has recovered completely from possible previous loads and that no demands are currently made on the systems under study.

Destabilization during the load process of the psycho-biological systems concerned involves changes in the psychophysiological state of the operator. These changes induce feedback to the actual mobilization of abilities and thereby to the effort to be made. Under the influence of behavioural changes in reaction to load, also fluctuations

in the character and the actual level of task demands and environmental factors may occur. Hence, the scheme in Figure 2.1 shows feedback to occur from the short-term reactions to the actual level of the task load. Section 4.2.2 will give some relevant examples.

A still functional adaptation response to a single and moderate load can develop through continued exposure and insufficient recovery into negative load effects, which may persist for a longer period of time or may even become irreversible. An (extremely) high momentaneous load can have similar effects. So the (negative) load effects are related to less transitory or even permanent symptoms that manifest themselves as a consequence of continued exposure to one or more load factors as more structural, negative changes of physiological or psychological functions. They bring about changes in the biological constitution and in the psychological dispositions. Thus, feedback takes place to work potential. In Figure 2.1 feedback is also shown to occur from the load effects to the work demands block. At first sight, this seems an unlikely relationship. However, load effects developed as a result of previous workloads, may in turn be conditional to the acceptability or "bearableness" of certain work aspects. This is very clearly illustrated in the situation in which an impairment has developed, which leads to functional limitations, which in turn results in a handicap in certain work situations. Thus, a back injury due to heavy physical work may render a person unsuitable for work on a forklift truck because of its mechanic vibrations affecting the back (Bongers & Boshuizen, 1990; Verbeek, 1991). Other examples are chronic stress complaints or depressive complaints due to mentally demanding work (Schellart et al., 1989, 1990), which make people less suitable to work under a high production pressure or without socio-emotional contacts and support.

In the next section we will discuss the various determinants and effects separately while also paying attention to the various forms of feedback presented in Figure 2.1.

4   WORK DEMANDS

4.1. Formal aspects of the work situation

The following formal aspects of the work situation are distinguished: work assignment, work conditions, work environment and facilities, and work relations.

The work assignment specifies the result of the work activities as well as the standards the result should meet. However, the specifications are often vague and the standards will often become clear only after the task has been completed. This vagueness may in itself function as a stress factor of the work situation. The work conditions concern the agreements regarding the assignment. The most important are the remuneration and the various time aspects, like production times, length of a working day, break schedules and the (ir) regularity in work-rest schedules. Remunerative aspects play a key role in regulating the work activities and the appreciation of their results (Thierry & de Jong, 1991; see also Volume 3, Chapter 8 and Volume 4, Chapter 12 of this Handbook) and therewith in the willingness to

spend capacity on the work task and to exert the required effort. The study of the temporal aspects of a work task provides the foundation for workload research. For this study can be used to determine the duration and intensity of the exposure to various load factors, as well as the periods of time between different kinds of exposures and the opportunities for recovery. The work environment and facilities concern the available aids and tools as well as aspects of the design of the workplace, the physical and chemical factors in the work situation, hygiene, canteens, etc. Work relations involve social and organizational aspects, such as hierarchical relationships, contacts with colleagues, etc.

4.2   Task demands and environmental factors

Task demands are the manifestations of the above-mentioned aspects in a concrete situation. They can be formulated as formal work aspects: "such and such has to be done", "within such and such a time", etc. At the same time task demands have to be considered from the perspective of the demand they make on the work abilities and their mobilization. Each study of workload sets out to determine the task demands for which various methods of task analysis are available (Karg & Staehle, 1982; Drury et al., 1987; Landau & Rohmert, 1989; Algera, 1991; Van Ouwerkerk et al., 1994).

Task demands are always met in a specific environment. Partly the environmental factors are stucturally determined by the formal aspects of the work situation, e.g. the physical-chemical factors inherent to the production process concerned. For another part they are coincidental, like the temperature of today, the burst of noise outside, someone having a bee in his bonnet, etc. Load research should also establish the character and level of these environmental factors. Ergonomics and industrial hygiene have thereto developed methods appropriate for workplace analysis (Klinkhamer, 1979; Schuffel, 1989; Van der Heide & Kragt, 1989; Voskamp, 1994).

4.2.1   Some complications

Classical theories in work psychology assumed that there is a one to one relationship between work demands and abilities or mental functions needed to meet these demands. As early as 1928 Baumgarten discussed the naivety of this theory. She argued that because of compensation mechanisms people may meet the same demands in completely different ways with similar results, without resorting to the same skills and mental processes. The relationship between the demands and abilities depends on the work procedure followed. This has at least two important consequences for the practice of the psychological study of workload. First, a task taxonomy based on basic abilities (Fleishman & Quaintance, 1984) is of limited value when it has not been established whether the abilities in question are indeed involved in the task performance, as different abilities may be involved in different working procedures with the same results. Second, the complication in the relationship between demands and abilities poses a methodological problem (Bainbridge, 1974). It concerns the distinction between external load and functional load. This distinction may be important from an analytical point of view, but in practice it may be hard to maintain. Thus, it is quite common to define mental load in terms of a specific information processing mode: the attention-demanding or controlled mode (see also section 5.2). The mental task load could then be determined on the basis of the time during which, in the task performance, demands are made on this particular processing mode (Mulder, 1980). As a consequence it is impossible to determine load independent of the way the task is performed and the mental processes involved in the performance. This poses a special problem which can probably best be illustrated by an example taken from Gopher & Donchin (1986). Under normal conditions, most of us are able to walk a 1-foot-wide plank that is placed just above the floor. However, if the plank is suspended between two houses at 50 feet, the same task will require much more effort and may even be impossible. The load decreases if we do not have to walk the plank between the houses upright but try to reach the other side of the street on all fours. For someone who has had too much to drink, the task will be impossible to perform even if the plank is laid on the floor. In short, the context in which a specific demand is made, makes a lot of difference to the question of load in work psychology. So, load is a relative notion, in which the external load and the capacity to meet the ensuing demands can hardly be defined independent of one another.

4.2.2 Fluctuation of work demands

One of the practical consequences of the above-mentioned is that the task demands and environmental factors cannot be regarded as static factors in the study of workload. Fluctuations in the demands may be coincidental. A catch in the production process may occur occasionally, or today it is warmer than yesterday. Such influences are usually regarded as "error-variance". There is no objection to that if it indeed concerns coincidental fluctuations. However, it becomes objectionable if fluctuations in the task demands and the environmental factors are related to changes in the state of the operator that result from the work activities themselves. This will be illustrated by some examples. The design of office furniture may meet anthropometrical standards. However, fatigue developed in the course of the task performance makes people change their posture behind the word processor, thus disturbing the optimal ergonomical proportions. As a consequence all kinds of load effects can develop which may manifest themselves among other things as backpain and headache. Another example is taken from industrial toxicology. The uptake of dust particles through the bronchial tubes depends, among other things, on the frequency and depth of breathing. Changes in breathing, e.g. due to physical exertion, also result in changes in the uptake of dust particles even if repeated environmental monitoring measures the same concentrations in the work room. Industrial toxicology distinguishes, therefore, between environmental exposure and intake versus internal exposure and uptake, or the concentration of a substance as measured in a room versus the levels of uptake and circulation in the body (Zielhuis & Henderson, 1986). Behavioral factors, connected among other things with differences in working procedures between people, play a vital role in the relationship between environmental exposure and intake (Van Dijk et al., 1988). Ulenbelt (1991) showed that the uptake of lead dust with the same environmental concentrations in the work room may differ considerably between people depending on person-related and task-related differences in working procedures and related hygienic work behaviour.

5   WORK POTENTIAL

5.1   Introduction

The demands people are confronted with at work may stem from very different sources. They have in common that they always activate the adaptive systems of the organism. Relevant to the present discussion are those adaptive systems that play a role in the mental functioning or the information processing in a broad sense. This does not merely include perception and cognition, but also the emotional, motivational and psychomotor aspects of information processing. Two kinds of adaptive systems are important, i.e. the computational and the energetical processes in information processing (Mulder, 1979, 1986; Sanders, 1981 and 1983; Hockey, 1993; Revelle, 1993). Computational processes pertain to the storage of information and the operations executed on it. They include processes that receive input information, transform it and process it further. Energetical processes play a role in making and keeping computational processes available, given the individual's current mental and physical state. They pertain to the intensity of information processing and to its emotional and motivational control. That is to say, knowledge of computational processes is needed to answer the question whether someone is able to cope with a certain task, or has the competence to do so. Capacity and attention are central notions in the concept of competence. To answer the question about the willingness to perform requires knowledge of energetical processes. Central to willingness are notions like effort and the costs at which an effort is made.

5.2   Computational processes

The information that reaches us through the senses is subjected to a series of operations before it results in a specific, overt or covert reaction. Theories on the architecture of the system in which these processes take place, distinguish three kinds of memories, i.e. the sensoric memory, the long-term memory and the working memory (see for overviews Kyllonen & Alluisi, 1987; Cowan, 1988). Information enters the sensoric memory. This is a very short-term memory, that retains the information in a more or less sensory form for a few seconds. This raw information is then identified, coded and processed further in the working memory of which the main feature is its limited capacity. In discussions on the working memory, the notion of attention plays a key role (see section 5.2.2). In the long-term memory knowledge is stored in a sort of dormant form.

Research into the electric and magnetic activities of the brain and the cerebral blood flow during information processing tasks showed it to be possible to identify the brain mechanisms that are mobilized during the performance of computational processes (Mulder et al., 1989; Wijers, 1989; Kosslyn & Koenig, 1992; Posner & Raichle, 1994). A considerable number of these computational processes are not accessible to consciousness. They are fast and automatic. They cannot be made measurable by subjective methods, and only partly so by behavioural methods through reaction time research. In contrast, computational processes that appeal to the working memory are slower and partly accessible through self-reports.

5.2.1   Long-term memory

The long-term memory comprises two forms of knowledge: declarative and procedural knowledge (Anderson, 1993). Declarative knowledge comprises the "what" of our knowledge. In a network with knowledge elements as nodes, this knowledge is stored in an organized way (Tulving, 1991). The declarative memory has a hierarchical structure and its central representation form is directed at concepts and schemes (Rumelhart & Ortony, 1977). They reflect the contents of the statement or the general meaning of an occurrence rather than the surface structure of the original message. On the basis of concepts and schemes it is possible to draw inferences that were not part of the original message or occurrence.

Procedural knowledge comprises the "how" of our knowledge. We know how to ride a bicycle, how to comb our hair, etc. Most of the time this knowledge is hard to explain to others. Habituation and other forms of conditioning are examples of procedural learning. Procedural knowledge can best be represented in terms of "if-then" or "condition-action" rules. The entire set of such rules for a certain task is referred to as a production-system. The if-part of the production does not need to be task-specific but may comprise a general aspect. In such a case a general rule or action programme has been developed that can be applied in different situations. There are indications that the declarative memory and the procedural memory make use of different brain mechanisms (Squire, 1987) and that the declarative memory develops later in the ontogeny than the procedural memory.

5.2.2 Working memory

All information that is subjected to momentary cognitive processes is part of the working memory. Working memory is the locus of attention-demanding operations, like (1) selecting information that needs attention, (2) scanning the current contents of the working memory itself, (3) retaining relevant information in working memory for a short period of time, and (4) searching for information in the declarative memory.

The central notion with regard to working memory is attention. Its meaning is best illustrated by two metaphors: the metaphor of the search light (Cowan, 1988, 1993) and the metaphor of the resource (Navon & Gopher, 1979; Wickens, 1991 and 1994). The former describes attention as some sort of light beam with the thing we are currently conscious of at its focus. Everything within the light beam is processed, whether we want it or not, and everything outside the light beam is not processed. The search light metaphor emphasizes the indivisibility of attention, while the resource metaphor emphasizes its divisibility. Performing mental tasks involves various mental operations, such as perceiving, repeating the information perceived and interpreted thus to avoid loss from working memory, selecting and programming movements, etc. Performing all these activities requires certain resources. Because the capacity of these resources is limited, the resource metaphor explains the failure to perform simultaneously two or more tasks that appeal to the same resources.

However, if there is sufficient reserve capacity, two or more tasks can be combined successfully. According to some theoretical models, each processing stage can fall back on a general, limited-capacity resource (Moray, 1967; Kahneman, 1973). Only then the term reserve capacity is aptly used (Kantowitz, 1987). Other models assume that each stage or cluster of stages has command over its own resource which is basically not interchangeable with the resource of a different stage or cluster of stages (Navon & Gopher, 1980; Gopher, 1986). Finally, there are also hierarchical models (Sanders, 1981, 1983; Mulder, 1986) which assume that in addition to stage-specific resources there is also a general, non-stage-specific resource.

At all of these points the theory is still being developed; therefore its main value is at present of a heuristic nature. It is, however, generally accepted that information in the working memory may assume two codes, i.e. acoustic or spatial (Wickens, 1987). These codes seem to involve two subsystems that hardly interfere with one another. New spatial information interferes with present spatial information and the same applies to acoustic information. Furthermore, if nothing is done with it, information in the working memory declines rapidly.

5.2.3 Processing modalities

The distinction between automatized and controlled cognitive processes, which dates as far back as 1890 (James, 1890), has had a considerable influence on the development of the theory on mental load. The seventies showed a revival of this distinction (Shiffrin & Schneider, 1977). Controlled processes comprise a sequence of nodes in the long-term memory which is temporarily activated in working memory. This occurs under the influence of a central executive system which directs the attention and has a limited capacity. In principle only one such sequence can be activated at a time. In sum, controlled cognitive processes require attention, they are relatively slow, flexible, (consciously) controlled by the person, and serial.

An automatized process can be seen as a more or less permanent sequence of closely integrated associative links in the long-term memory that becomes active only in response to a specific input configuration. Practice under consistent conditions leads to automatization and renders the task increasingly independent of the limited-capacity systems of working memory. Dominant features of the automatized processes are: (1) the high speed and the limited variability of the activity, (2) the stimulus-specific character of the activity, (3) the uncontrollability of the process, once the process has been started, it is hard to slow it down or stop it, and (4) the decreased cognitive effort.

5.2.4   Cognitive processing levels

Work tasks differ as to the level in which they appeal to the attention-demanding operations in working memory and make use of knowledge from the declarative memory and the procedural memory. That is to say, they differ in the degree of mental effort that has to be spent in the task performance. In this respect work tasks can be classified into three broad categories of processing levels: skill-based, rule-based, and knowledge-based (Hacker, 1973; Rasmussen, 1987).

The processing level is called rule-based when the task performance is chiefly based on the application of general rules or relatively uniform action programmes in otherwise varying situations. It mainly employs knowledge from the procedural memory. Tasks performed at this level require some, but not excessive, mental effort. If a concrete stimulus situation usually yields the same response, the process can be automatized. Such automatization is the result of a mostly long-term learning process under consistent conditions. The task performance is then called "skill-based". In such cases, the various parts of the task performance require little to no mental effort. In contrast, tasks performed at a "knowledge-based" level appeal strongly to the knowledge in the declarative memory and to the attention-demanding (controlled) processes in working memory. Such tasks cannot be performed without expending mental effort.

The level of processing is determined by the variability of the work task in the situation concerned. This is characterized by three features (Matern, 1984; de Vries-Griever, 1989): (1) the stability of the working situation, (2) the number of task elements, and (3) the complexity of the

relationships between the various task elements. The first feature pertains to the variability of the work assignment and the performance conditions. The second feature concerns the number of subtasks or elements of the task assignment concerned. The third characteristic involves the relationships between the various task elements. Important questions in this respect are: Is the order of the relationships always fixed, thereby guiding the course of action in the work situation, or, do their mutual relationships differ from situation to situation according to relatively complicated, and possibly unpredictable patterns? Tasks that have little stable assignments and comprise many different task elements with complex mutual relationships will require a "knowledge-based" level of processing. In such cases procedural knowledge will be hard to acquire and the operator will have to make a sustained appeal to the declarative knowledge and attention-demanding operations in working memory. The same applies to new situations or to tasks that are difficult to learn. In general, a "rule-based" level of processing is possible when a task consists of a limited number of elements with little complicated and relatively stable, mutual relationships. Stable situations in which the task elements have a fixed relationship and are more or less automatized or can be performed "absent-mindedly" generally allow for a "skill-based" level of processing.

5.2.5   Changing processing levels

The same work task is not always performed at the same processing level. This depends on: (1) the available time, (2) the level of the task demands, (3) the changes in the situational context, and (4) the psychophysiological state of the operator.

It should be noted that people often get satisfaction from performing tasks at a "knowledge-based" level. This is most evident in people who in order to relax solve complicated puzzles, chess problems, and so on. So, exerting mental effort in itself does not necessarily have to lead to negative effects. The risk becomes manifest only if the task demands exceed or threaten to exceed the capacity of the required computational processes. For then there is a conflict between the task load and the processing capacity. Whether this will occur in real task situations depends very much on the relationship between the time needed for a proper task performance on a "knowledge-based" level and the available time. This relationship is affected by the task demands, as higher demands tend to require more processing time. It is also likely to be affected by changes in the performance conditions, e.g. noise during tasks that require a relatively high level of concentration. The relationship may also change when in addition to the main task, secondary tasks require the operator's attention. And finally, the relationship may be affected by changes in the state of the operator him/herself, as a consequence of which the actual level of performance capacity and/or willingness to perform may be lowered.

In general, it can be said that changes in the work procedure will occur when the task load and the processing capacity are or threaten to be in conflict. These changes come down to the operator trying to switch to a different level of cognitive processing: from "knowledge-based" to "rule-based" or to "skill-based" (Hacker, 1973). Thus the operator will try to keep the mental effort needed to perform the task within limits and still reach an acceptable performance (Welford, 1978). The possibility of making such a switch and its effectivity depend on control over the stringency of the task demands and the standards regarding the quality and the quantity of the product, in particular the temporal aspects. That is to say, having and exercising control is of overriding importance in the protection against mental (over) load, which the operator can get at his disposal by changing to another work procedure.

Various studies may illustrate the above-mentioned aspects. The first example pertains to a switch in processing levels during the performance of the same task in relation to fluctuations in the task load. Coeterier (1971) and Sperandio (1972) investigated the work procedures of air traffic controllers subjected to fluctuations in the number of airplanes to guide down. With a relatively low number of planes, they made them approach in complicated patterns thus to get each plane down in the most efficient way. While doing so the air traffic controllers deployed flexible, "knowledge-based" strategies. This requires a relatively high level of mental effort and is possible only with not too high a workload so that each plane can be given individual attention. When asked in Coeterier's study, the air traffic controllers remarked that this was the most satisfying work procedure. With an increasing number of planes the work procedures changed. The air traffic controller switched to a procedure that treated all planes in a uniform pattern: "park in pancakes, have them fly in circles and get them in one after another". In this way the treatment of individual planes requires less attention because it meets an uniform rule. The work procedure has obtained a "rule-based" character. It protects the air traffic controller against overload, but it is little flexible towards individual planes and is perceived as less satisfying. Quite interestingly, Sperandio found also that less experienced air traffic controllers switch to "rule-based" strategies with a lower number of planes than their more experienced colleagues.

The study of fatigue provides other examples of such shifts in relation to changes in the state of the operator. In the course of a working day, with an objectively constant task load, crane drivers (Wendrich, 1973) are changing from a quite complicated, but flexible work procedure to a less complex and uniform procedure which makes a lesser appeal to attention-demanding information processing. Rasmussen & Jensen (1974) observed that fatigue made maintenance personnel change their search strategies for failures from complex and attention-demanding decision processes that could lead more quickly to a solution to work procedures that involve a sequence of successive and often mutually redundant, simple yes–no decisions. Holding (1983) described a similar phenomenon in a series of laboratory studies. The test tasks in these studies consisted of locating and repairing failures in an electrical circuit. To this end the subjects could apply alternative work procedures that differed in effort and expectable success. The more effortful work procedure resulted in a faster success. In separate sessions the subjects were made familiar with these alternative work procedures. The study showed that the subjects, under physical as well as mental fatigue conditions, both brought about by special pretreatments, preferred the work procedure that required less effort to the one that required more effort.

Carver and Scheier (1990) is important. According to this theory, during the performance continual comparisons are being made between the desired speed for obtaining a goal consistent with an intrapersonal standard and the actual speed with which the goal is obtained. If the actual speed is higher than the desired speed, positive affects would arise, while a lower actual speed would give rise to negative affects. The latter will occur if the time needed to perform a task or a task element would (threaten to) exceed the available time. They will also occur when the operator has to perform a task or a task element which exceeds the current capacity of the computational system and the time and/or possibilities to find solutions are lacking. In this respect, the occurrence of disturbances or interruptions in the work process is of great importance (Leitner et al., 1987), because with specified standards and times they can seriously slow down or even prevent the goal from being obtained.

5.4.2   Mental efficiency

With a given work assignment and under the present work conditions, self-regulation usually aims to maintain the required level of performance against an acceptable effort expenditure (Welford, 1953, 1978; Bainbridge, 1978). This efficiency point of view is of great relevance to the study of workload. As far as can be gathered, Dodge (1913) seems to have introduced this point of view in the study of task performance. Thorndike (1914) applies it in his discussion of the classical German study on mental fatigue. He pointed out that people are able to maintain the same level of performance by investing additional effort, even under extreme conditions like sleep deprivation or after hours of gruelling work. In contrast, they may fail to perform under conditions in which such failure is not expected. According to Thorndike, the question in the study of mental load and fatigue does not so much pertain to people's abilities to deliver a certain effort, but rather to their willingness to do so, and at what costs. In his opinion, the latter could best be measured by means of physiological arousal- and activation-measures. Although it seems an obvious thing to do, the efficiency point of view has been little applied in the study of mental load. Relevant

empirical studies were described by Tent (1962), Heemstra (1988) and Paas and Van Merrienboer (1993). The principle will be illustrated by some results from our own study (Meijman et al., 1989).

Eighteen city bus drivers perform a visual memory search task under different conditions of prior workload. The efficiency of information processing in the task is defined as the relation between the performance and the effort expenditure it requires. Figure 2.4 presents the results. The test is always performed at 12.30 hours. At that time, the drivers in the morning shift have worked for eight hours, in the day shift for four hours, and in the late shift they are about to start working. As a fourth condition, the drivers are studied during their day off.

The test involves recognizing a character, one of a set of four characters that has been memorized in advance, which is displayed on a screen surrounded by three characters that were not included in the memory set. The entire task consisted of 40 trials, 20 of which contained a character from the memory set and 20 that did not. Performance is measured by response latency in recognizing the character from the memory set. Effort is measured by the heart rate variability, the so-called 0.10 Hz component (G. Mulder, 1980; L. Mulder, 1988). This physiological measure is one of the standard indicators in the study of mental load (see also section 2.1). It is based on the phenomenon that the variability of the heart rate interbeat interval times is relatively low when a person is involved in an attention-demanding information processing mode and in that sense is expending mental effort.

It appears that on their day off performance is delivered (reaction time 620 milliseconds and 8% wrong responses) against a certain amount of effort (standardized 0.10 Hz: 35). Just before the start of the late shift, the drivers deliver more or less the same performance as on their day off (reaction time 585 milliseconds and 9% wrong responses) against an equal amount of effort compared with the day off (standardized 0.10 Hz: 30). So, under both conditions the mental task is performed equally efficient. After four hours working in the day shift, the efficiency of the information processing drops considerably. For, although the drivers invest the same effort

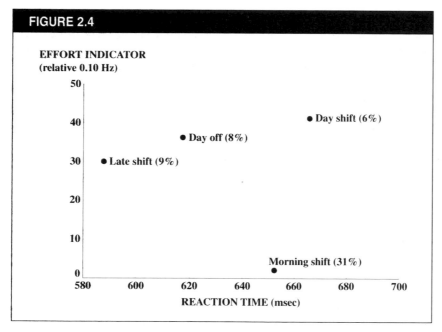

FIGURE 2.4

EFFORT INDICATOR
(relative 0.10 Hz)

Efficiency (reaction time by effort) in a visual memory search task; 18 bus drivers; differentiated to conditions of workload (for further explanation see text).

(standardized 0.10 Hz: 41) as on their day off or before the late shift, their performance is (statistically significantly) worse, i.e. 665 milliseconds with 6% wrong responses. Quite remarkably, after eight hours morning shift and after four hours day shift the levels of performance are virtually the same, but under the former condition it seems to take the drivers less effort while the percentage of wrong responses is considerably higher, i.e. 31%. The drivers seem to have adopted a different strategy that allows them to maintain the reaction time but not the quality of the reaction. Such a shift in strategy, that shows in changes in the efficiency of information processing, is characteristic of the phenomenon called mental fatigue. It may be assumed that mental fatigue will occur after working for eight hours in the morning shift, which often involves sleep deprivation.

5.4.3 Mental fatigue

The problem of fatigue as a work psychological issue does not so much concern the lack of competence, but rather the decision regarding its availability (Meijman, 1991). To allocate attention to a task and proceed to action is predominantly the outcome of strategic decisions. What the outcome will be depends on the person's appreciation of his current psychophysiological state in relation to the character and level of the demands the task and the task situation make on it. Several options are open to the person when to his judgement his actual state and the demands made on it are or threaten to be at conflict (Hockey, 1986a, 1986b). The person can (re)interpret the demands so that the (threatening) conflict is solved or at least becomes less serious. As a result he may not comply with the task assignment or he may comply with the assignment in a way that matches the appreciation of his actual state by following a less strenuous strategy or by not making an optimal effort. The bus drivers appeared to do just that when performing the visual memory search task after eight hours working in the morning shift. As a second option, the person can adjust his actual state in the direction of the required state by investing compensatory effort. Fatigue pertains to the decision regarding these options and the way in which this decision is acted upon. Looked at in this way, fatigue points to a distinct programme of action or strategy, i.e. not to adopt or having to adopt the above-mentioned, second option. The extent to which this programme is in fact realized depends above all on the personal interpretation or redefinition of the task assignment. At the same time, this also depends on the extent to which the performance to be delivered has been standardized and is as such compulsory or is considered to be so. For this determines whether, and if so to what degree, self-regulatory mechanisms are deployed to minimize the discrepancies between the actual state and the state an adequate task performance requires, that is to say, whether compensatory effort is invested or the necessary attention is devoted to a task. According to Bartlett (1953), the characteristic psychological feature of fatigue, i.e. the feeling of "aversion", or as Thorndike (1914) describes it "the intolerance of any effort", is associated with this process of self-regulation in real task activities.

6   DECISION LATITUDE

6.1   Objective and subjective decision latitude

The choice of a specific processing strategy and work procedure depends primarily on the possibilities of control which the situation allows. Therefore, and because of its great interest to the study of workload, decision latitude has been included as a distinct determinant in the effort-recovery scheme (Figure 2.1), although it is to an important part included in formal work aspects like assignment, conditions, facilities and relations.

It should be noted that, although decision latitude may objectively be included in the task assignment and work situation, the operator has to perceive it as such for him/her to utilize it. That is to say, that the utilization of decision latitude depends on the operator's abilities and his/her actual mobilization. If the operator fails to recognize the opportunity he/she objectively has, it is hard to take it. And even while being aware of the opportunity for exercising control, he/she may currently lack the required skills or willingness to do so.

It is important to note that subjective decision latitude is restricted as a consequence of the load itself. Thus, the Cambridge studies (Bartlett, 1943) showed that operators—pilots in a simulator in which very long flights were simulated—when tired not only persist in applying inefficient or even wrong strategies but also restrict their visual field and fail to notice signals from the periphery. As a consequence, they no longer utilize the decision latitude they objectively have.

6.2   Decision latitude and effort

The study of work stress has shown the great importance of having decision latitude (Karasek, 1979; Karasek & Theorell, 1990). Work situations with little decision latitude are particularly stressful because, among other things, they do not allow shifts in task performance strategies or hamper such shifts. We already pointed to the significance of such shifts in manipulating the load. The significance for the operator of having control over his work procedure is illustrated by the following laboratory experiment (Zijlstra et al., 1990).

This experiment aimed to investigate the relationships between, on the one hand, the task load in combination with the operator's state of fatigue and him having control over the task situation, and on the other hand, the effort the task requires. The task to be performed is a visual memory search task. Characters have to be memorized and subsequently recognized when displayed on a screen between other characters. Sixteen subjects, male students, performed the task in an imposed pace of work, i.e. they were unable to determine the work pace themselves. Another group of 16 students performed the task in a self-determined or free pace of work. All subjects were examined on two different days, at four o'clock in the afternoon. On one day the subjects were manipulated and worn out prior to the experimental session. For six hours they had to perform mentally demanding exams, which were repeatedly corrected and marked by the test supervisor. On the other day they could spend the time prior to the session as they liked, as long as they abstained from heavy, physical and mental activities. During the experimental session the task was performed twice, with varying task loads, i.e. with the two character sets containing either one or four characters. After the performance of each task, the subjects scored the amount of effort expended on the task on a standardized rating scale, the RSME (Meijman & Zijlstra, 1989; Zijlstra, 1993). The entire task consisted of 40 trials, 20 of which contained a character from the memory set and 20 did not.

In Figure 2.5 the mean reaction time of the correct answers is plotted against the mean effort score. In addition, it differentiates between the two levels of task load, i.e. one or four characters, and between the condition "worn out" (the black symbols in the figure) and the condition "not worn out" (the open symbols in the figure). The results of the tests with an "imposed pace of work" and with a "free pace of work" are presented next to each other.

First, it appears that a low task load (one character) requires hardly more effort than a higher task load (four characters) if the subjects are allowed to determine their own pace of work. Under the "free pace of work" condition, the differences between the effort scores for the four tasks are not statistically significant. This is not the case if the subjects have to work in an imposed pace of work. Then the increased task load is evaluated as (statistically significantly) more effortful as appears from the differences in scores

between the four character trials and the one character trials. Second, fatigue appears to have little effect on the effort when the subjects are allowed to determine their own pace of work, especially with a low task load. For no statistically significant difference was found between the perceived effort scores in the "worn out" condition versus the "not worn out" condition. With a higher task load and a free pace of work, however, there seems to be a difference, though not statistically significant, between the two fatigue conditions.

With an imposed pace of work the outcome is completely different, with fatigue clearly playing a role. In both task load conditions, the perceived effort scores for the task are (statistically significantly) higher under the "worn out" condition as compared to the "not worn out" condition. Finally, in the imposed pace of work condition, subjects appear to react more quickly than in a free pace of work condition. However, in the first condition they make a lot more mistakes (70% correct answers) than in the second condition (95% correct answers). So, it is inapt to say that a higher

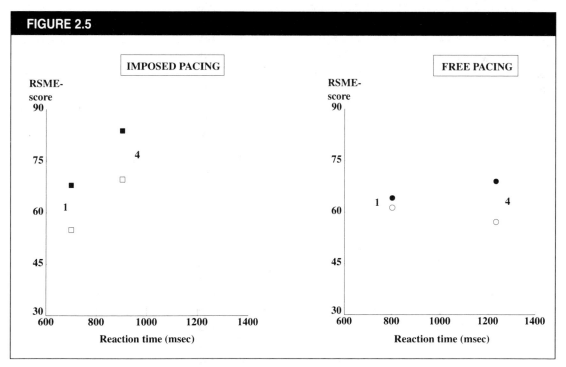

FIGURE 2.5

IMPOSED PACING

FREE PACING

RSME-score

Reaction time (msec)

Efficiency (reaction time by effort) in a visual memory search task; differentiated to memory load (one or four characters), pretreatment (open symbols = "not worn out" pretreatment; closed symbols = "worn out" pretreatment).
Figure left: 16 students working in paced condition; figure right: 16 students working in unpaced condition.

level of effort expenditure will always result in an overall better performance.

The outcome of this experiment shows that making an effort is very much a dynamic process, depending on the task load in combination with the operator's state and the amount of active control he has over the relationship between his performance and the effort to be expended.

6.3   Mental load and stress; the impact of decision latitude

As long as control is possible, thereby preventing the task demands from exceeding the possibilities of self-regulation, the effort will remain within limits acceptable to the individual and will not necessarily elicit a tension reaction (see also section 5.3.4). So, mental load and stress are related. In both cases the adaptive systems are activated. However, mental load does not necessarily have to lead to stress. This happens only when the operator has no or insufficient possibilities for adequate coping and is incapable of developing these possibilities on short notice, while he/she cannot withdraw from the task, or only on pain of sanctions. Under such conditions the load may turn into a threat because the operator is forced to expend an amount of effort which is almost or entirely beyond her/his ability and which he/she is neither emotionally nor motivationally willing to expend. Being confronted with such a situation or just anticipating it, generates the typical reaction pattern with specific physiological and emotional components, which may be characterized as a tension or stress reaction.

So, essential to the occurrence or non-occurrence of such a reaction is the possibility of control (Fisher, 1986; Furda & Meijman, 1992). If there is no or insufficient possibility during the exertion of a mental effort, a physiological mechanism is activated, which Selye (1956) described as the classical stress reaction. Characteristic of this mechanism is an increased secretion of the hormone cortisol next to the secretion of catecholamines, in particular adrenaline. The latter hormone is also secreted as part of the sympatic activity that is characteristic of expending mental effort with the possibility of control.

7   NEGATIVE EFFECTS AND HEALTH CONSEQUENCES

7.1   Introduction

Expending effort yields the short-term reactions mentioned in Figure 2.1. These reactions involve responses of the organism's adaptive mechanisms that are already observable during the load period. In principle these responses are measured as changes in the physiological and psychological processes concerned with respect to a baseline value. At a physiological level, they may involve an increased secretion of a specific hormone that plays a role in activating the organism, like adrenaline. At a mental level, they may involve changes in mood or motivation. Such reactions are in principle reversible. This takes a certain amount of time in which no or little use is made of the systems concerned. This process of reversion is called recovery. The significance of recovery, in which time is the crucial variable, was very early recognized in the work psychological study of load. Both its founders, Mosso (1894) and Kraepelin (Rivers & Kraepelin, 1896), devoted attention to it. In theories on decrements in well-being and health due to mental workload and workstress, the concept of recovery takes a prominent place, because the (im)possibility to recover is essential to short-term load reactions turning into negative load effects. As was said in section 3, the load effects are related to the negative symptoms that may manifest themselves in the long run due to prolonged exposure to one or more load factors without sufficient time for recovery. They manifest themselves as more structural, negative changes in physiological and/or psychological functions and possibly as impairment, disorder or illness.

7.2   Cumulation and effects on well-being and health

Daily work usually involves loads which measured at a certain moment do not necessarily exceed a minimum level of harmfulness. However, because they recur daily and consequently function as a continued and therefore uncontrollable source of tension, loads may in the long run have negative effects. As was said earlier, for this to happen depends primarily on the opportunities for recovery between successive periods of exposure. If the opportunities for recovery after the exposure period are both quantitatively and qualitatively sufficient, the physiological and psychological processes activated while expending the daily work effort will stabilize at a baseline value. However, if these systems are again activated subsequent to insufficient recovery, the organism, which is still in a sub-optimal state, will have to make additional, compensatory effort. This will show in an increased intensity of the load reactions, which in turn will make higher demands, both quantitative and qualitative, on the recovery. Thus, a cumulative process may be started yielding negative load effects such as feelings of prolonged fatigue, complaints about chronic tension and sleep deprivation, and other psychosomatic complaints. Under unchanged conditions, these symptoms may develop into manifest health problems. Such a process has been described in various theories (Kagan & Levi, 1974; Frese et al., 1978; Gardell, 1980).

The question whether an elevated risk of psychosomatic complaints and illnesses may be caused by an increase in the intensity and duration of effects due to mental and emotional workloads, can empirically be answered only by a longitudinal study over a succession of years. Besides longitudinal studies (Johnson et al., 1991), transversal studies involving large-scale, epidemiological research by means of questionnaires (Caplan et al., 1975) indicate psychosocial workload factors and health indicators to be related. It should be noted that the relationships involve mainly indicators that in some way or another provide information on a high work pressure (House et al., 1986), possibly in combination with a low work autonomy or decision latitude (Karasek, 1979; Karasek et al., 1981). But the reported relationships tend to be low. This is not merely due to methodological weaknesses of the studies concerned (Kasl, 1978, 1986; Lazarus et al., 1985; House, 1987), but in particular to the multicausality of health problems (Frese, 1985). However, as yet much is still in the dark regarding the mechanisms underlying these relationships found in epidemiological studies. Animal experiments suggest that a chronic (over)activation of the neuro-endocrine systems due to prolonged exposure to threatening and hence uncontrollable events play an important role (Henry et al., 1981; Bohus et al., 1987). (Work)stress research among humans also indicates that continued exposure over a succession of years to sources of tension, as in the work situation, may cause chronically elevated levels of adrenaline and noradrenaline, and of corticosteroids (Knardahl & Ursin, 1985; Levine, 1986; Frankenhaeuser, 1989). As a consequence, changes may occur in the regulation of the organ systems affected by these substances, e.g. catecholamines affect the cardiovascular system, in particular the regulation of blood pressure (Sterling & Eyer, 1981; Majewski & Rand, 1986; Marmot & Theorell, 1988; Dienstbier, 1989). A prolonged confrontation with stressors which are more or less beyond control, can lead to the development of decrements in the normal functioning of parts of the immune system which may persist over longer periods of time (Ballieux & Heijnen, 1988; Brosschot, 1991; Kaplan, 1991). Chronically elevated levels of corticosteroids are assumed to play a role in this development. Although these decrements have not as yet been shown to have a direct relationship with an increased susceptibility to colds and other infectious diseases, their role in situations of an already elevated susceptibility should be taken into account (Cohen & Williamson, 1991).

7.3 After effects of work pressure

In thinking about the development of negative load effects consequent to prolonged activation of neuroendocrine systems, it is of major interest that the secretion of a certain hormone as a response to workload does not stop immediately after the exposure.

Such after effects or "spillover" were found after periods of working excessive overtime (Rissler, 1977, 1979). Frankenhaeuser (1980) calls it "slow unwinding" when the hormone levels elevated in the course of the task performance drop to their baseline levels only several hours after the end of the performance. Our own field study among driving examiners under three work conditions confirmed this effect (Meijman et al., 1992). The work conditions differed as to the number of exams to be held during a working day from 08.00–16.00 hours, i.e. nine, ten or eleven exams, respectively. The duration of the exams did not differ between conditions. In other words, in this field study the level of work pressure or work intensity was manipulated systematically. On a "9-exams" day, a light working day, the examiners were directly productive, i.e. holding exams for 75% of their working day. In the "10-exams" condition, a normal working day, productivity amounted to 80%, and in the "11-exams" condition, an intensified day, it amounted to 86%. In the last condition, the examiners did not have a moment to spare between successive exams versus about five minutes on a "9-exams" day and two minutes on a "10-exams" day.

On these working days and after work, in the evening, the excretion levels of adrenaline (in nanograms per minute: Ng/min) in urine were determined. The same was done on a Sunday, when the examiners had a day off. Figure 2.6 presents the pattern of adrenaline excretion levels.

Adrenaline excretion levels are found to be higher on the working days than on the day off. Strikingly, on the working days the levels are the same for the three conditions. However, at the end of an intensive working day, at 16.00 hours, the adrenaline excretion level is (statistically significantly) higher than on the two other working days. Furthermore, and this is of great interest, after an intensive working day this increased level persists throughout the evening. Apparently, the organism remains activated for quite some time after a period of intensive load, even if it is not exposed to any special loads during the period of recovery. This condition of increased activation caused the examiners to be troubled by sleep complaints, in particular falling asleep, during the nights after the intensified working days. The following morning they reported increased feelings of tension. This study serves to illustrate the mechanism which may lead to the development of a state of prolonged neuroendocrine activation which eventually may lead to complaints.

7.4   Load effects and health

In a series of transversal field studies among city bus drivers (Mulders et al., 1982, 1988) indications were found of a relationship between workload-related elevated hormonal levels and health status. Epidemiological analyses (Kompier, 1988) showed this occupational group to be at an elevated health risk attributable to a combination of a high work pressure and insufficient recovery. As was argued above, prolonged disruption of the complementary relationship between load and recovery could start a process of increasing dysfunctioning. The field studies aimed to find out whether an apparently decreased resistance, measured by frequency of absenteeism, also manifest itself in an elevated hormonal reactivity in the normal work situation. Therefore, the drivers were examined both on working days and on days off. During the days off, no differences in the adrenaline excretion levels in urine were found between drivers with a high frequency (five times or more) of short sick leave in the year prior to the study and drivers of the same age and sex who had been absent only once or less. Both groups showed an elevated level of adrenaline on working days as compared to days off. However, on working days the excretion levels of the group with a relatively high absenteeism were considerably higher than the levels of drivers with a low absenteeism.

Absenteeism, however, is a complex measure, which cannot simply be used as an indicator of general health. That is why a series of new studies were started to investigate the relationship between the level of perceived health measured by a standard Dutch questionnaire (the VOEG; Dirken, 1969) and the reactivity in adrenaline under a normal workload. The adrenaline excretion levels on a normal working day and on a day off of 168 men from a wide variety of occupational backgrounds were compared. They had filled out the VOEG a few weeks prior to the physiological examination. The subjects were divided by their VOEG-scores and age. Figure 2.7 presents the results (Meijman et al., 1990).

As can be seen in Figure 2.7, all groups show an elevated excretion level on the working day as compared to the day off. However, in the older age groups, people with many perceived health complaints show a significantly higher excretion level than people with little to no complaints. On the day off, no difference was found between the two groups. So, it does not involve a habitual difference in general activation of the hormonal system,

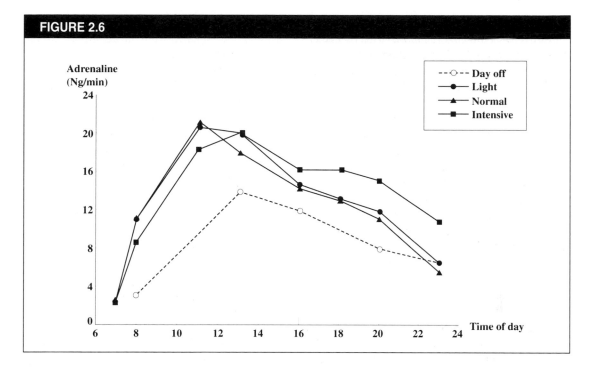

FIGURE 2.6

Excretion rate of adrenaline, in urine, during working days (light: five-minute breaks; normal: two-minute breaks; intensive: no breaks) and a day off. 27 driving examiners.

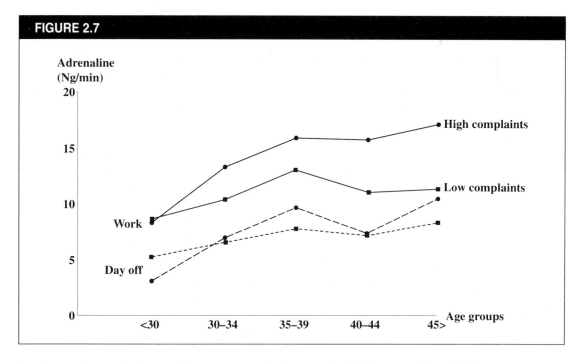

FIGURE 2.7

Excretion rate of adrenaline, in urine, during a normal working day and a day off (both between 900 and 1230).
Data of 168 men, from various occupations, differentiated to age (<30 N=36; 30–34 N=53; 35–39 N=36; 40–44 N=25; 45 > N=18) and to level of psychosomatic complaints. 102 subjects "low complaints", 66 subjects "high complaints".

but a difference in reactivity to the daily workload. This difference in hormonal reactivity is related to perceived health and occurs especially at an advanced age, i.e. after the age of 35 when most people have been exposed to daily workloads for over 15 years.

8   SOME CONCLUDING REMARKS

The work psychological study of workload concerns the changes in structure and regulation of work activities under influence of the demands made in the work situation. It comprises the study of changes in performance as well as the study of changes in the willingness to expend effort and of the costs involved. These changes are studied in functional relationship with the character and the level of the loads the worker is exposed to in the actual work situation. The demands that are thus made on the processing capacity are met by the mobilization of resources and therefore required activation of psycho-biological adaptive systems. This process of expending effort causes changes in the systems concerned, which can be observed as reversible load reactions. Under the condition of sufficient recovery, they stabilize at a baseline level within a short period of time after the end of the load period. Sustained load and insufficient recovery may lead to negative load effects which may persist for longer periods of time or may even be irreversible, which shows in a loss of function, impairment or illness.

The effort-recovery relationship—given the demand to expend a certain minimum effort—is pivotal to the work psychological study of workload. For, in case of no or insufficient recovery, the effort process may obtain a cumulative character in the course of a working day and in the course of a succession of working days. This process determines the costs in terms of decrements in work capacities and in the long run in well-being and health. In the final analysis, the study of workload does not concern the question whether a person is able to cope with a specific level of task demands but the short-term and long-term costs involved in coping with loads in actual work situations. This has to be investigated from the perspective of the cycle of effort and recovery.

REFERENCES

Algera, J.A. (Eds.) (1991). *Analyse van arbeid vanuit verschillende perspectieven* (Approaches to task analysis). Amsterdam/Lisse: Swets & Zeitlinger.

Anderson, J.R. (1993). *Rules of the mind*. Hillsdale, NJ: Lawrence Erlbaum Associates.

Astrand, P.O., & Rodahl, K. (1986). *Textbook of work physiology: Physiological basis of exercise*. New York: McGraw-Hill.

Bainbridge, L. (1974). Problems in the assessment of mental load. *Le Travail Humain*, *37*, 279–302.

Bainbridge, L. (1978). Forgotten alternatives in skill and workload. *Ergonomics*, *21*, 169–185.

Ballieux, R.E., & Heijnen, C.J. (1988). Stress and the immune system. In D. Hellhammer, I. Florin, & H. Weiner (Eds.), *Neurobiological approaches to human disease*. Toronto: Hans Huber Verlag.

Bartlett, F.C. (1943). Fatigue following highly skilled work. *Proceedings of the Royal Society*, *131*, 247–257.

Bartlett, F.C. (1953). Psychological criteria of fatigue. In W.F. Floyd, & A.T. Welford (Eds.), *Symposium on fatigue*. London: H.K. Lewis.

Baumgarten, F. (1928). *Die Berufseignungsprüfungen*. München/Berlin: Oldenbourg.

Bohus, B., Benus, R.F., Fokkema, D.S., Koolhaas, J.M., Nyakas, C., van Oortmerssen, G.A., Prins, A.J.A., de Ruiter, A.J.H., Scheurink, A.J.W., & Steffens, A.B. (1987). Neuroendocrine states and behavioral and physiological stress responses. In E.R. de Kloet, V.M. Wiegand, & D. de Wied (Eds.), *Progress in brain research*, *72*, 57–70.

Bongers, P.M., & Boshuizen, H.C. (1990). *Back disorders and whole-body vibration at work*. Dissertation, University of Amsterdam.

Bonjer, F.H. (rap.) (1965). *Fysiologische methoden voor het vaststellen van belasting en belastbaarheid* (Physiological methods for the study of workload). Assen: van Gorcum/CargoTNO.

Brosschot, J.F. (1991). *Stress, perceived control and immune response in man*. Utrecht: ISOR; Dissertation, University of Utrecht.

Burger, G.C.E. (1959). De betekenis van kwantitatieve meting en functionele beoordeling van arbeidsbelasting en belastbaarheid voor de practische bedrijfsarts (The measurement of workload and capacity in occupational health practice). *Tijdschrift voor Sociale Geneeskunde*, *37*, 377–387.

Caplan, R.D., Cobb, S., French, J.R.P. Jr., Harrison, R. van, & Pinneau, S.R. Jr. (1975). *Job demands and worker health*. Washington DC: NIOSH.

Carver, C.S., & Scheier, M.F. (1990). Origins and functions of positive and negative affect. A control-process view. *Psychological Review, 97*, 19–35.

Coeterier, J. (1971). Individual strategies in ATC freedom and choice. *Ergonomics, 14*, 579–584.

Cohen, S., & Williamson, G.M. (1991). Stress and infectious diseases in humans. *Psychological Bulletin, 109*, 5–24.

Cowan, N. (1988). Evolving conceptions of memory storage, selective attention and their mutual constraints within the human information-processing system. *Psychological Bulletin, 102*, 163–191.

Cowan, N. (1993). Activation, attention and short-term memory. *Memory and Cognition, 21*(2), 162–167.

Dienstbier, R.A. (1989). Arousal and physiological toughness: implications for mental and physical health. *Psychological Review, 96*, 84–100.

Dijk, F.J.H. van, Meijman, T.F., & Ulenbelt, P. (1988). Towards a dynamic model of exposure, susceptibility and effect. In W.R.F. Notten, R.F.M. Herber, W.J. Hunter, A.C. Monster, & R.L. Zielhuis (Eds.), *Health surveillance of individual workers exposed to chemical agents.* International Archives of Occupational and Environmental Health, Supplement. Berlin/Heidelberg: Springer Verlag.

Dijk, F.J.H. van, Dormolen, M., Kompier, M.A.J., & Meijman, T.F. (1990). Herwaardering model belasting-belastbaarheid (The load-capacity model revisited). *Tijdschrift voor Sociale Gezondheidszorg, 68*, 3–10.

Dirken, J. (1969). *Arbeid en stress* (Work and stress). Groningen: Wolthers-Noordhoff.

Dodge, R. (1913). Mental work: A study in psychodynamics. *Psychological Review, 20*, 1–43.

Drury, C.G., Paramore, B., van Cott, H., Grey, S., & Corlett, E.N. (1987). Task analysis. In G. Salvendy (Ed.), *Handbook of human factors.* New York/Chichester, UK: Wiley & Sons.

Ettema, J.H. (1967). *Arbeidsfysiologische aspecten van mentale belasting* (Physiological aspects of mental load). Assen: van Gorcum.

Ettema, J.H. (1973). Het model belasting en belastbaarheid (The load-capacity model). *Tijdschrift voor Sociale Geneeskunde, 51*, 44–54.

Fisher, S. (1986). *Stress and strategy.* Hove, UK: Lawrence Erlbaum Associates Ltd.

Fleishman, E.A., & Quantaince, M.K. (1984). *Taxonomies of human performance.* Orlando, New York: Academic Press.

Frankenhaeuser, M. (1979). Psychoneuroendocrine approaches to the study of emotion as related to stress and coping. In H.E. Howe, & R.A. Dienstbier (Eds.), *Nebraska symposium on motivation, 1978.* Lincoln: University of Nebraska Press.

Frankenhaeuser, M. (1980). Psychobiological aspects of life stress. In S. Levine, & H. Ursin (Eds.), *Coping and health.* New York: Plenum Press.

Frankenhaeuser, M. (1989). A biopsychosocial approach to work life issues. *Journal of International Health Services, 19*, 747–758.

Frankenhaeuser, M., & Lundberg, U. (1985). Sympathetic-adrenal and pituitary-adrenal response to challenge. In P. Pichot, P. Berner, R. Wolf, & K. Thau (Eds.), *Psychiatry, Vol. II.* New York, USA/London, UK: Plenum Press.

Frese, M. (1985). Stress at work and psychosomatic complaints: a causal interpretation. *Journal of Applied Psychology, 70*, 314–328.

Frese, M. (1987). A concept of control: implications for stress and performance in human-computer interaction. In G. Salvendy, S.L. Sauter, & J.J. Hurrell (Eds.), *Social, ergonomic and stress aspects of work with computers.* Amsterdam, The Netherlands/Oxford, UK: Elsevier Science Publishers.

Frese, M., Greif, S., & Semmer, N. (1978). *Industrielle psychopathologie.* Bern: Hans Huber Verlag.

Furda, J., & Meijman, T.F. (1992). Druk en dreiging, sturing of stress (Demands and threat: The impact of control). In J. Winnubst, & M. Schabracq (Eds.), *Handboek arbeid-en gezondheids psychologie.* Utrecht: Lemma.

Gardell, B. (1980). Psychosocial aspects of industrial production methods. In L. Levi (Ed.), *Society, stress and disease, Vol. IV: Working life.* London: Oxford University Press.

Gopher, D. (1986). In defence of resources: on structures, energies, pools and the allocation of attention. In G.R.J. Hockey, A.W.K. Gaillard, & M.G.H. Coles (Eds.), *Energetics and human information processing.* Dordrecht: Martinus Nijhoff Publishers.

Gopher, D., & Donchin, E. (1986). Workload: An examination of the concept. In K.R. Boff, L. Kaufmann, & J.P. Thomas (Eds.), *Handbook of perception and human performance, Vol. II: Cognitive processes and performance.* New York/Chichester: Wiley & Sons.

Graf, O. (1954). Der Begriff der Leistungsbereitschaft. *Zentralblatt Arbeitwissenschaft, 8*, 141–144.

Hacker, W. (1973–1978). *Allgemeine Arbeits und Ingenieurspsychologie.* Berlin: VEB Deutscher Verlag Wissenschaft.

Hacker, W. (1986). *Arbeitspsychologie.* Bern: Huber.

Heemstra, M.L. (1988). *Efficiency of human information processing. A model of cognitive energetics.* Dissertation, Free University, Amsterdam.

Heide, H. van der, & Kragt, H. (1989). Quick scan ergonomie. *Maandblad Arbeidsomstandigheden, 65*, 25–29.

Hellinga, P. (1985). *De constructie van de groninger adjectief checklist, de GACL* (The construction of the Groningen Adjective Checklist). Groningen: Heijmans Bulletin, HB-85-771-Ex.

Henry, J.P., Ely, D.L., & Stephens, P.M. (1981). Medical ethology in relation to occupational health. In L. Levi (Ed.), *Society, stress and disease, Vol IV: Working life.* London: Oxford University Press.

Hockey, G.R.J. (1984). Varieties of attentional state: The effects of environment. In R. Parasuraman, & D.R. Davies (Eds.), *Varieties of attention*. New York: Academic Press, Inc.

Hockey, G.R.J. (1986a). Changes in operator efficiency as a function of environmental stress, fatigue and circadian rhythms. In K.R. Boff, L. Kaufmann, & J.P. Thomas (Eds.), *Handbook of perception and human performance, Vol. II: Cognitive processes and performance*. New York/Chichester: Wiley & Sons.

Hockey, G.R.J. (1986b). A state control theory of adaptation to stress and individual differences in stress management. In G.R.J. Hockey, A.W.K. Gaillard, & M.G.H. Coles (Eds.), *Energetics and human information processing*. Dordrecht: Martinus Nijhoff Publishers.

Hockey, G.R.J. (1993). Cognitive-energetical control mechanisms in the management of work demands and psychological health. In A. Baddeley, & L. Weiskrantz (Eds.), *Attention: Selection, awareness and control. A tribute to Donald Broadbent*. Oxford: Clarendon Press.

Hockey, G.R.J., Gaillard, A.W.K., & Coles, M.G.H. (Eds.) (1986). *Energetics and human information processing*. Dordrecht: Martinus Nijhoff Publishers.

Holding, D.H. (1983). Fatigue. In G.R.J. Hockey (Ed.), *Stress and fatigue in human performance*. New York/Chichester: Wiley & Sons.

House, J.S. (1987). Chronic stress and chronic disease in life and work: Conceptual and methodological issues. *Work and Stress, 1*, 129–134.

House, J.S., Strecher, V., Metzner, H.L., & Robbins, C.A. (1986). Occupational stress and health among men and women in the Tecumseh community health study. *Journal of Health and Social Behavior, 27*, 62–77.

James, W. (1890). *The principles of psychology*. New York: Holt.

Johnson, J.V., & Johansson, G. (Eds.) (1991). *The psychosocial work environment: Work organization, democratization and health*. Amityville, NY: Baywood Publishing Co.

Johnson, J.V., Hall, E.M., Stewart, W., Fredlund, P., & Theorell, T. (1991). Combined exposure to adverse work organization factors and cardiovascular disease: Towards a lifecourse perspective. In L.D. Fechter (Ed.), *Proceedings of the 4th International Conference on the Combined Effects of Environmental Factors*. Baltimore: John Hopkins University School of Hygiene and Public Health.

Kagan, A.R., & Levi, L. (1974). Health and environment-psychosocial stimuli: A review. *Social Science and Medicine, 10*, 225–241.

Kahneman, D. (1973). *Attention and effort*. Englewood Cliffs NJ: Prentice Hall.

Kalsbeek, J.W.H. (1967). *Mentale belasting: Theoretische en experimentele exploraties ter ontwikkeling van een meetmethode* (Mental load: A theory and measurement method). Assen: van Gorcum/CargoTNO.

Kalsbeek, J.W.H., & Ettema, J.H. (1964). Physiological and psychological evaluation of distraction stress. *Proceedings of the 2nd International Ergonomics Congress*, Dortmund.

Kantowitz, B.H. (1987). Mental workload. In P.A. Hancock (Ed.), *Human factors psychology*. Amsterdam, The Netherlands/Oxford: Elsevier Science Publishers.

Kaplan, H.B. (1991). Social psychology of the immune system: A conceptual framework and review of the literature. *Social Science and Medicine, 33*, 909–923.

Karasek, R.A. (1979). Job demands, job decision latitude, and mental strain: implications for job redesign. *Administrative Science Quarterly, 24*, 285–307.

Karasek, R.A., Baker, D., Marxer, F., Ahlbom, A., & Theorell, T. (1981). Job decision latitude, job demands, and cardiovascular disease. *American Journal of Public Health, 71*, 694–705.

Karasek, R.A., & Theorell, T. (1990). *Healthy work: Stress, productivity and the reconstruction of working life*. New York: Basic Books.

Karg, P.W., & Staehle, W.H. (1982). *Analyse der Arbeitssituation: Verfahren und Instrumente*. Freiburg i/B: Rudolf Haufe Verlag.

Kasl, S.V. (1978). Epidemiological contributions to the study of workstress. In C.L. Cooper, & R. Payne (Eds.), *Stress at work*. Chichester: John Wiley & Sons.

Kasl, S.V. (1986). Stress and disease in the workplace: a methodological commentary on the accumulated evidence. In M.F. Cataldo, & T.J. Coates (Eds.), *Health and industry, a behavioral medicine approach*. Chichester: John Wiley & Sons.

Klinkhamer, H.A.W. (1979). *Beoordelingslijst ergonomie* (Ergonomics checklist). Deventer: Kluwer/NIVE.

Knardahl, S., & Ursin, H. (1985). Sustained activation and the pathophysiology of hypertension and coronary heart disease. In J.F. Orlebeke, G. Mulder, & L. van Doornen (Eds.), *Psychophysiology of cardiovascular control*. New York/London: Plenum Press.

Kompier, M.A.J. (1988). *Arbeid en gezondheid van stadsbuschauffeurs* (Work and health of city bus drivers). Delft: Eburon; Dissertation, University of Groningen.

Kosslyn, S.M., & Koenig, O. (1992). *Wet mind: The new cognitive neuroscience*. New York/Oxford: The Free Press.

Kuiper, J.P. (1985). Vertoont het belastingsmodel ideologische trekken? (Ideological aspects of the load-capacity model). *Tijds. Soc. Gezondhz., 63*, 579–580.

Kyllonen, P.C., & Alluisi, E.A. (1987). Learning and forgetting facts and skills. In G. Salvendy (Ed.), *Handbook of human factors*. New York/Chichester: Wiley & Sons

Landau, K., & Rohmert, W. (1989). *Recent developments in job analysis*. London: Taylor & Francis.

Lazarus, R. (1966). *Psychological stress and the coping process*. New York: McGraw-Hill.

Lazarus, R.S. (1991). *Emotion and adaptation*. New York/Oxford: Oxford University Press.

Lazarus, R.S., DeLongis, A., Folkman, S., & Gruen, R. (1985). Stress and adaptational outcomes: The problem of confounded measures. *American Psychologist, 40*, 770–779.

Lehmann, G. (1962). *Praktische Arbeitsphysiologie, 2 Aufl*. Stuttgart: Georg Thieme Verlag.

Leitner, K., Volpert, W., Greiner, B., Weber, W.G., & Hennes, K. (1987). *Analyse psychischer Belastung in der Arbeit*. Köln: Verlag TüV Rheinland.

Levine, P. (1986). Stress. In M.G.H. Coles, E. Donchin, & S.W. Porges (Eds.), *Psychophysiology: Systems, processes and applications*. Amsterdam, The Netherlands/Oxford: Elsevier Science Publishers.

Lundberg, U., & Frankenhaeuser, M. (1980). Pituitary-adrenal and sympathetic-adrenal correlates of distress and effort. *Journal of Psychosomatic Research, 24*, 125–130.

Majewski, H., & Rand, M. (1986). A possible role of epinephrine in the development of hypertension. *Medical Research Review, 6*, 467–486.

Marmot, M., & Theorell, T. (1988). Social class and cardiovascular disease: the contribution of work. *International Journal of Health Services, 18*, 659–673.

Matern, B. (1984). *Psychologische Arbeitsanalyse*. Berlin/Heidelberg: Springer Verlag.

Meijman, T.F. (1988). Belasting en herstel, een begrippenkader voor het arbeidspsychologisch onderzoek van werkbelasting (Load and recovery: A conceptual frame for the study of workload). In B.G. Deelman, & G. Mulder (Eds.), *Nederlands psychologisch onderzoek, deel 3*. Lisse: Swets & Zeitlinger.

Meijman, T.F. (Eds.) (1989). *Mentale belasting en werkstress, een arbeidspsychologische invalshoek* (Mental load and workstress: A work psychology approach). Assen: van Gorcum.

Meijman, T.F. (1991). *Over vermoeidheid, arbeidspsychologische studies naar de beleving van belastingseffecten* (On fatigue: The perception of workload effects). Studiecentrum Arbeid en Gezondheid University of Amsterdam; Dissertation University of Groningen.

Meijman, T.F., & O'Hanlon, J. F. (1983). Arbeidsbelasting, een inleidend overzicht van psychologische theorieën en meetmethoden (Workload: An introduction into psychological theories). In P.J.D. Drenth, Hk. Thierry, P.J. Willems, & C.J. de Wolff (Eds.), *Handboek arbeids en organisatiepsychologie*. Deventer: van Loghum Slaterus.

Meijman, T.F., Ouwerkerk, R. van, Mulder, L.J.M., & Vries-Griever, A.H.G. de (1989). Hartslagvariabiliteit, het onderzoek van mentale efficiëntie (Heart rate variability: The study of mental efficiency). In T.F.

Meijman (Ed.), *Mentale belasting en werkstress, een arbeidspsychologische invalshoek*. Assen: van Gorcum.

Meijman, T.F., Mulders, H.P.G., Kompier, M.A.J., & Dormolen, M. van (1990). Individual differences in adrenaline/noradrenaline reactivity and self-perceived health status. *Zeitschrift zur Gesammte Hygiene, 36*, 413–414.

Meijman, T.F., Mulder, G., Dormolen, M. van, & Cremer, R. (1992). Workload of driving examiners: A psychophysiological field study. In H. Kragt (Ed.), *Enhancing industrial performance*. London: Taylor & Francis.

Moray, N. (1967). Where is capacity limited? A survey and a model. In A.F. Sanders (Ed.), *Attention and performance, Vol. 1*. Amsterdam: North Holland Publishing Co.

Mosso, A. (1894). *La fatigue intellectuelle et physique*. Paris: Felix Alcan.

Mulder, G. (1979). Mental load, mental effort and attention. In N. Moray (Ed.), *Mental workload: Its theory and measurement*. New York: Plenum Press.

Mulder, G. (1980). *The heart of mental effort*. Dissertation, University of Groningen.

Mulder, G. (1986). The concept and measurement of mental effort. In G.R.J. Hockey, A.W.K. Gaillard, & M.G.H. Coles (Eds.), *Energetics and human information processing*. Dordrecht: Martinus Nijhoff Publishers.

Mulder, G., Wijers, A.A., Smid, H.G.O.M., Brookhuis, K.A., & Mulder, L.J.M. (1989). Individual differences in computational mechanisms: A psychophysiological analysis. In R. Kanfer, P.L. Ackerman & R. Cudeck (Eds.), *Abilities, motivation and methodology*. Hillsdale, NJ: Erlbaum.

Mulder, L.J.M. (1988). *Assessment of cardiovascular reactivity by means of spectral analysis*. Dissertation, University of Groningen.

Mulders, H.P.G., Meijman, T.F., O'Hanlon, J.F., & Mulder, G. (1982). Differential psychophysiological reactions of city busdrivers to workload. *Ergonomics, 25*, 1003–1011.

Mulders, H.P.G., Meijman, T.F., Kompier, M.A.J., Broersen, J.P.J., Westerink, B., & O'Hanlon, J.F. (1988). Occupational stress in city busdrivers. In J.A. Rothengatter, & R.A. de Bruin (Eds.), *Road user behavior, theory and research*. Assen: van Gorcum.

Navon, D., & Gopher, D. (1979). On the economy of the human information processing system. *Psychological review, 84*, 214–255.

Navon, D., & Gopher, D. (1980). Task difficulty, resources and dual task performances. In R.S. Nickerson (Ed.), *Attention and performance, Vol. 8*. Hillsdale, NJ: Lawrence Erlbaum.

Ouwerkerk R. van, Meijman, T.F., & Mulder, G. (1994). *De analyse van arbeidstaken op cognitieve en emotionele eisen* (The analysis of tasks: Cognitive and emotional demands). Utrecht: Lemma.

Paas, F.G.W.C., & Merrienboer, J.J.G van (1993). The

efficiency of instructional conditions: An approach to combine mental effort and performance measures. *Human Factors, 35*, 737–743.

Posner, M.I., & Raichle, M.E. (1994). *Images of mind*. New York: Scientific American Library.

Pribram, K.H., & McGuinness, D. (1975). Arousal, activation and effort in the control of attention. *Psychological Review, 82*, 116–149.

Rasmussen, J., & Jensen, A. (1974). Mental procedures in real-life tasks, a case study of electronic trouble shooting. *Ergonomics, 17*, 293–307.

Rasmussen, J. (1987). The definition of human error and a taxonomy for technical system design. In J. Rasmussen, K. Duncan, & J. Leplat (Eds.), *New technology and human error*. New York/Chichester: Wiley & Sons.

Revelle, W. (1993). Individual differences in personality and motivation: "non-cognitive" determinants of cognitive performance. In A. Baddeley, & L. Weiskrantz (Eds.), *Attention: Selection, awareness and control. A tribute to Donald Broadbent*. Oxford: Clarendon Press.

Rissler, A. (1977). Stress reactions at work and after work during a period of quantitative overload. *Ergonomics, 20*, 13–16.

Rissler, A. (1979). A psychobiological approach to quality of working life: Costs of adjustment to quantitative overload. In R.G. Sell, & P. Shipley (Eds.), *Satisfaction in work design: Ergonomics and other approaches*. London: Taylor & Francis.

Rivers, W.H.R., & Kraepelin, E. (1896). Uber Ermüdung und Erholung. *Psychologische Arbeiten, 1*, 627–678.

Rohmert, W. (1983). Formen menschlicher Arbeit. In W. Rohmert, & J. Rutenfranz (Eds.). *Praktische Arbeitsphysiologie*. Stuttgart, Germany/New York: Georg Thieme Verlag.

Rohmert, W. (1984). Das Belastungs-Beanspruchungs Konzept. *Zeitschrift der Arbeitswissenschaften, 38*, 193–200.

Rumelhart, D.E., & Ortony, A. (1977). *The representation in memory*. San Diego, CA: University of California, Center for Human Information Processing.

Sanders, A.F. (1981). Stress and human performance: A working model and some applications. In G. Salvendy, & M.J. Smith (Eds.), *Machine pacing and occupational stress*. London: Taylor & Francis.

Sanders, A.F. (1983). Towards a model of stress and human performance. *Acta Psychologica, 53*, 61–97.

Schellart, A.J.M., Deynen, W., van, & Koten, J.W. (1989, 1990). Beroep en ziekte in de WAO, I, II en III (Occupation and diseases of disabled people). *Tijdschrift voor Verzekerings Geneeskunde, 27*, 166–172, en *28*, 6–10 en 39–42.

Schuffel, H. (1989). *Richtlijnen ten behoeve van werkplek-ergonomie* (Prescriptions for the design of workplaces). Den Haag: Ministry of Social Affairs SoZaWe/DGA, rapport S59.

Selye, H. (1956). *Stress of life*. New York: McGraw-Hill.

Shiffrin, R.M., & Schneider, W. (1977). Controlled and automatic information processing: II. Perceptual learning, automatic attending and a general theory. *Psychological Review, 84*, 127–190.

Sluis, H. van der, & Dirken, J.M. (1970). *Dagelijks energieverbruik van de Nederlandse industriearbeider: methoden ter bepaling en normen* (Daily energy use of the Dutch industrial worker). Leiden/Groningen: Ned. Instituut voor Preventieve Geneeskunde TNO/Wolthers-Noordhoff.

Sperandio, J.-C. (1972). Charge de travail et régulation des procèssus operatoires. *Le Travail Humain, 35*, 85–98.

Squire, L.R. (1987). *Memory and brain*. New York/Oxford: Oxford University Press.

Sterling, P., & Eyer, J. (1981). Biological basis of stress related mortality. *Social Science and Medicine*, 15E, 3–42.

Tent, L. (1962). Untersuchungen zur Erfassung des Verhältnisses von Anspannung und Leistung bei vorwiegend psychisch beanspruchenden Tätigkeiten. *Archives zur Gesammte Psychologie, 115*, 106–172.

Thayer, R. (1978). Factor analytic and reliability studies of the activation-deactivation adjective checklist. *Psychological Reports, 42*, 747–756.

Thayer, R.E. (1989). *The biopsychology of mood and arousal*. New York/Oxford: Oxford University Press.

Thierry, Hk., & Jong, J.R. de (1991). Arbeidsanalyse ten behoeve van beloning (Function analysis for remuneration). In J.A. Algera (Ed.), *Analyse van arbeid vanuit verschillende perspectieven*. Amsterdam/Lisse: Swets & Zeitlinger.

Thorndike, E.L. (1914). *Educational psychology, Vol. III: Mental work and fatigue and individual differences and their causes*. New York: Teachers College Columbia University.

Tulving, E. (1991). Concepts of human memory. In L. Squire, G. Lynch, N.M. Weinberger, & J.L. McGaugh (Eds.), *Memory: Organization and locus of change* (pp. 3–32). New York: Oxford University Press.

Ulenbelt, P. (1991). *Omgaan met blootstelling aan chemische stoffen: grenswaarden, hygiënisch gedrag en regelmogelijkheden* (Coping with the exposure to chemical substances at work). Amsterdam: Studiecentrum Arbeid en Gezondheid University of Amsterdam; Dissertation University of Amsterdam.

Verbeek, J.H.A.M. (1991). *Arbeidsongeschiktheid op grond van rugklachten en andere aandoeningen van het bewegingsapparaat* (Disability due to low back pains). Amsterdam: Studiecentrum Arbeid en Gezondheid University of Amsterdam; Dissertation University of Amsterdam.

Voskamp, P. (Ed.) (1994). *Handboek ergonomie. De stand van de ergonomie in de ARBO wet* (Handbook of ergonomics). Alphen a/d Rijn: Samson BedrijfsInformatie.

Vries-Griever, A.H.G. de (1989). De methode van psychologische arbeidsanalyse (Psychological analysis of tasks). In T.F. Meijman (Ed.), *Mentale belasting en werkstress, een arbeidspsychologische invalshoek*. Assen: van Gorcum.

Welford, A.T. (1953). The psychologist's problem in measuring fatigue. In W.F. Floyd, & A.T. Welford (Eds.), *Symposium on fatigue*. London: K. K. Lewis.

Welford, A.T. (1978). Mental workload as a function of demand, capacity, strategy and skill. *Ergonomics, 21*, 151–167.

Wendrich, P. (1973). Methodische Probleme bei der Anwendung von Algoritmen zur Strukturanalyse von Arbeitstätigkeiten bei Belastungsuntersuchungen. In W. Hacker, W. Quaas, H. Raum, & H.J. Schultz (Eds.), *Psychologische Arbeitsuntersuchung*. Berlin: VEB Deuts Verlag Wissens.

Wickens, C.D. (1984). Processing resources in attention. In R. Parasuraman, & D.R. Davies (Eds.), *Varieties of attention*. Orlando: Academic Press.

Wickens, C.D. (1987). Information processing, decision making and cognition. In G. Salvendy (Ed.), *Handbook of human factors*. New York/Chichester: Wiley & Sons.

Wickens, C.D. (1991). Processing resources and attention. In D.L. Damos (Ed.), *Multiple-task performance*. London: Taylor & Francis.

Wickens, C.D. (1992). *Engineering psychology and human performance (2nd ed.)*. New York: Harper-Collins Publishers Inc.

Wijers, A.A. (1989). *Selective visual attention: an elektrophysiological approach*. Dissertation, University of Groningen.

Zielhuis, R.L. (1967). Theoretisch denkraam voor hygiënisch beleid, I, II en III (Theoretical framework for occupational health research). *Tijdschrift voor Sociale Geneeskunde, 45*, 345–352, 392–397, 427–423.

Zielhuis, R.L., & Henderson, P.Th. (1986). Definitions of monitoring activities and their relevance for the practice of occupational health. *International Archives of Occupational and Environmental Health, 57*, 249–257.

Zijlstra, F.R.H. (1993). *Efficiency in work behavior*. Dissertation, Technical University of Delft.

Zijlstra, F.R.H., & Meijman, T.F. (1989). Het meten van mentale inspanning met behulp van een subjectieve methode (Measuring mental effort by means of a subjective method). In T.F. Meijman (Ed.), *Mentale belasting en werkstress: een arbeidspsychologische benadering*. Assen: van Gorcum.

Zijlstra, F.H.R., Cavalini, P., Wiethoff, M., & Meijman, T.F. (1990). Mental effort: Strategies and efficiency. In P.J.D. Drenth et al. (Eds.), *European perspectives in psychology, Vol. I*. New York: John Wiley & Sons.

ogists know about and appreciate each others contribution. In addition there is overlap. One example concerns the area of complex decision-making and of decision-aiding tools. More generally, a somewhat more complex organisation may easily suffer from a deficient general structure, due to problems of command, control and communication (C3), which may be related to aspects of industrial psychology as well as of ergonomics. The same may be said of questions on training and re-training which are still always underestimated in today's second industrial revolution. Moreover, the rapid developments in society and industry are accompanied by a range of new problems, both in industrial psychology and ergonomics, which may well lead to further contacts. Hence, a chapter on ergonomics is clearly relevant to this Handbook. It will present a general, and hence, superficial helicopter view, much of which is treated in much greater detail in the well-known handbooks, which are listed in the references. One chapter is obviously not enough, and therefore some issues such as work load and safety, are discussed elsewhere in greater detail.

There are no detailed references in this chapter, which should not be taken to imply that the forthcoming discussion reflects the author's contributions. Instead, much has been derived from many texts and papers, which provide much more detailed references. The author's contributions are actually minor and can be found in Sanders (1997), which is concerned with basic and applied issues of reaction processes and attention.

1.2 Development

Ergonomics may still always be described in terms of adaptation of work to human capabilities or, more colloquially, "fitting the job to the worker". This is the opposite of fitting man to the job, as aimed at by selection, classification and training. Although the early beginnings of ergonomics stem from before World War II—for example, research on environmental effects such as noise and illumination on performance—the main emphasis during the prewar period was on mental testing. Ergonomics showed a rapid growth during and following World War II, since most newly developed military systems were often difficult to

handle by a human operator, and did less well than expected, therefore. Research on the design of the cockpit of the Spitfire—the famous "Cambridge cockpit"—and on vigilance in operating sonar and radar echoes belong to the classical examples from World War II, to which the names of Bartlett, Drew, Mackworth, Fitts and McFarland are connected as pioneers.

Thus, the relevance of ergonomics was first recognised in defence research. In the postwar industrial problems the field was originally received with some hesitation, and, even now, one may maintain that ergonomics has not yet reached the status it deserves. There are of course reasons for this state of affairs. One is undoubtedly the lack of basic knowledge, so that many ergonomical problems required expensive experimental research, and could not be solved by simple recommendation or best guess about the optimal design. The lack of basic knowledge was due to the fact that psychological theorising of the prewar period—Gestalt theory and behaviorism—could not address the issues of man-machine interaction. Hence, the major ergonomical applications came initially from sensory psychophysics and from workphysiology—disciplines which, at least in Europe, were hardly seen as domains of psychology but rather of physics and engineering.

The early fifties witnessed a revolution in experimental psychology away from the above research traditions to a conception of the human as an information-processing system. For the ergonomical practice, this provided initially not much more than some theoretical background for designing "knobs and dials" in control rooms. This was still rather peripheral and remote from the ideal to take part in the total concept of system design. However, much progress was made in the course of the recent decades, which is, among others, reflected in the successive editions of McCormick's textbooks, which are now continued by Mark Sanders. This does not mean, though, that there is now sufficient knowledge about human capabilities and optimal usage in automated systems. The point is that the technological advances raise new issues, which, in turn, require other basic research. This has become evident in the increasing emphasis in experimental psychology on complex cognitive issues, relating to problem solving, knowledge acquisition and representation, and internal mental models about the environment. The counterparts in ergonomics are human-computer interaction, design of expert systems, process control and decision aiding, all issues which were fully unknown during the sixties.

1.3 Methodology

The relation between basic and applied research is faced with a methodological problem which is more serious as the involved human-machine system is more complex. The problem may be summarised by saying that human performance in real life consists of more than the sum of elementary skills. It is rather a matter of complex interactions, so that it is hazardous to predict performance in complex systems on the basis of research on elementary mental functions. The alternative is that human behaviour in complex systems is merely studied in realistic simulations with a considerable physical validity. This is not only expensive but there is also the problem that results of simulation studies cannot be generalised either. Hence, studies in simulators under realistic conditions have often rendered disappointing results, although for specific purposes, such as training, they have proven to be highly useful. Field studies suffer from even stronger constraints, in view of problems with experimental control and variation.

Thus, there remains the dilemma that, methodologically, serious objections can be raised to laboratory research on elementary functions as well as to field studies on total work situations. It would be incorrect, though, to sharpen the contrast between these two extreme options too much. Basic as well as field research may be of interest, given a specific set of conditions. In addition there are interesting mixtures, and they do not exclude each other either. Thus, it may be useful to develop a design on the basis of suggestions derived from basic research and, then, to test the adequacy in a simulation. Yet, the trend in ergonomics develops into the direction of specialisms, such as traffic, aviation, robotica etc, which expresses the need of special domain-specific knowledge. In addition there remains a need for generalists, in particular with respect to embedding new developments of a more general nature.

1.4 Human-machine systems

It is now almost trivial to mention the fact that, due to automation, much manual labour is being replaced by supervisory inspection. This is not to say that the problem of physical load has disappeared. The number of back complaints is still increasing, albeit probably due to problems with sitting rather than with carrying heavy loads. Supervisory control means that computer systems and connected equipment perform the task, while the human operator merely watches whether the processes develop satisfactorily. This may be somewhat exaggerated but still contains a great deal of truth. It has been suggested that ergonomics may outlive itself in fully automatised systems, which are fully self-supporting, including issues of trouble shooting and supervisory control. As will be argued in the section on system analysis, this suggestion is wrong. Here it is only noted that the design of total systems always raises the issue which tasks should be performed by human operators and which by machines. In view of the advances in computer technology, this question cannot be answered in any absolute way. Yet, it is interesting to repeat some traditional replies: With regard to routine actions and to remembering large amounts of statistical information the computer is clearly superior. The human is still always better in pattern recognition, although the computer is making rapid progress in this area. When flexible responses to unforeseen and new events are a characteristic of a task, the human operator is still far superior. Yet, the operator cannot be expected to do the impossible, and certainly not when a system is constructed in a way which does not correspond to natural human skills.

This has led to attempts to frame human skills in simulation programs, which, in turn, can be connected to simulations of the machine part of the system. This would enable advance probe trials on total performance of a human-machine system. Although this approach is preferred to total neglect of "the human factor"—as still happens too often—a warning against computerised human performance models should be issued as well. So far the models are too static and sometimes too optimistic about what a human can accomplish. Thus, in some, fatigue and motivation are not taken into account, while, in others, errors is that one cannot assume that they are understood by those who need the information most. Abbreviations, but also numbers and color codes, are only permissible when one can be sure that users know or can easily retrieve their meaning.

Abbreviations are often used on computer screens in order to save space, but the disadvantage is that, although one has acquired their meaning, reactions remain slower and error proportions higher. An example is buying KPN instead of KNP shares or vice versa. There are some general rules for presenting information on screens which are all related to optimal organisation of data with the aim of facilitating search for a relevant target. First, there are the classical Gestalt principles for grouping visual categories. Grouping may be accomplished through spatial separation but also through inserting common features such as colour or contrast. Although combinations of these rules—e.g. spatial organisation together with colour differences within each spatial category—may further facilitate search, one should avoid too many categorical distinctions, since the positive effect of organisation may easily turn into a negative effect of disorganisation. Moreover, the categorical differences should be perfectly valid: When a red colour has a certain categorical meaning, say a type of ship in a listing of all ships embarked in a harbour, an exception to this rule will be difficult to detect. A taxonomy for categorisation should obviously correspond to well-known or natural differences. This is related to the internal representation or mental model of a system which will be returned to in the context of software ergonomics.

2.2   Presentation of non-verbal visual information

The design of non-verbal displays, such as indicators, pictograms, and other icons like arrows, belongs to the classical issues of hardware ergonomics. For example, the optimal design of indicators was an early application of information theory, in which the question was raised how many alternatives could be distinguished on a continuous scale. Meanwhile, there are a number of general design principles: More categories can be distinguished in a single glance on a circular than on a horizontally or vertically shaped display.

It is obvious that the accuracy of a pointer display is determined by the threshold for absolute perceptual discrimination. In line with the Gestalt principles, it is wise to group scale markings by using variation in marker length. A moving pointer usually leads to better accuracy than a moving scale. If quantitative accuracy is the only thing that matters, a digital scale is unsurpassed.

It is not recommended, though, to apply these principles rigidly, since the optimal shape is determined by the total context in which the display is positioned. In the case of a display panel, in which rough deviations of an optimal reading have to be detected, circular moving pointer displays are optimal, provided that the optimal position of all pointers is the same. For detecting direction circular displays are also optimal. As said, a digital indicator is best for a precise quantitative reading, but for estimating aircraft altitude, and in particular for changes in altitude, a vertically moving pointer display is superior due to the spatial correspondence between display and distance from the ground.

This last principle is usually coined "display compatibility", since it refers to the experienced location in space, with regard to body posture. Application of the same principle in representing the attitude of an aircraft with respect to the horizon leads to a peculiar paradox. Thus, one may display the horizon straight and the aircraft oblique—which is the real situation or, alternatively, one may display the aircraft display straight and the horizon oblique—which is the perceived situation, with the exception of rapid changes in attitude. Research (see Wickens, 1992) suggests that neither display is optimal. The best solution is something in between, in which rapid changes in attitude are reflected by an oblique display of the aircraft, whereas slower and smaller changes are expressed by an oblique horizon. In fact, this mixture corresponds best with the combination of experienced proprioceptive and visual information and, hence, is most "display compatible".

The concept of "display compatibility is also applied to comprehension of pictograms or icons, which have the advantage that they do not require specific language skills and that they are better legible, which makes them particularly attractive as information signs in traffic or in buildings. It is evident, though, that their meaning should be self-explanatory. A standard for international acceptance of an icon is that the proposed symbol should be studied in at least six different countries, with at least 66% correct interpretation in any test. An excellent set of icons is presently used in Dutch railway stations (Zwaga & Boersma, 1983).

Recent years have witnessed an increasing interest in so-called integrated or diagnostic displays. The point is that, for many years, an indicator, like a pointer display, provided only information about a single parameter of a system, whereas usually a diagnosis is needed about the state of the total system, which requires an integrated evaluation of all indicators. This raises serious problems in diagnosing complex and rapidly changing processes, which will be returned to in the section on system analysis. Integrated displays aim at summarising the state of a number of indicators into a single value, so as to facilitate the diagnosis of the state of the system. In the design of integrated displays the basic research on perceiving integral dimensions (Garner, 1974) has been particularly useful. Integral dimensions have the property that the resulting perceptual pattern is more than the sum of the variations on the individual dimensions, so that a unique perceptual pattern may arise for each particular diagnosis.

Apart from indicators or icons, non-verbal information is found in warning signals, such as stroboscopic movements at railway crossings or flashing lights on police cars or ambulances, in advertisements and in codes. In the first two cases, non-verbal conspicuity is aimed at. Thus a moving advertisement attracts attention, provided it is the only moving element in the visual scene. Besides movement, one may use colour, form and size as coding principle, single or in combination with verbal information. For instance, a signposting system in a building, a hospital or a campus may encode rooms in terms of a combination of verbal and non-verbal information. Corridors, wings or even whole units, may be indicated by a colour, while the rooms which belong to the specific colour group are assigned a number. One should be careful, though, to limit the number of colors to a maximum of some three or four. Despite the fact that many colours can be distinguished in a comparative judgement, people perform poorly in absolute judgement of perceptual dimensions. An additional advantage of using a limited number of colours is that colour deficient people have no problems, in particular not when colour and brightness covary.

2.3 Visual ergonomics

The discussion of visual information presentation will be concluded with some general remarks about visual factors which should be taken into account in a design. The relevance of proper illumination and contrast was already briefly touched upon. In addition, there is the issue of reflection of shining surfaces or screens. This leads to competition between the reflected image and the text on the screen as soon as the contrast of the text is less than ten times that of the reflection, False reflections can be avoided by using mat surfaces or by positioning lightsources in a way that no reflections are caused. Frequent interaction with computer screens may cause serious visual complaints in the sense of visual fatigue, headache and irritant eyes. There are indications that these complaints may be due to problems with eye convergence, which system takes care of fusing the images from both eyes. If the distance from the eyes to the screen does not correspond with the natural convergence distance—and there are pronounced individual differences in optimal distance—the convergence system is forced to adapt all the time which would cause the above mentioned complaints.

Working on computer displays has a number of other potential problems such as angle of regard and continuous shifts of focus from the screen to a handwritten text and back, which may imply frequent shifts between light letters and a dark background and dark letters and a light background. It is obvious that such shifts should be avoided in the design of the task. Shifts in focus may also subtend a large visual angle, which creates problems of integrating information from successive percepts. Finally, older screens still suffer from flicker. Glare is still always a main problem in traffic and is caused by sunlight as well as headlights.

processes, but also on workstations in offices and work benches for manual labour. The present discussion will not elaborate on issues of presentation and control of individual elements, which were already touched upon in the previous sections. Rather the discussion is concerned with the total configuration which, until recently, used to be characterised by a large number of displays in a complex system, such as a cockpit of a modern aircraft or the control room of a chemical or nuclear plant. There are some intuitively appealing principles with respect to the relative positioning of individual displays or indicators. Thus, important or frequently used displays and controls deserve a central position in the visual field. Moreover, the sequence of use principle states that functionally coherent displays should be close together. Another principle is that clusters of displays should be well separated and distinguished from each other. In this context, the Gestalt rules find a natural application

What is the maximum permissible angle of regard for the information presented in a workstation? Given the prerequisite that the operator should be able to efficiently monitor all displays, the heuristic is that the total panel can be inspected without head movements, which means an angle of regard of no more than 45°. The same is true for relevant information while driving a car—note the position of side mirrors!—and for a typist who should be able to type and read text without making head movements. The heuristic can obviously not be maintained in the case of complex control panels, which, however, means a loss in efficiency. One may admit head movements, which means that the panel may subsume some 120° without turning the upper part of the body. One may resort to swivel chairs when 120° does not suffice—which is still better than to require an operator to walk around. The distance from the operator to the panel is determined by the range of the arms so as to reach controls on the panel and, of course, by the necessary space for the legs. If this leads to an unacceptably small distance between operator and panel—a striking example was the older personal computer which had a combined keyboard and screen—displays and controls might be separated, although this may mean a loss of S-R compatibility.

A horizontal distance of some 60 cm from the panel is still within the reach of the arm, although 40 cm is preferable. This last figure is also the optimal reading distance for verbal information. Another relevant aspect is the type of force that is required to operate the control: 60 cm is appropriate for pulling, while the distance from the panel should be less for an upward or downward movement. When operating a keyboard, the forearm should be perpendicular to the body so that the keys should be no more than 20 cm from the body. In the vertical dimension, the most important controls should never be farther than 50 cm above or below the horizontally stretched arm position—the actual location depending obviously on whether the operator stands or is seated. The type of control is also a relevant factor. A steering wheel should always be below the horizontal forearm position while a discrete response key may well be higher. Since it requires a push response a key may be pressed with the arm stretched, whereas a steering wheel should not be operated with a stretched arm. It is highly important that response keys have sufficient spatial separation and are functionally connected with their corresponding visual information. A separation of minimally 3 cm is needed to minimize errors.

Frequently used visual displays should be about 15° below eye level and perceived at a right angle. Desk height should be in between 65–80 cm and chair height some 40–50 cm, the optimal value depending on the length of the operator. The difference in height between desk and chair should provide the necessary space for the legs. If the task requires the operator to stand—which should be avoided whenever possible—the optimal height of the operating space does not basically differ from what is required when the operator is seated. The relevant factors are the height of the elbow and the required precision of the movements. When great precision is required the operating surface should be some 10 cm above the height of the elbow, while it may be 10 cm below elbow height in the case of less precise movements. As mentioned, one should always attempt to realise a workstation in which the operator is seated. There are of course tasks which require too much mobility to satisfy this requirement, but whether mobility is really needed or the consequence of a poor total design is another issue.

The above considerations are largely a matter of functional anatomy and biomechanics, disciplines which are of prime relevance in workstation design. This is also true for the macro aspects of workstation design, such as the distances and locations of machines, including their display and control elements, in order to guarantee that they can be reached at all. In designing engine rooms for ships this aspect is often neglected. A reasonable passage requires a width of 60 cm and a height of 195 cm but minimally 160 cm is needed. The 60 cm width means that people cannot pass each other. This would require an additional 50 cm. All these figures depend of course on individual differences. All too often workstation design has been based on "design for the average" so that smaller and larger people may experience problems. This was realised and has led to adjustable chairs, desks etc.

A discussion of the requirements for stairs, ladders or chairs is beyond the scope of this chapter, but they are obviously relevant for a proper ergonomic design. The same can be said for the "science of seating". In fact, this is a highly specialised area, among others characterised by the optimal distribution of forces on various parts of the body, which cannot be summarised in a couple of paragraphs. The same is the case for body posture during manual labour. A frequent adverse body posture—such as stooping with stretched legs, resulting in a lot of force on the lower parts of the back—asks for back complaints. However, equally adverse but less recognised body postures are met when seated in poorly designed chairs.

Besides the configuration of displays and controls and the role of human posture and movement, workstations often suffer from suboptimal illumination, which leads to unwanted reflections and unacceptable differences in contrast. False reflections from blackboards are a notorious example! This may be avoided by appropriate positions and shapes of the light sources—avoid a direct point of view of light—and by regulating outside sunlight. It is difficult when sunlight cannot be regulated—e.g. the outside view may be essential to the task. Yet it may fully block perception of

task-relevant information. False reflections from blackboards are a notorious example! Another problem is that one does not want to lose "outside contact", which means that the elimination of sunlight is not accepted. A combination of perceiving outside information and reading from a computer screen—say, when controlling navigation in a harbour—often suffers from an unsurmountable problem of strong differences in contrast due to light from outside. In the case of shipping traffic one may wish to use both direct outside information and radar information, but the light intensities of either task are highly incompatible. In the other extreme, all light has to be excluded to improve contrast on a radar or sonar screen or of electronic plots in a command centre—which should be legible at a somewhat larger distance. Yet, a total dark is not acceptable either, since it excludes reading or writing notes or instructions. Local illumination cannot be recommended since it spoils dark adaptation which is essential to reading the above mentioned low contrast screens. A better solution is a diffuse low level of coloured—preferably blue—illumination, which neither affects contrast nor dark adaptation, while still permitting reading and writing.

Besides the physical properties of a workstation, there is the social element. Many tasks require formal communication among people, which should be possible without distracting those which are not involved. This means another functional requirement of the total configuration of workstations. In addition, though, informal communication plays a part, which should not be neglected either. At least, the issue should be addressed whether one wants to promote or avoid informal communication A distance of some 45 cm between people provides a perfect opportunity for informal contact. The relevance of informal contacts in particular in manual labour, follows from research showing that noise complaints may be due to the fact that informal communication is masked.

To account for all the above factors it is recommended to construct a static simulation of a proposed workstation design—or of a set of work stations—which may serve the role of a blueprint. The static simulations used to be built as full-size electromyogram, (EMG) although the value of the EMG should not be overestimated, at least not in dynamic situations.

The amount of energy consumption—and, thus, physical work efficiency—depends on the way the work is actually carried out. Transport of a load by means of a backpack, which mainly and about equally loads the two shoulders, costs much less than when the same load is carried manually by way of two suitcases. When working on the surface, as in gardening or on floors, posture affects energy consumption. Bending with stretched legs takes about twice as much energy as kneeling. The same work takes less when sitting than when standing. Hence, it makes sense to find the most efficient form, and in particular when faced with a heavy load. It should be stressed again, however, that caloric consumption is certainly not the only criterion for physical load. Merely loading weak spots of the body—and in particular the lower area of the back—by unfavourable postures is gaining weight in an era in which much work is carried out in seated position.

In the case of a somewhat longer lasting heavy physical load—as when running—the demands on oxygen consumption exceed the natural supply which results in an "oxygen debt", the symptoms of which are a painful muscle fatigue and heavy panting. It makes sense, therefore, to avoid too much load. It is hard, though, to define strict criteria for what makes up a heavy load. This depends, among others on state of training, age and sex.

3.2 Mental work load

In many cases, manual demands have been replaced by operating machines or, when the task has been fully automatised, by supervisory monitoring. This development belongs to the main reasons for the interest in hardware ergonomics, in which context the issue of mental work load has been studied since the fifties. There are two main avenues: One may be too busy or too bored.

Intuitively, a work load problem arises most logically from too heavy demands on information processing. Provided one has a certain fixed capacity for information processing, it is evident that certain limits should not be exceeded, and this

has been the leading notion in developing work load measures. A first measure is the so-called timeline analysis, a modern version of time and motion study, which consists mainly of recording the time taken by any activity required by the task, both in the sense of observable actions and of thinking and deliberation. Besides an estimate of the total amount of time taken by the task, timeline analysis is interested in overlapping activities. The idea is that one may not do more than "one thing at a time", so that too much overlap implies overload. Recent applications of timeline analysis use computer programs, such as SAINT and MicroSAINT.

A second measurement technique is by way of a so-called secondary task, which equally starts from the idea that one can do only one thing at a time. The second task serves as a loading task, in that the better it can be carried out the less the load of the main task. Various second tasks have been proposed, among others production of a regular interval (tapping), generation of a random letter sequence, reacting to incidentally occurring stimuli and simple arithmetic. Although the second task is sometimes found to be a fair reflection of the demands of the main task—e.g. in car driving on different types of road—the method is only rarely used for a number of good reasons. First, one should have the guarantee that the second task has no negative effect on the main task. In particular in the case of time-critical main tasks a suspicion would render the technique unacceptable. Second, there are doubts about the sensitivity of the secondary task technique. The main problem is that the technique may not be insensitive to the nature of the main task. The point is that there is accumulating evidence in favour of so-called "multiple resources" or qualitatively different types of processing capacity, which correspond to the specific demands of main and secondary tasks. If this is the case, performance on the same loading task would be better in combination with some than with other main tasks, depending on whether or not a particular combination taps different or the same resources. The consequence would obviously be that a simple secondary task performance measure would be inappropriate as an estimate of mental load.

A third method for measuring work load aims at estimating the amount of spare capacity by increasing the usual demands of the main task until performance failures can no longer be avoided. An important restriction of this technique is that one should have a valid simulation of the main task, since committing errors in the real task is usually not permissible. One task in which this method was successfully applied was air-traffic control. Increasing the number of aircraft to be controlled within a constant period of time led to an estimate of the capacity limits of the system, as well as an estimate of the usual work load—also in terms of number of aircraft. The advantage of testing the limits over a second task is that, albeit at various levels of actual demands, subjects perform only the main task, the load of which is actually the main interest of the study.

Much research has been devoted to the feasibility of estimating work load by some psychophysiological measure, with measures of heart rate, and in particular heart rate variability, as prime candidate. More recently, evoked brain potentials have been considered as well. Yet, there is little chance that a standard practical application will be successful. In this regard, there has been considerable progress with measurement of subjective judgements. In particular the SWAT technique—Subjective Workload Assessment Technique—has proven its merits in a variety of perceptual-motor tasks, among bus drivers and helicopter pilots. The method simply consists of the regular production of a set of three estimates, by way of the digits 0–2 (e.g. 2–0–1) to indicate respectively (a) the degree of being busy (b) the complexity of the present activity and (c) the experienced stress. Prior to the actual judgment the method demands individual calibration of the weights of the three dimensions by conjoint measurement so as to arrive at a single load score. A disadvantage of the technique is that it does not say anything about the question whether a certain level of estimated work load is acceptable from the perspective of actual performance. A fairly high load, but not high enough to lead to performance failures, is already likely to elicit a 2–2–2 estimate, so that the SWAT is insensitive to differences at the high side of the load continuum and does not indicate whether the main task can be completed

without errors. On the other hand, the SWAT has the advantage of a high sensitivity at the low side of the load continuum, where performance measures are of little value since the demands can be met anyway.

In summary, it can be said that, given the present state of the art, work load can be determined best by a combination of a subjective evaluation technique and a behavioural index. Normally, the behavioural measure will consist of some type of timeline analysis, although, if possible, a measure of spare capacity by testing the limits should be preferred.

3.3 Boredom

The above measurement techniques were all engaged with determining the upper limit, in order to determine to what extent the operator can cope with high task demands. In so-called vigilance tasks the issue is reversed since, apart from some incidental adjustments, the operator is idle. Research on vigilance has shown that underload leads equally to suboptimal performance, in that simple but somewhat faint target signals tend to be missed. Signal detection analysis has shown that the effect is not merely a matter of a decrement in perceiving signals but also due to a tendency to be passive—i.e. adopt a higher response criterion. Knowledge of one's performance—hits as well as misses—is a good method for counteracting the decrease in vigilance and, more generally, the effect of monotony. In practice this may be impractical or impossible to do, in which case one may consider presenting artificial signals and limit knowledge of results to the latter category. It should be noted that boredom and loss of motivation, to which the vigilance effect is thought to be due, has a similar effect in short cycled repetitive work.

3.4 Noise, sleep-loss and psychotropic drugs

Noise is a frequently studied adverse environmental condition which has a number of potential effects. The first effect concerns hearing impairment which is found to occur when regularly exposed to intensities beyond 90 dBA. Continuous noise is not necessary to bring about a hearing loss. Regular exposure to brief intensive bangs, as on a military shooting range, is sufficient to cause the effect. The common countermeasure is wearing protective noise attenuating ear plugs. A second effect of noise, which occurs at intensities over 60 dBA concerns masking of speech which hampers social communication. The effects were already touched upon in the discussion on auditory information processing. Furthermore, noise has psychophysiological effects, which are most easily demonstrated in the case of sudden bursts. The ensuing startle response consists of a general sympathetic reaction including muscle contraction, increase in heartbeat frequency, pupil dilatation and an increase in skin resistance. However, this pattern of reaction disappears soon after the startle response has passed, so that it is quite uncertain whether regular exposure to short-lasting noise—as in the vicinity of a busy airport—inflicts direct physiological damage. There are epidemiological data which suggest that living near an airport is mentally unhealthy but it is uncertain to what extent startle responses contribute. It may as well be due to annoyance, sleep-loss or anxiety which may all arise from aircraft noise.

Much research has been devoted to potential effects of noise on performance with mostly inconclusive results. If any, the effects are usually minor and dependent on specific task demands, such as short-term memory load and sustained attention. In either case, brief periods of distraction are damaging. It has also been found that perceptually loading tasks are more sensitive to noise than primarily motor tasks, and that noise tends to have the effect that decisions are made less carefully. This last effect has been sometimes ascribed to an overactivating effect of loud noise. According to the activation hypothesis noise has a stimulating effect when a person's activation level is low and a disintegrating effect when it is already high. Indeed, there are results suggesting that in a state of low activation, due to, say, sleep-loss or monotonous work, noise has a positive effect on performance and in particular when the task demands are sensitive to activation as in predominant motor activity. From this perspective it is not surprising that accompanying music is particularly appreciated when the task demands are mainly motor and much less when they have a

strong perceptual or cognitive component. In these last cases, the distractive effect of noise may be dominant.

Of all adverse environmental conditions, sleep-loss has by far the strongest effects on performance. Both perceptual and motor activity appears to slow down. It should be noted that the decrement is not gradual, but that brief periods of inefficiency and normal functioning alternate. In the case of monotonous work, such as in quality inspection, targets are liable to be missed, whereas reaction time increases when targets are clear but unexpected. Lack of sleep induces passive behavior in the sense that one tends to react rather than to anticipate on forthcoming events, which is particularly dangerous in dynamic tasks as driving, where sleepiness may well account for a considerable proportion of accidents.

Yet, the effects of sleep-loss are less general than might be suspected. Thus, central cognitive functions of reasoning and decision making seem to be less affected than perceptual-motor functions. For instance "interesting" work is still done quite well after a night of sleep loss. It has been suggested that interesting work activates, thus counteracting the deactivating effect of sleep-loss. The problem with this view is that variation of cognitive load—by varying S-R compatibility—in an otherwise equally monotonous task is little sensitive to sleep-loss, whereas a larger perceptual load—by degrading the visual signal quality—or a larger motor load—by introducing unprepared reactions—appear quite sensitive to sleep-loss. Obviously, this should not be taken to imply that the central functions are never affected by sleep-loss. Research on performance "round the clock" for 72 hours has revealed a sharp decline in more complex tasks as well, but performance is surprisingly little affected during the first 24 hours.

Effects of sleep-loss can be counteracted by stimulant drugs, such as amphetamine and caffeine, but also by motivational stimuli. A nice example of a motivational effect concerns knowledge of results which has the effect of eliminating most of the effect of 24 hours sleep-loss. When performing over a longer period of time—e.g. a half hour period of continuous work—there is little evidence for an effect of sleep-loss during the first five or ten minutes of work, the effect rising sharply during the remaining period. The conclusion is that one is not simply governed by deactivation but that, at least temporarily, effort investment may compensate performance impairment.

The last paragraph leads to consideration of effects of psychotropic drugs, such as stimulators, tranquillizers and sedatives. The effects of clinically prescribed doses are certainly measurable but they are minor in comparison with a night's sleep-loss. It is interesting that the size of the effect of stimulants depends on the level of activation. They have little effect on performance after a night of normal sleep, whereas the same dose may fully annihilate the performance decrement caused by a night of sleep-loss. In other words amphetamine has no absolute but a relative effect, depending on the distance to the optimal activation level. It is known that the effects of amphetamines and tranquillizers are mutually compensatory and that the thrust of the effects is on motor functions. In contrast a sedative—e.g. a barbiturate—has its main effect on perceptual processing. This type of result leads to a cognitive-energetical theory in terms of two major energetical supply systems: One (arousal) is phasic, dependent on outside stimulation and particularly relevant to perceptual processing. The second system (activation) feeds mainly motor processing, its effects are tonic, and it is only indirectly related to outside stimulation. Both systems are coordinated by a third hierarchically supraordinate system, which is under conscious control and may be coined "effort". A main task of the effort system is to guarantee an equilibrium of the lower order arousal and activation systems. Thus, it is capable of compensating for too little or too much arousal or activation. In this context, stimulants and tranquillizers affect activation, barbiturates have their prime effect on arousal, whereas sleep-loss affects both systems. Negative effects can be modulated by effort, which has the consequence that the laboratory effects—where subjects know that their performance is being monitored—are probably much smaller than those in everyday life (Sanders, 1997).

The last suggestion may also explain why effects of alcohol are much less dramatic when tested in the laboratory than may be expected on the basis of observation or epidemiological data. Many laboratory studies show only a minor performance effect, even after considerable alcohol consumption. Again, effort might compensate the negative effects, and certainly in short-term tests. One may of course compensate as well in real life conditions, but it is possible that there is not always sufficient motivation to do so. This suggests laboratory conditions in which a normal situation is approximated as much as possible. As said, little effect should be expected in short-term tests; however, effort is supposed to decline as a function of time-on-task so that the real effects of the drug should become more visible as time proceeds. One should be obviously careful to eliminate any implicit or explicit encouragement to do well and abstain from knowledge of results. Yet, the minor alcohol effect in the laboratory may as well have a different background. It could be that in real life the effect of alcohol is more pronounced due to an interaction with other deactivating stimuli. Thus, the depressant effect of alcohol when consumed in combination with a tranquillizer is considerably stronger than the effect of either drug as such. Again, the disinhibiting effect of alcohol may be much stronger when consumption is accompanied by party-like social stimulation than when consumption occurs in the quietness of the laboratory. In the same way the effects of long-term performance and vigilance on performance are minor after normal sleep in comparison with 24 hours sleep-loss. Combinations of adverse conditions—or more generally of conditions which affect energetics, as knowledge of results and motivation—strengthen or weaken the individual effects, depending on whether they activate or deactivate.

3.5 Stress reactions

The notion that the state of the basal mechanisms of arousal and activation are controlled by effort suggests a number of divergent stress reactions (see also Chapter 7 of this Volume). A stress reaction occurs whenever effort falls short of achieving the desired equilibrium in arousal and activation so that there is an obvious lack of optimal energetic supply. A first deficient state concerns situations in which arousal is overstimulated, as in the case of unexpected emotional or threatening stimuli, which cause panic. Stress arises when effort is incapable of inhibiting the arousal level, which has the effect that performance control is considerably weakened. In contrast, monotony has the effect of too low a level of arousal, in which case effort should increase arousal. If failing, the stress response reflects the perceived performance loss. A similar reasoning leads to another two stress responses when effort cannot compensate over- or under-activation, while, finally, effort may have a direct energetic effect on the central processes of reasoning and decision making, which could fall short as well.

A direct application of the model is found in the analysis of work situations with a paced or self-paced rate of work. In a paced condition the speed is prescribed by the system which has the effect that a previous unit should be completed when the next unit arrives. In other words one cannot afford brief periods of inefficiency due to fluctuations in activation. In turn this requires continuous effort investment. A range of studies has indeed shown that paced work elicits harmful physiological stress reactions. Hence, paced work should be avoided, unless the rate of pace is sufficiently low or the work spell is sufficiently brief to forgo effort investment.

3.6   Temperature and motion

Responses to heat and cold are fully described by heat exchange between the human body and its environment. In the case of a high temperature (30°) exchange occurs mainly through transpiration. The contribution of transpiration is negligible at temperatures of less than 20° in which case exchange occurs primarily by direct radiation and indirect air transmission. Heat exchange is determined by a combination of factors, namely air temperature, humidity, wind and temperature of objects in the direct environment. This is acknowledged in the definition of heat, i.e. an effective temperature (ET) of 21° implies a heat sensation of 21° at a humidity of 100%. In comparison ET is about 27° when humidity is only 10%. In addition the role of wind is taken into account in the ET definition.

From a human factors' perspective, the effects of heat on body temperature are of course most relevant. The general heuristic is that, during manual labour, the body temperature should not exceed 38° because body temperature appears to rise relatively fast once this temperature is reached. The effects of heat on physical labour have been well established: Given a reasonable humidity and a temperature of 30°, continuous physical labour should not last more than 30 minutes, not even in the case of moderate caloric demands. The effects of heat on mental tasks depend also on duration and, again, a fairly sharp performance loss should be expected when ET exceeds 30°.

The notion of a comfortable temperature has the problem that people acclimatise, so that subjective comfort may be optimal in a range between 17° and 22°. However, when ET drops below 15° most people find the environment cold, at least without protective cloths. Accurate and detailed motor tasks are negatively affected at an ET below 15° whereas there is little evidence for a negative effect on cognitive tasks. Effects of lower temperatures can be usually prevented by adequate clothing—again with the exception of fine motor movements.

The effects of motion are concerned with a range of issues among which are vibration, acceleration, deceleration and motion sickness. Vibrations can be regular or varying and vary in frequency and amplitude. The intensity is a combination of amplitude, displacement, velocity and acceleration of motion. In the case of varying vibration it is common to determine the frequency spectrum, in which intensity is plotted as a function of frequency. Thus, cars and aircraft have an about equal spectrum at the low frequencies, whereas higher frequencies (10–30 Hz) are much stronger in a car. Vibration may be a problem in truck driving and in operating equipment such as a pneumatic drill. The problem is physiologically reflected in an increased muscle tonus, which has the effect that manual tracking is less precise. The continuous displacement of the body as a result of vibration has the effect of a degraded visual perception. Yet, the effects on cognitive and perceptual-motor tasks are minor so that the above effects may be fairly direct and subject to compensation. Yet, there could well be an accumulating effect as a function of time-on-task, and much depends on the actual characteristics of vibration:

When in the range from 4–8 Hz, they are particularly hard to endure, even when they are low intensity, since the body tends to follow the movements. Higher frequencies are easier to bear and as frequency increases, intensity may increase as well.

Effects of acceleration and deceleration (g-forces) are mainly a problem for professions such as military pilots and astronauts. They have serious effects on a wide range of performance tasks. Moreover, there are illusions in regard to movement direction, in particular in the case of a combination of acceleration and movement of the head into the opposite direction (Coriolis illusion). Motion sickness refers to a general feeling of depression and nausea, and is found to occur in the case of regular motion with a frequency of less than 1 Hz. It is a common problem on ships, but may occur as well in cars or airplanes The effects are usually ascribed to incongruity of information from different senses, and in particular vision, kinaesthesia and equilibrium. Motion sickness can lead to severe disfunctioning on a ship.

3.7 Domain of application: Shift work

When discussing energetic factors, the notion of biological rhythms was not yet raised, notwithstanding the fact that they strongly contribute to work efficiency. Normally, the level of activation increases during the morning, decreases somewhat in the early afternoon—the so-called post-lunch dip, although actual food intake appears to have little effect on the dip –increases again in the course of the afternoon, reaches its highest level in the early evening, decreases strongly late at night and reaches a low in the early morning. The level of activation has a clear relation with performance in high speed tasks. It should be noted, though, that this picture applies in particular to extraverts. It is much less pronounced with introverts, who are typically more activated during the morning and less during the afternoon. The effects of rhythm increase after sleep-loss, in that, following a night sleep-loss, a poor performance in the early morning improves considerably during the late morning, which is followed by a much more pronounced post-lunch dip and a much stronger decrement during the evening.

The above results are relevant to shift work, which is characterised by working at unusual hours of the day or of the night (see also Chapter 5 of this Volume). In the case of three shifts, a usual scheme is 7.00–15.00 (the day shift), 15.00–23.00 (the evening shift) and 23.00–7.00 (the night shift). One may conceive of a wide variety of schemes—including one in which a person is always working in the same shift—but it is common practice to rotate, so that a changing rhythm is asked for. The rotation can be slow, in which case a change in working hours occurs after a week, interrupted by a few days off, or fast, in which case the shifts follow each other in rapid succession, albeit usually a fixed one. An important element is whether the shifts continue during the weekends. It is evident that the problems aggravate in air traffic where a shift implies a shift in time zones as well.

From the perspective of biological rhythms, it is not surprising that most problems arise with the night shift, since one is supposed to work at the low point of activation and is expected to retire when activation is rising again. This is among the reasons that the night shift people sleep less than those of the other shifts, which results in an accumulation of sleep-loss. The prime question is of course whether and to which extent a rhythm may adapt to the change in conditions. There are indications that, even when a person always works at night, the rhythms do never adapt completely. One reason could be that, when a couple of days off duty, most people return to their common day scheme. Both night shift and shift rotation are harmful, the extent of which depends on personal characteristics and on type of work. If night shift as such is viewed as the main problem one may decide to introduce a shorter cycle—i.e. less consecutive nights. Alternatively, if rotation is seen as more adverse one may wish to rotate less frequently. Although there are preferences for either a short or a longer cycle, there is no convincing evidence in favour of either one, although, when viewed merely from the perspective of biological rhythm, a show cycle is less disadvantageous. A slow cycle is also preferable for older employees (>40 years), who have gradually more problems in adapting to change and suffer more from sleep disturbance. One may also hold that older employees should be completely exempted from night shift. However, biological rhythms are not all important. For instance, is it possible to sleep well in a society which is mainly active during the day? If sleep-loss accumulates a long period of night work is obviously hard. How well may one maintain social contacts, when involved in evening and night shifts? Social events are primarily during the evening so that both the evening and the night shift are at a disadvantage. Which cycle permits optimal arrangement of spare time? This requires the possibility of planning ahead and of trading shifts. These arguments favour a short cycle. Yet, studies on employee's preference show a slight trend in favour of a somewhat longer shift. It should be admitted, though, that the results are not fully consistent, and are likely to be dominated by personal habits.

In regard to the literature, there is the somewhat older but still very useful book of Edholm (1967). The work of Tichauer (1978) is also recommended. There is an extensive literature on effects of environmental conditions, which might be entered by reading the papers in Hockey, Gaillard and Coles (1986) and, on psychotropic drugs, in O'Hanlon and De Gier (1985). With respect to shift work one is referred to Folkard and Monk (1985), and with respect to noise, to Davies and Jones (1982).

4 SOFTWARE ERGONOMICS

Software ergonomics is concerned with the dialogue between the human and a computer-controlled system. Each system has a set of operating rules which operators should have at their disposal in order to control the system. It is a matter of software when the operating rules do not directly follow from the system components as such but from system programs. The basic issue of software ergonomics is the extent to which these rules are adapted to the characteristics of the operator with special reference to memory, learning, knowledge representation and reasoning. It is evident that this type of dialogue is not exclusively found in human-computer interaction. Hence, the notion of software ergonomics is often extended to include any ergonomical question related to processes of memory and thought. In this wider sense it includes computer simulation of mental processes—the so-called expert system—as well as the areas of system analysis and decision making, which will be discussed separately in this chapter.

4.1 Short-term memory

It is common in theories of memory to distinguish between short- and long-term memory. Short-term memory is always concerned with memorising a limited number of cognitive elements, which should be available for a brief period of time. In contrast, long-term memory refers to issues of meaning, knowledge and established action procedures. Short-term memory is sometimes conceived of as an interaction between perception, attention and memory, since aspects of all three of these mental functions play a part. Thus, the capacity of short-term memory depends on the availability of acquired codes, on relations among these codes, but also on the degree to which the codes are phonologically similar, and on the readiness to keep the codes under cognitive control. Short-term memory is of prime relevance for any mental process. It retains the surface structure of what has been perceived most recently, thus enabling extraction of essentials and integration with earlier encoded contents. When short-term memory is deficient—usually a clear sign of dementia—it is hard to keep track of a line of thought. Short-term memory is often connected to the "magical number seven"—the size of the memory span—which is actually a fairly arbitrary number. It has been known long since that a much longer sentence can be perfectly reproduced, whereas retaining three or four items may raise a problem. A typical everyday example concerned the introduction of the secret code for bank passes. Initially, many people proved to have problems in reproducing their four-digits code, despite the fact that this number is much less than the magical number seven. The problem is that, irrespective of their number, items are rapidly forgotten when they are not continuously rehearsed or intentionally learned by heart, in which case the four-digits code is added to the database of knowledge. It is evident, though, that retention is increasingly poor as the number of items is larger. Most people do not know their bank account or car registration number. Moreover, due to their sheer length, many errors are committed when copying an account or dialling a telephone number. Error rates are reduced when different cognitive categories are involved: A series of letters should be preferred above a series of digits, in particular when the letters permit recoding of the series into a meaningful or even into a pseudo word. A combination of letters and digits—e.g. KGS385—is superior to a digit combination, such as 217385, whereas a list of three digits followed by three letters is retained better than a combination like KG28SL. Application of these principles in assigning alphanumerical codes is obviously useful.

As mentioned, when forgetting has to be avoided, codes should be added to the database or remain under continuous attentional control. The problem is that learning alpha-numerical codes belongs to the most unfavourable ways of knowledge acquisition, namely paired associate or simply rote learning. This is relevant to the design of programming languages and text processing systems which employ a lot of alpha-numerical codes. Linking these codes to natural language or to other compatible representation modes prevents a lot of artificial and cumbersome learning. For efficiency reasons, designers of programming languages tend to use meaningless codes such as "i" and "x" rather than, say, Next and Max, despite the fact that these last codes correspond more closely to the existing knowledge of the user. This is only a simple example, which will be further elaborated in the discussion of using meaningful codes in text processing.

4.2 Navigation in programming

Programming languages may be classified as navigational versus non-navigational. In the first category, the user should not only describe the actions but also the relations between actions by using the syntactic elements of the programming language. In this way, the user instructs the system how to solve the problem which obviously requires a great deal of skill in handling the syntactics of the programming language. In the non-navigational approach the program has more control; it presents the user a menu of questions among which a choice should be made; the choice, then, leads to a new and more detailed set of questions, and so forth. The menu approach makes full use of the natural language, which has the effect that the user does no longer program the solution himself but merely follows the path as recommended by the system. This may be achieved by a menu but equally well by a sequence of questions which all require a simple answer.

Navigational and non-navigational methods have both their own merits. The advantage of the non-navigational method is that the user finds solutions without actual demands on programming knowledge. The disadvantage is obviously that the possible solutions are strictly limited to the domain of the menus. Another problem concerns the degree of detail in the sequence of menus. A slow build-up, each small step of which has to be completed, is annoying when a user is capable of taking larger steps. Moreover there is the objection that the user does not gain real understanding of the system and its potential, although one may doubt whether this is really needed for solving the problem at hand. Yet, a navigational language is more suited as the users are more skilled, since it creates the operating space which a skilled user wants to have. In the case of a navigational procedure one is required to issue a sequence of verbal instructions; alternatively there is the option of a combination of verbal instructions preceded by a flow diagram. The benefit of a flow diagram may depend on the degree of detail: In general a flow diagram is made up of somewhat larger steps, so that each step requires its own program. This is usually better than a very much detailed flow diagram in which each element corresponds to a single instruction. In the case of an experienced programmer, it is unnecessary to structure the problem by means of a flow diagram, but for the less experienced one it is a perfect aid. In addition it is very useful as a demonstration of the logic of a program. Another valuable aid concerns specified computer comments following each instruction. The computer informs about the consequences of the instruction, so that the programmer can evaluate whether it actually contributes towards achieving the desired aims. Thus, it plays the role of immediate feedback. Direct indication of errors—instructions which violate the rules of the programming language—serves a similar aim.

It is evident that similar principles are applied in computer-aided instruction, in which the computer plays the role of a teacher. There are rapid developments in this area that will strongly affect the didactics of all kinds of subjects. A particular point is that the programs require precise specification of which types of didactic aids are most beneficial to learning and skill acquisition. Among the examples of didactic principles are various kinds of feedback of results, error analysis, non-verbal illustrations, and return to earlier covered material that has been insufficiently understood or assimilated. Besides the expectation that pupils will learn faster, since they are immediately informed about errors and their nature, it has been well established that feedback is motivating. The evidence that faster learning is achieved notwithstanding, there are still serious problems with respect to the quality and scope of the programs, which rapidly gain complexity as the issue is more complex. For example, the program must be aware of all types of errors and potential misunderstandings of a problem. Besides application to teaching in schools, computer-aided instruction has a promising future in retraining courses in industry.

4.3 GOMS

Experience is a decisive element in human-computer interaction. Experience refers to the degree of knowledge that a user has about the system, which determines the scope of the aims that can be achieved and which is part of the well-known GOMS model. GOMS is shorthand for Goals, Operators, Methods and Selection rules. Aims are determined by the task and vary in complexity; operations refer to the control potential of the system; methods are production systems which lead to a specific result; finally, given the aims of the task, the selection rules determine which methods are optimal. Experience is mainly a matter of availability of elaborate methods and selection rules.

The advantage of GOMS as an abstract conceptual model is that it emphasises the potential gap between a user and a specialist who actually has the task of developing a programming language. The specialist tends to overestimate the user's

level of experience, which problem is, for that matter, not uniquely connected to human-computer interaction but plays a role as well in composing users' manuals for controlling and operating equipment, such as an oven or a video-recorder. The indications are almost invariably technical and declarative-explanatory and fail to provide the appropriate procedural "methods" so as to accomplish the desired aims. There are poignant examples of incomprehensible manuals, which has the effect that many options of technically excellent equipment remain unused. The best strategy for constructing a manual is to carry out a micro task analysis of the actions required for achieving a certain goal, followed by definition of the production rules for each separate action. It is of prime importance that the manual aims at transferring procedural rather than declarative knowledge. Moreover, the texts should be as brief as possible and be supplemented by illustrations and videotapes. This is particularly relevant for instructing emergency procedures, such as in the case of a hotel fire or of problems during a flight. It is highly doubtful whether the present practice suffices in cases of stress and panic.

4.4 Search in external memories

An important aspect of human-computer interaction is concerned with a search for files, which becomes an urgent problem when files are poorly defined or when their number exceeds manageable limits. Searching for a limited set of papers on a specific subject in a library is a good example. In that case, detailed search should be preceded by a retrieval specification of the category features to which the desired file belongs. Human memory may not be the appropriate metaphor for optimal construction of data file systems. The problem is that, at least thus far, external memories are serially searched, whereas search in human memory has strong parallel components as well. When searching for a poorly specified file, one may use a list of key concepts, some of which contain features of the desired file. A proper combination of relevant key concepts, then, may either directly lead to the desired item or to more detailed key concepts, which contain more concrete features of the item and, thus, limit the number of alternatives. In this way the model for data file search has the following steps: (1) determine the features of any desired file; select a list with key concepts which together determine the area in which the file should be; (3) specify further features—and hence new key concepts—whenever the earlier ones proved too general or incomplete; (4) determine a list of possible files which obey a particular subset of key concepts. If this list turns out to be too large, step 3 should be repeated, until the number of alternatives has become manageable.

This may sound simple but, in fact, constructing a well functioning system is highly complex. It depends heavily on the quality of the key concepts, which, in turn, depend on whether they are prototypical for the corresponding items. Suppose the question is to retrieve which diplomats took part in undersigning the Camp David agreement. One may decide to consult a key concept such as "diplomatic agreements". On itself, this keyword would produce a multitude of agreements so that it should be accompanied by a number of additional key concepts which together permit retrieval of the Camp David one. The Camp David file may tell that the agreement was between Israel, Egypt and the USA and the date it was signed, but not mention the names of those taking part. Yet, the newly available information may deliver new features, such as the nations involved and the date on which the agreement was signed, so that in combination with a further key concept such as "diplomats", the names of the actual undersigners can be retrieved. Thus, the accessibility of data depends very much on how well key concepts cue the data. This means that redundancy in the system is quite relevant. When designing a data search system it is recommended to decide on the set of features by logical analysis as well as by empirical checks.

4.5 Expert systems

In an expert system the computer takes over intelligent tasks, and assists in analysing problems, reaching a diagnosis and recommendations for subsequent action. Thus, in the area of medical diagnosis a computer may ask routine questions, analyse the answers, transmit the data from laboratory tests and generate hypotheses for the ultimate diagnosis. In the case of deciding whether a client is creditworthy, a bank has to arrive at a diagnosis as well, in which case the computer may state a number of questions and arrive at a recommendation. An important task for software ergonomics in building expert systems is the so-called knowledge elicitation, i.e. determining the way in which experienced experts arrive at their final judgement and translating expert knowledge into elements which are manageable for the computer.

4.6 Domain of application: Text processing

Text processing is probably the most widespread application of the computer. There are various systems available, which are all in continuous development so that ergonomical evaluation is always dated soon afterwards. Various factors play a part in the evaluation of text processing systems. One is the way in which a system can be mastered by the average user. A satisfactory system must be easy to comprehend, which has the additional advantage that the usual fear for computers is eased. Rapid mastering and user friendliness are of course related but should be separately mentioned. Does the text as it appears on the screen correspond with the ultimately printed text? This should be expected from a user friendly system. What is the potential of the system? This is of course a relevant aspect, but a system with more options is not necessarily superior. The question is rather what is needed by the user, which has to be determined by task analysis. Thus far, the potential of a system has been too much a matter of the personal taste of computer scientists, who design systems but have little feeling for what the average user can manage and needs to do. Unfortunately, this is not only the case for text processing!

In the following two—now dated—systems will be compared since they had fully different starting points, i.e. the traditional WordPerfect system under MS-DOS 2.11 and a traditional Apple text processing system, such as MacWrite. Either system has now new versions, which tend to become more and more similar—but the initial principles of the Apple text processing philosophy remain unchallenged. The typical feature of the Apple programs is that all procedures can be carried out with spatially organised movements through controlling a mouse, so that the keyboard is completely available to typing verbal text. Hence, function keys are not found on a typical Apple keyboard. In contrast, WordPerfect required keypress responses for any action; the connections between responses and actions are listed and should be acquired by mere rote learning. In regard to procedures general ones—such as choosing, arranging, copying, starting, stopping and deleting—can be distinguished from direct procedures—such as saving, choosing of letter font and formatting. In regard to general procedures MacIntosh has the so-called desktop metaphor; there are files with documents on the desktop and there is a waste paper basket. The advantage is that the organisation of data files corresponds to what the operator is used to do when writing and filing papers on the desk. With respect to direct procedures there are menus with clear texts, such as "cut" and "paste", which can be operated by simple aiming movements of the mouse. Again, the text appears on the screen in the same format as it is ultimately printed.

Thus, the Apple programs have a large correspondence between action and effect, which avoids paired associate learning of meaningless codes. Moreover, the correspondence between text on the screen and in print prevents errors from occurring. The result is that the basics of the program can be mastered in a couple of hours, and—perhaps more importantly—are resistant against disuse. This is also due to the separation between verbal and spatial actions, which utilises a larger variety of human cognitive potential. In contrast, at least in its original forms, WordPerfect was highly incompatible; even verbal codes were inconsistent. One could maintain that pressing a "P" for "print" is a fair option, but how about "E" for "renaming", "O" for "copy" and "Y" for "delete"? Moreover, there was a lack of consistency for the various levels of the menu: In the main menu "Del" meant that a character was removed, whereas Ctrl-T implied that a word was removed. Once on the submenu, removal of a character was now achieved by Ctrl-S! This is the more serious, because the human internal representation of the processing system does not correspond to the potentials on the level of the menu but on the structure of a coherent set of actions, which together achieve a goal. This means

action sequences which run through all levels of the menu.

It is hard to understand why, the ergonomical inferiority notwithstanding, the MS-DOS systems have managed to survive throughout the years. It is correct that the MacWrite program had less options, but, as said, it is doubtful whether a wide variety of options is really utilised by the average user. It has been shown that, when keyboard commands have been mastered, the execution time is less than for mouse commands, so that skilled operators might prefer key press commands for procedures. Yet, the time needed for mastering the commands is excessive and largely a waste. The argument that carrying out mouse commands leads to "less knowledge of the system" does not convince either. It may well be that the preference for MS-DOS operated systems was due to commercial interests, which did not take ergonomical aspects into account. In this regard, the trend is rapidly changing since user friendliness is becoming a prime issue in getting a wide public ready for the computer era.

A wide variety of applications of memory research can be found in Baddeley (1990). In regard to human-computer interaction there is, among others, the classical work of Card, Moran and Newell (1983) and the edited volume of Van der Veer and Mulder (1988).

5   SYSTEM ANALYSIS

5.1   Supervisory control

This section is closely connected to the previous one. The main difference is that, whereas software ergonomics is foremost concerned with the individual interaction between man and computer, system analysis refers to process control in computer operated complex systems. Examples include nuclear and chemical plants but also more and more tasks like flying aircraft. The operator has the task of error detection and correction and one may correctly wonder whether this may not be automatised as well, so that the human operator is fully excluded. There remains the problem, though, of potentially unknown or unexpected failures, which the computer is unable to solve. In fact, the task of a process controller is unattractive since (1) (s)he has the left-overs which are hard to automatise, (2) (s)he has a boring task in which nothing happens as long as the system functions properly and (3) (s)he is expected to find the correct solution in case of emergency. Besides the potential of reacting creatively and flexibly, this type of task is not very well suited to the human operator. One problem is that the operator has excellent knowledge of the processes and possible error sources, while the usual supervision task does not involve any practice.

What does it mean to know an automatised process? The operator receives data about the flow of events by means of values of process variables, on the basis of which (s)he should construct a judgement about what is going on. In order to evaluate the data, one should have a correct internal model of the total process. The first question then is whether the operators have this at their disposal. Engineering models on process control sometimes assume that a correct internal model consists of a set of mathematical formulas with parameter values which should not exceed a certain safety margin. In everyday reality, people appear to have a more functional model, consisting of a set of heuristics which cover the normal functioning of the processes. The problem is of course that the functional model may fail in unusual conditions, in which case no adequate solution can be found. The most common procedure for counteracting the lack of experience with a malfunctioning system is to practise simulated emergency procedures; among others this is a normal routine for civilian aircraft pilots. There remains the problem, though, that unknown conditions may arise but the hope is that simulator training leads to a sufficiently differentiated internal model, which enables creative solutions for unknown situations. It is evident that this implies the implicit but unproven hypothesis that the trained scenarios provide prototypic procedural knowledge, which can be generalised to new situations. However, the available evidence suggests that neither declarative nor explanatory knowledge leads to procedural knowledge; again, experience in process control does not lead to skill in manual control.

One of the main problems in the study on mental models is a lack of tools for analysis. It is not surprising that attempts towards solving this issue have given a new impetus to classical techniques, such as introspective reports and protocol analysis. The attempts have not been completely unsuccessful, although they have shown that non-verbally represented components of internal representations are hard to mould into a verbal description. Thus, the proper methodologies are still a matter of research and debate, so that, its impact on the adequate form of simulator training programmes notwithstanding, a reliable analysis of the structure of a mental model remains problematic. There are presentation techniques, though, which promote obtaining an optimal model of a process. One is presentation of a composite flow diagram of the main process components and their interactions in a single dynamic scheme. The issue is always how detailed the diagram should be and according to which principles it should be constructed. One option is direct correspondence with the real flow of processes, whereas, alternatively, one may decide in favour of a diagram depicting the functional effects of process components and their mutual interaction. A flow diagram is already an example of a diagnostic or integrated display, which has the characteristic that it summarises the combined status of a set of parameters, which together, suggest an essential property of the system. Another option is construction of tests about the status of the system, which have the additional advantage that the operator is more active. One should be warned, though: The Chernobyl nuclear disaster was, among others, due to the fact that a planned test was carried out, while the system was already malfunctioning! This suggests a highly relevant problem in process control, namely that malfunctioning is so rare that one tends to neglect indications about errors.

Even when operators have a good internal model, the data on the displays may be ambiguous and lead to an incorrect interpretation. One example was the display about the safety valve of the cooling system of the Three Mile Island nuclear plant, which indicated the command—open! close!—rather than the actual status. This meant that a situation could arise in which the display suggested that the valve had closed—i.e.

safety records, in order to identify what went wrong. Practically all research into safety criteria is of this second type. A third strategy is the most logical, comparing safe and unsafe companies in order to see where and why they differ. We know, unfortunately, of no such study. As a result it is on purely practical grounds that we start by following the "in search of misery" tradition, studying accidents as a way of understanding safety. As our argument develops, however, we will move towards an "in search of safety" approach, in which accidents play a minor role in determining how safety is to be assessed and managed.

3 WHAT IS AN ACCIDENT?

To study accidents one must first define what an accident is. Definitions may involve the requirement for medical treatment, the undesired release of energy or hazardous substances or even just the creation of unwanted situations. An accident may involve a cut finger, but could also involve losing in excess of a billion dollars without the loss of life or limb. One can philosophise deeply over the issue, but such discussions are of little value in practice. This is not to say that there are no definitional problems in the real world. On the contrary, the practical definition of what constitutes an accident is a major determinant of the accident statistics, so much so that without a deep insight into the definitions used the statistics are almost absolutely meaningless. Comparing different companies, whether in the same or different branches, in the same or different countries, the same or different sizes etc., is impossible in practice, because it is obvious that different definitions will have been applied.

Often accident statistics distinguish between fatal accidents and those that lead to at least one day off work (lost time incidents or LTIs). One can also register smaller accidents (restricted work cases or RWCs) and near misses where no one gets hurt. Most organisations still do not do the latter, at least not systematically. At first sight fatal and LTI accidents appear to be clear categories, but even applying those criteria creates difficulties. Someone just avoids being hit by a falling piece of concrete, but dies shortly thereafter of a heart attack that *might* not have happened without the shock of the falling block. Is this a fatal accident to be registered by the safety department, or a case of illness to be registered by the medical department? A child, despite all warnings, plays on a construction site, is run over by a truck and dies. The child wasn't even on the payroll of the construction company! A typist traps several fingers in a drawer, and, as a result, cannot type for three days. The typist can, however, still work as a receptionist. Is this an LTI or an RWC? In our own field studies we have seen how a victim was unceremoniously deposited outside the "fence", because accidents "outside" don't count; we have seen people after they have had an accident being redeployed for two weeks as a "guard" on a location where there was nothing to guard, just because this ensured that the accident was recorded as a less serious RWC rather than an LTI! This latter redefinition was important because a significant bonus was promised for each group that reached a million man-hours worked without an LTI.

Definitions can be extremely important in determining what happens in the workplace. It is even possible for victims to be withheld medical assistance because calling in a doctor automatically leads to registration of an incident as an accident. Problems of definition are less important when accidents are not the principal measure of safety, but only provide one of a number of measures. This is the reason why, in our own research, we have used a simple rule of thumb: an incident is treated as an accident when the company provides it to us defined as such. In this case it is at least being defined as an event the organisation would rather avoid and researchers who place themselves at the service of industry have no reason to disagree with such a clear wish. Furthermore, it will become clear in what follows that ordinary observations also provide vital insights into the criteria for safe work.

4 THE GENERAL CAUSAL CHAIN

When studying accidents it proves worth while to develop a general conceptual framework, so that more general facts can be obtained from individual and highly variable events. Discovering such a general framework requires a cyclical process. Before one starts one has no idea what analytic structure might prove effective. Initial hypotheses about what is important need to be proposed, refined and rejected. After a number of accidents one begins to develop a vague notion of what might prove effective, by the thousandth one has acquired the necessary insights. But, this approach requires regularly revisiting the first accidents to see if the latest proposal actually works. The structure proposed in this chapter was developed using such an iterative approach. There are many other structures; researchers tend to follow their own tastes and preferences. There is nothing wrong with that, so long as their structures meet a number of requirements. A more detailed description of the general causal chain we use is described in Wagenaar, Hudson and Reason (1990) and Wagenaar (1991).

Figure 4.1 represents the general accident causal chain. By *general* we mean that it is applicable to every accident; by *causal* we mean that it describes the necessary conditions for the occurrence of accidents. Eliminating any one of the links in the chain breaks the chain, so that the accident no longer happens. We treat the diagram in reverse, from right to left, backtracking from the accident to the original decisions that led to it.

5 THE ACCIDENT ITSELF

An accident is the final result of the causal chain. It is, nevertheless, not always clear exactly which event one should choose to regard as the accident. Is it the fall or the injury? Is it the explosion or the ensuing deaths? Often people think of prevention in terms of the placing of some barrier between the physical event (the explosion) and the consequence (the fatality). Examples of such last-ditch preventative measures are safety helmets, seat belts, lifeboats, ejection seats, escape routes etc. The absence of such a final line of defence may be the result of a structural shortcoming in the safety policy or its implementation. This is why for our definition the accident is the fatality, not the

explosion that led to someone dying, the injury rather than the fall. This definition, framed in terms of the general pathway, allows us to analyse accidents, near misses and, even, situations in which nothing has yet gone wrong in a consistent and systematic way.

6 DEFENCES

This approach makes it immediately clear what we mean by the second element, the defences, represented in Figure 4.1 as a shaded barrier interpolated between unsafe acts and the actual accident. Defence mechanisms are there to ensure that explosions do not result in accidents. Nuclear power plants are usually constructed with a so-called containment, a very strong concrete construction capable of withstanding an explosion, in order to prevent the release of radioactive material. Of course, there is no intention that the reactor be allowed to explode in the first place, but *should* it happen, such a containment represents a good defence. Where people work and hazards are involved, defences are always necessary. If and when people do fail, that should not lead inevitably to a disaster. This consideration is so important just because people most certainly will fail. Relatively simple actions, such as pushing a button on a control panel, reading a meter, opening the right valve or performing a sequence of five actions in the correct order, are performed incorrectly at least once every thousand times (Swain & Guttmann, 1983). When work is so organised that such errors lead inevitably to accidents, the necessary defences must be missing. It is not for nothing that the computer asks, before you delete everything in a directory, "Are you sure?".

There is one form of defence that we know really does not work, that is the use of specific instructions and procedures in which errors are not allowed, but no further preventative measures are taken other than telling people not to do it. When an error can result in disaster, there is little to be gained from simply forbidding that error. People do not, on the whole, make errors willingly, so forbidding unintentional errors is of little effect. See section 7.

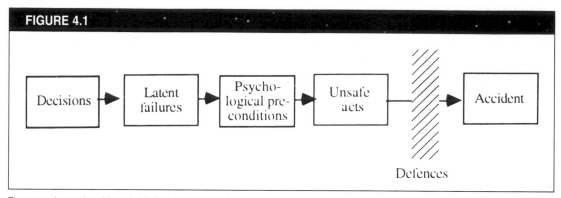

FIGURE 4.1

The general causal accident chain. Accidents are at the end of a long chain starting with a fallible decision.

6.1   Inherent weaknesses in defences

The major problem with defences is that no one defence system is completely safe. Alarm systems can be turned off and, sometimes, must be disabled. The Chernobyl nuclear accident is a good example as performing the safety test, which is what they were doing when things went wrong, required negating the normal alarms. People take pride in beating the system; in such cases defences can increase rather than decrease the dangers. For instance, in a certain location, work may only be carried out when the fire brigade is present. Therefore there are two locks on the door, the key to one is held by the firemen, the other is held by the maintenance department. The intended effect is that the door should only be opened when the fire brigade is present. In practice the door forms a challenge to the maintenance men to prove that, with their technical ability, they are not to be held back by a simple lock. Winning means opening the door, *without* the firemen.

Even so-called inherently safe systems are never completely safe. Here we are talking about systems that, with any disturbance, fall into a safe state as a result of the application of the laws of nature. A simple example is an "automatic level crossing half-barrier". The boom is held open by the application of a voltage on an electrical circuit. Should the electricity fail for any reason, the barrier will automatically fall into place as a result of gravity. But, this requires that the hinge is not rusted solid, that saboteurs have not propped the boom open, that, just as the boom is falling, no large vehicle is passing underneath which is subsequently trapped. Guaranteed safe is not even a characteristic of inherently safe systems; the only pure guarantee is provided by not undertaking the activity.

The design of defences requires that one has sufficient insight into the kinds of errors people make. The problem is that some errors are hard to envisage in advance. Who would have thought that a qualified electrician would have touched a 10 kV switch gear without first checking to see if it was live (cf. Wagenaar et al., 1990)? Who would have imagined that construction fitters would remove so many bolts from a steel bridge that it would fall down on its own (cf. Bignell, Peters & Pym, 1977, ch. 5)? Who would have predicted that the operators at Chernobyl would withdraw all the control rods in the reactor so that the process became uncontrollable (cf. Report of the USSR State Committee, 1986)? One cannot expect to design and construct defences such that the effects of human error will be totally eliminated.

6.2   Defences may induce errors

Defence strategies can lead to extremely fundamental discussions within organisations. The best example is the Automatic Train Control System. In principle that is a system that allows the driver to perform all the control functions of the train, but which intervenes whenever the driver makes an error. Drivers could get the feeling that they are being observed by such a system. There is also an anxiety that drivers might be sloppier because they know the system will always correct their errors. A driver could, as it were, consider passing through a red signal at full speed, because the system will still stop the train. This discussion has led to the situation that in The Netherlands the automatic system now only checks whether drivers brake for amber warning signals, not whether they stop for red. Driving through red has, as a result, become a daily occurrence. The error, once made, is not corrected by the defence that should have been there.

There is even the chance that a defensive system actually reduces overall safety. For example, an operator does not attend closely when warming a liquid in a pressure vessel. The automatic pressure protection fails to work and the vessel explodes. As a result it is decided to make the vessels much stronger. The result now is that the next time there is an explosion it will be considerably larger than the first one. The safer method, surprisingly, is to make the vessel *weaker*, so that in case of failure there will be a smaller explosion. Many defences have this counter-intuitive consequence, of making smaller accidents less likely, but when they *do* occur, the accidents are now more devastating. Train crossings are no longer manned, but shut automatically, resulting in fewer open crossings that should have shut. Because the safety margin is no longer seen as necessary, the delay between closing the crossing and the train arriving can be significantly reduced; this reduction can be so much that a train cannot stop once the track is blocked (cf. Bignell et al., 1977, ch. 8).

In summary, we can state that while defences against error are necessary, at the same time we cannot expect that they provide sufficient protection against all errors. An effective safety policy needs to encompass both defences and measures intended to make those defences unnecessary, in practice.

7 UNSAFE ACTS

Practically all accidents are preceded by unsafe acts that we identify with human errors. That does not mean that the acts will have been recognised as unsafe, let alone dangerous. In the majority of cases that is just what happens. Unsafe acts may be regarded as those acts that, with hindsight, we would regret had things turned out badly. In order to understand this we have to go in depth into the sort of errors we can distinguish.

7.1 Reason's GEMS model

Reason's (1990) model of operator behaviour (GEMS = generic error-modelling system) synthesises the theories of Norman (1981) and Rasmussen (1982, 1983). The diagram in Figure 4.2 summarises the theory. In the first instance behaviour is seen as being determined at three levels. At the lowest level, the *skill-based* or automatic level, actions are performed as reflexes. Here we have sequences of actions organised hierarchically in schemas. An example is going home after a day's work. I pack up my briefcase, leave the room, exit the building, find my car and then drive home. Each piece of the "mother" schema consists of a "daughter" schema. Leaving my room involves a sequence of putting on my jacket, picking up the briefcase, turning off the light, opening the door, stepping through the door, locking the door. The daughter schemas themselves consist of "granddaughter" schemas, so locking the door requires finding my keys (mostly in the right-hand jacket pocket), finding the correct key, the one with the two separated holes on top, inserting it into the keyhole, turning (clockwise), removing the key, replacing the keys in the jacket, checking if the door is really locked. Inserting the key, in its turn, requires moving the key towards the keyhole, minimising the distance until contact is made, pushing until resistance is felt etc. GEMS proposes that each of these actions is performed automatically and then automatically calls up the next in the sequence once there is satisfaction that the step has been completed successfully, according to the expectations carried in the schema. At this basic automatic level extremely complex sequences of actions can be performed, punctuated by control checks on success.

The transition to a higher level, the *rule-based* level, occurs when the control check reveals that not all has gone to plan. For instance, when the key fails to fit the hole, the sequence cannot proceed. A solution to this problem must be found. At the

FIGURE 4.2

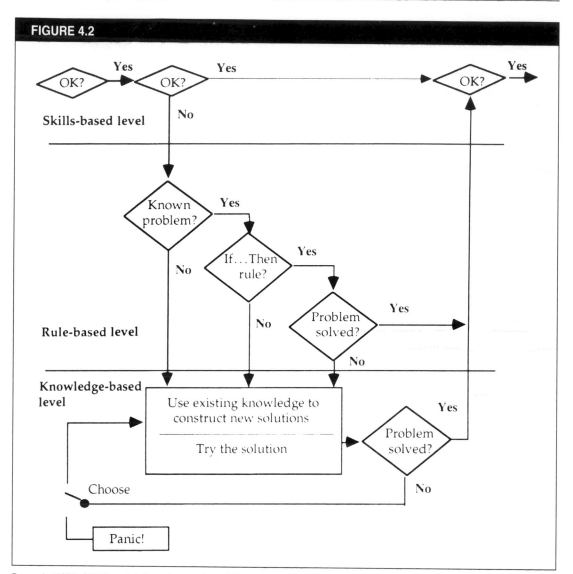

Reason's (1990) GEMS model. Operation on three different levels involves dropping from the skills-based to the rule-based level in case of an identified failure, while dropping to the knowledge-based level is caused by inability to solve at the rule-based level.

rule-based level, solutions are found to be appealing to *if. . . then* rules. *If* the key does not fit, *then* try another. A study of solutions to everyday problems (Wagenaar, 1992) revealed that people have the same rules in their heads. In the case that the key fails to fit, people have the following rules:

1. use a bit more force;
2. check to see if you have the correct key;
3. check to see if the key is damaged;

4. look to see what is wrong with the lock.

The rules are based upon what previously helped in similar situations, rather on any fundamental insight into the nature of the problem. The most frequently successful is tried first (using more force) even when it might have negative consequences (the lock on my car is now broken).

When the situation is not recognised as belonging to a known type, or the rules fail to solve the problem, then behaviour is shifted to the *knowledge-based* level. At this level a new solution is sought for based upon insights, often from first principles. Therefore it is necessary to diagnose the nature of the problem, discover the cause and finally think of a way to remove that cause or circumvent the problem. If I find the wrong bunch of keys in my pocket, I still have to work out how to get the door locked. This may involve working out where my keys really are, how and whether I can get them and, if not, knowing who has a copy key (we share room keys within the department so this problem now becomes, who is left in the building?).

7.2   The GEMS error taxonomy

The most important advantage of the hierarchical organisation of actions, as is used in GEMS, is that the majority can be performed without directing any attention to them. There is no alternative possible, because the majority of actions have to occur in parallel. This parallel character ensures that most of our actions can be carried out highly successfully and rapidly. With a parallel architecture, however, overt attention can only be directed to one process, rather than be directed simultaneously over all the processes, which means that the others are not attended to, which in turn can lead to problems. The parallel architecture provides the system with enormous capacity, but the downside is that errors can occur in those processes that run without attention. The system is designed to detect and correct error, by predicting what is expected to happen in a purely feed-forward manner and checking progress against those expectations. But, such checks will not always happen or will themselves be erroneous and an error may be the result.

7.2.1   Skill-based errors: slips and lapses

Errors at the skill-based level are distinguished into *slips* and *lapses*. Slips are errors of commission, failures in the performance of a plan that is itself good. They arise for all sorts of reasons. The best known type is the double-attention slip. The situations in which this occurs are when one is following a plan where at first a known scheme is followed, but which is meant to diverge at a certain point in the sequence. At the point of choice the

attention is diverted (thus "double-attention") and the execution follows the old scheme. A clear example of a "double-attention" slip is : "We now have two refrigerators in the kitchen and yesterday we moved all the food to the new one. This morning I kept opening the old one" (Reason, 1990, p. 48). A second type of error at the skills level is the "lapse after an interruption". Whenever a scheme is interrupted ("someone called me on the phone") it is difficult to pick up the task execution at the same point. A third type of error at the skills level is loss of intention: "I was going upstairs to get the stapler, but when I got up there I could not remember why I had come upstairs".

Lapses form a crucial type of unsafe act, because they are much harder to detect and, therefore, to counter. Controlled "flight into terrain", more obviously the result of mistaken behaviour of pilots and, occasionally, air traffic controllers, remains the prime direct cause of air crashes. Analyses of the causes of aircraft crashes show that the second major cause is maintenance-related. In an analysis of 276 in-flight engine shut-downs, Boeing found that 34% were due to incomplete installation after maintenance and a further 11% were due to equipment not having been installed, or left out. While the omitted items seem trivial, such as fastenings left undone or washers missing, these may be more than enough to cause a crash.

7.2.2   Mistakes: rule-based and knowledge-based errors

At the rules level completely different errors occur, which are mostly called "mistakes". It is typical of mistakes that the plan is wrong, not the execution of it. The best explanation of mistakes is therefore wrong planning. When the plan is executed, at the skills level, then it is impossible to detect the error at that level; all that is being checked for is deviation from the expectations built into the plan. At the rules level mistakes always have something to do with the applied rule. This is true when the situation is classified incorrectly. For example, the situation during the accident at Three Mile Island (Rogovin, 1979) was incorrectly identified as a less important problem which had been ongoing for several weeks. The rule applied led to a worsening of the situation instead of to a solution. It is often the case that before the signals which indicate what is actually happening are received the problem has been explained away. Rules are ordered in a certain hierarchy: rules that are often applied successfully, become more powerful and win the "race" more easily for application in a concrete case. General rules are usually stronger than special rules, for example: *use water to extinguish fire*. However, when there is a fire in a pan with oil, water only makes it worse; *do not use water but cover the pan*. This special rule is difficult to apply, because the general rule is applied almost impulsively. This is an example of errors of the sort *strong* but *wrong*, in which what are usually the best solutions turn out to be the wrong ones. Another problem in the application of rules is that the use of "bad rules" is often systematically rewarded. The life threatening procedure that the crew of the *Herald of Free Enterprise* used for loading vehicles is a good example of a bad rule. The use of that rule, however, formed the only possible way for the ship to keep to its timetable and it was therefore systematically rewarded. The application of such a bad rule leads in the course of time to accidents, but whilst being used that can remain hidden for a long time.

At the knowledge level once again completely different errors arise. Unlike rule-based processing, knowledge-based reasoning involves starting from scratch and working things out from first principles. We often call failures to find the right solution at this level "mistakes" as well, but here the origin is entirely different. Mistakes at the knowledge-based level arise because a reasoned solution to a problem is incorrect, because too little of the problem space has been considered in the solution (Evans, 1983), because the quality of the solution was not critically investigated (Nisbett & Ross, 1980), or because of too much self-confidence (Wagenaar & Keren, 1986).

A complete review of the various types of errors at the different levels can be found in Reason (1990). The brief overview given in Figure 4.3 will have to suffice here. The most important point in the figure is the clear distinction into four

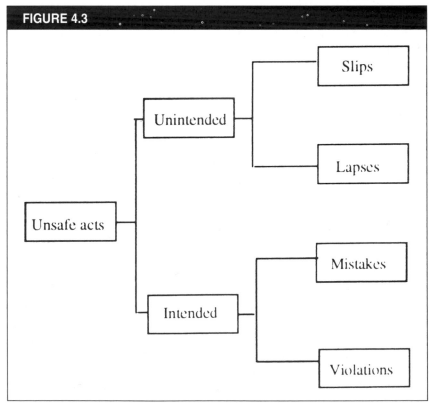

FIGURE 4.3

Four sorts of unsafe acts. The four sorts of human error each constitute different types of unsafe acts.

categories of human error: slips, lapses, mistakes and violations. The first three of these cannot be avoided by instruction, or persuasion, by making personnel aware of the importance of safety nor by motivating them in special courses.

7.3 Violations

Only the last category, violations, consists of errors which people make consciously. Violations are deliberate, and therefore intentional, actions. Programmes intended to increase safety consciousness are mostly expected to have an influence on violations, but that influence is limited. The best known example is the wearing of seat belts in the car. Approximately 25% of car drivers/passengers do so voluntarily. Following the introduction of legislation making it compulsory the percentage of wearers rises to 50–60% (according to Slovic, 1985). Through checks and punishment this percentage can become even higher. Ninety per cent is certainly obtainable, but the investment in control is then considerable and has to be maintained. The reason is that some people find the seat belt uncomfortable, unnecessary and ineffective. This attitude is difficult to change and obedience of the law must therefore be enforced.

Contrary attitudes form an important problem in the compliance with rules, but not the only problem. It is a common occurrence that rules are simply not known or are wrongly interpreted. The minimum condition for the use of rules and regulations is that there should be regular checks to see whether the rules are known and understood. This precaution is no more than the regular check carried out on fire extinguishers, but is in practice little used. One of the most important causes of the fatal disaster on the Piper Alpha oil and gas production platform (Cullen, 1990) was that an employer of a maintenance company did not know the work permit rules. The fire on the Dutch submarine, *Walrus*, whilst it was under construction is mostly likely to have been caused by a foreign welder who, through his lack of knowledge of Dutch, did not know what precautions had to be taken when welding on board (*Report on Cause of Fire on Walrus*, 1987).

Another important reason why rules and regulations are not followed is that following them is impossible. Occidental, the owner of *Piper Alpha*, had prescribed that the head of a platform is in command of combating accidents. As a result of the explosion however the necessary equipment was knocked out so quickly that command within the *Piper Alpha* platform was impossible. Noone took over command, because the regulations had not foreseen this possibility.

Deliberate failures to follow procedures within the industrial setting are, unlike more everyday situations such as road traffic, not necessarily the result of poor attitudes to safety and bad intentions. Studies of offshore workers (Hudson & Verschuur, 1996) found that the intentions are not the problem, but expectations derived from previous experience are. If "impossible" procedures have not been improved and the quality of the planning makes corner cutting necessary to meet deadlines, violation is to be expected. Violators are also characterised by feelings of special competence, of being capable of bending the rules safely. This approach to the following of rules is seen as the exercise of initiative, when it is successful, and a violation only when things go wrong.

Violations, being deliberate, are not regarded as errors. Nevertheless they are not necessarily malicious and can be regarded more as mistakes by people who do not oversee the bad consequences or who sincerely believe that those consequences will not happen when they are in charge. Because of such beliefs violations form the most dangerous category of human error. In particular violators assume that everyone else is doing the right thing, carrying out the necessary checks and inspections. The fact is that while the intentions of others may be good, unintended errors can interact with violations and lead to disaster (Free, 1995).

7.4 The prevention of unsafe acts

From what has been stated above it will be clear that unsafe acts cannot always be prevented by forbidding them or by convincing people that they should, above all, work safely. Even violations are performed by well-meaning employees who are trying to get the job done. In a modern adult company, lack of commitment, motivation and even knowledge are seldom the cause of unsafe behaviour. An analysis of behaviours which lie at the foundation of hundreds of accidents on ships is shown in Table 4.1 (drawn from Wagenaar & Groeneweg, 1987). The table shows the successive steps in the decision process that lead to unsafe acts. In the first phase information must be received about the threatening danger; in 21% of the cases this information is missing, so that a decision cannot be consciously taken. In the second phase the information that is available must be understood to be an indication of danger; that is not the case in 27% of cases. In the third phase, when the danger has been recognised, a list of possible alternative plans of action must be drawn up; in 15% of all cases only one possibility is seen as plausible. In the fourth phase the alternative plans of action have to be evaluated for their possible risks; in 36% of cases the risk attached to the action plan that is finally opted for has not been recognised. Only in the remaining 1% of cases is there a consciously accepted risk. This analysis illustrates that accidents are seldom the consequence of deliberate violations, caused by lack of motivation or suchlike. In the majority of accidents the unsafe acts are slips and mistakes. The conditions in which slips and mistakes are, so to speak, provoked, follow directly from the description which is given above. Unsafe acts can, in particular, be prevented by taking away such conditions.

Example: double-attention slips occur when a task must be carried out in which the initial sequence is identical to that of a known task, but where the remainder is different. At the point at which there is divergence from the routine extra attention must be paid otherwise the known routine will be followed automatically. But at the skills level the routines unfold without any accompanying attention. A new task like this creates a working condition which provokes accidents. Whenever it is not possible to address the task in another way, then in order to actually carry it out correctly, at the point of choice extra precautions have to be taken, for instance a written checklist, extra supervision or an extra control afterwards.

7.5 Taking risks

When we look at the unsafe acts which people carry out, the illusion that easily arises is that people takes certain risks knowingly. It is then assumed that the possibility of a wrong outcome is appreciated beforehand, but that the chance is underestimated, or that it is assumed that operators incorrectly underestimate the importance of unsafe acts (according to Hofstee, 1987; Wagenaar, 1987). This conclusion has led to the introduction of programmes in which they attempt to alter the behaviour of the employees by persuasion. The premise is however incorrect; it is only seldom that the person committing the unsafe act realises what the possible consequences are. The impossibility of foreseeing the consequences of unsafe acts is based on the complex nature of accident scenarios (according to Wagenaar, 1986; Wagenaar & Groeneweg, 1987). Accident scenarios are in general very complex, even when the accident is a simple fall. The actors in the drama do not know the whole scenario; at the moment that the relevant events occur simultaneously to form

TABLE 4.1		
Decision phase	*Number of accident scenarios in which the decision went wrong*	
	Absolute number	*(%)*
1. Receipt of information	17	21
2. Detection of problem	21	27
3. Finding options	12	15
4. Evaluation of consequences	19	36
5. Conscious acceptance of risk	1	1

Where decisions about risky actions go wrong in 57 accidents at sea, reported by the Raad voor de Scheepvaart (Shipping Council) in 1984 and 1985 (some accidents are represented on more than 1 line: from Wagenaar, 1991).

the necessary coincidence, the concurrence comes as a complete surprise. Up until the last moment the accident, which happens in a very short period of time, is considered to be impossible. As soon as those involved realise that there is a real chance of an accident, they then take action. This means that "possible" accidents do not take place, and "impossible" accidents do (see also Jørgensen, 1988; Östberg, 1984).

In the previously mentioned analysis of ship accidents (Wagenaar & Groeneweg, 1987) it appeared that in 51% of the cases the necessary knowledge was divided between two actors in the drama, who did not know of each other's actions. In an analysis of 21 fatal accidents in oil production the comparable number was 86%. The number of unsafe acts that were necessary to cause an accident in both studies is shown in Table 4.2.

In the analysis of shipping accidents there were four more instances in which no clearly unsafe act was taken. In oil production this "act of God" situation did not occur at all. In the shipping industry on average 3.4 unsafe acts were needed, in oil production that was 8.0. These numbers do not mean that workers in the oil industry make more errors: on the contrary, in the oil industry there are far fewer accidents than in the shipping industry. The numbers mean only that through better organised safeguards errors in oil production do not lead so quickly to an accident: on average you need eight to create an accident. On the other hand it will, however, be clear that the limit has just about been reached in the oil industry: it is not likely that scenarios in which eight unsafe acts concur can be overseen by those present. Refraining from such acts cannot be expected in the basis of insight into the consequences. Reading the extremely complex scenarios of accidents such as the disaster in Bhopal, the fire in King's Cross Underground Station, the running aground of the *Exxon Valdez*, the explosion on *Piper Alpha*, the reader will realise that the actors in these dramas were not able to recognise their unsafe acts as such. On the contrary, they did what they usually did. Their actions were performed on the skills level or, at most, on the rule level. At both these levels the risks entailed in actions are not considered. A conscious analysis which leads to a choice for or against unsafe actions, as described in Table 4.1, can only be performed at the knowledge level. That is to say, the problem must first of all have led to a shift of control from the skills level to the rule level. There the insight has to have been that the situation does not fit into an existing category and that consequently no rule is available for the solution of the problem. This transition to the highest level generally only occurs after the accident is inevitable or has even occurred. For a more extensive discussion about risk estimation and the committal of unsafe acts we would refer you to Wagenaar (1990a, b, 1991).

7.6   Unsafe act auditing

The American process industry company Dupont has developed a safety strategy which is based on the prevention of unsafe acts. The basic idea behind it is that unsafe acts are recognisable as such and that employees can protect themselves and others against them. The technique consists of learning to recognise a number of sorts of unsafe acts. Thereafter at all levels within the organisation people have, as part of their task, to walk around and identify and report the unsafe acts they have observed. The technique has been introduced into many companies and has even become an important sales product of Dupont. It is always difficult to establish whether a strategy "works" without studies being performed with carefully chosen control groups. Dupont claims without

TABLE 4.2		
How many unsafe acts are necessary to cause an accident?		
Number of Unsafe Acts	*100 Shipping Accidents*	*21 Accidents in Oil Production*
0	4	0
1	3	0
2	22	1
	26	0
3	22	2
4	14	2
5	5	1
6	2	1
7	2	1
>7	2	14

much evidence that "unsafe act auditing" can bring about a dramatic improvement in the safety of a company. The only evidence to this effect is from Dupont's own accident statistics but, as stated, without having an insight into the precise definition of accidents a statistic can be difficult to interpret. In any case it can be said that the principle, according to which unsafe acts are always recognisable in advance, is not very plausible. The technique will be particularly effective where the personnel are committing many violations; that is to say, in companies which have a rather poorly developed safety policy. Slips, lapses and mistakes cannot however be prevented in this manner, because they are not committed consciously. They are caused by the manner in which the work is organised and unsafe act auditing cannot affect them. Unsafe act auditing is at its most effective when the *reasons* for the unsafe acts are analysed and attention is paid to the more underlying causes. The success of companies that have implemented unsafe act auditing may be attributed to their raised level of management commitment to safety, that led to implementing the behavioural technique. As the factors have never been partialled out, no firm positive conclusions can be drawn about the success of such an approach in the absence of other, deeper-seated, approaches.

8 PSYCHOLOGICAL PRECURSORS

Unsafe acts are difficult to combat when the conditions under which they take place are not known. These conditions demonstrate a clear system, which are directly linked to the three levels of Reason's GEMS model. The conditions under which errors arise in the execution of skills programmes are not the same as those in which the wrong rules are applied, in which analysis at knowledge level leads to incorrect solutions. In general we can state that performing tasks under conditions of haste, with insufficient communication and lack of necessary knowledge, are conditions that can be almost guaranteed to lead to error, despite the best of intentions.

In addition there are also conditions which force

the transition from lower to higher levels. For example: the execution of a complex task which is rarely performed. The low frequency means that factors which induce errors at knowledge level are now offered their opportunity. Such an observation leads to the reasoning that such infrequent tasks should be avoided. It is better to set up specialist teams which, wherever they are needed, come in to carry out such tasks. An example of this approach is the setting up of police arrest teams who take over the dangerous job, for arresting officers and the arrested alike, of making arrests. Completely in line with this is the increasing tendency of large companies to subcontract work to contractors; these are companies whose daily business is carrying out jobs that the parent company cannot specialise in. The disadvantage of such a working method is that naturally more actors are introduced who, not knowing about each other, can contribute to the elements of an accident scenario. On *Piper Alpha* 188 of the 226 on board were working for a contractor; employees of a maintenance contractor had removed the pressure safety valve from a compressor system, which was then started up by the operators working for the parent company. If the maintenance had been left solely to the operators, that almost certainly would not have happened.

8.1 Precursors of errors at skills-based level

The conditions that lead to errors at the skills-based levels cannot be exhaustively listed. But a few are important enough to be mentioned here.

- The execution of a new action which hides a highly automated scheme of action. For example: changing to go out to the theatre, but instead pulling on one's pyjamas.
- The execution of new action which in part is very similar to a highly automated scheme of action. For example: driving in a new car, in which the controls for the indicators and the windscreen wipers are reversed.
- The lack of a scheme of action that runs automatically. For example: being disturbed by the telephone when making coffee.
- The presentation of very similar stimuli, whereby an incorrect but highly automated scheme of action is started. For example:

walking towards the telephone when the kitchen timer rings.

- Executing two schemes of action simultaneously. For example: drinking a cup of coffee when eating chips, whereby the sugar is sprinkled onto the chips and ketchup is put into the coffee.
- Over-attention, whereby a highly automated scheme of action has to be performed at the rule or knowledge level. In section 9 we will indicate further when these precursors occur.

8.2 Precursors of errors at rule-based level

At the rule-based level errors occur when what are in fact good rules are applied in incorrect situations. Here are a number of examples.

- A situation occurs for the first time, so that the correct rule is not yet known.
- The situation is difficult to classify because there are many misleading signals.
- The situation is difficult to classify because there are too many signals.
- The situation strongly resembles another situation for which a "strong" rule exists.

Errors at rule level also occur when bad rules are applied. In this event we recognise the following situations.

- In some situations the *if* part of the *if . . . then* rule is too general or not sufficiently specific. An example: the crew of *Piper Alpha* had been taught that under no circumstances were they to jump from the platform. In the circumstances of the disaster it appeared to be the only way of saving life. All those who survived had, in the end, jumped from the platform into the sea.
- The *then* part of the *if . . . then* rule is incorrect. An example: *if* you suddenly see a car appear in front of you in the mist, *then* you have to brake strongly. *If* you want to keep the company running, *then* you have to economise on personnel costs.

The rule-based level may produce mistakes by being driven by the situation, represented by the *if* part. This is a feed-forward or forward-chaining mode of thought, as emulated by some expert systems. Alternatively, incorrect *then* parts may be applied in attempts to diagnose situations in a backward-chaining mode, such as used by MYCIN-type expert systems (Buchanan & Shortliffe, 1984). Rule-based mistakes of action or diagnosis are characterised by inappropriate rule selection followed by performance based upon the belief that the choices have all been made correctly.

8.3 Precursors of errors at knowledge level

At the knowledge-based level errors principally occur for two reasons: firstly because only a part of the problem is overseen; and secondly because incorrect knowledge is the basis on which action is taken. Here are several examples of typical errors at the knowledge-based level.

- *Selectivity* Attention is only given to part of the problem. The best known example is that in which a rule is thought up without asking oneself what kind of reaction this will produce in those involved. Example: A general prohibition on alcohol is introduced in a company without considering what the risk is of the various tricks that the personnel will use to get round that rule.
- *Out of sight, out of mind* Parts of a problem, which are not clearly presented, are easily missed. A risk analysis of a new industrial activity does not usually demonstrate how people contribute to accidents; those who take a decision on the basis of this analysis do not fill this deficiency in.
- *Preference for confirmation* People have the tendency to seek and select information which supports their own solution. Arguments to the contrary are ignored.
- *Unmotivated self-confidence* This occurs in particular when a lot of energy has been invested in looking for solutions (*sunk-cost effect*); when the solution is a compromise between various parties; when the solution is the product of a hidden agenda.
- *Halo effects* There is a tendency to rank solutions on only one dimension; for instance, in order to find the simplest (or the cheapest) solutions it is assumed that these are also the best.

- *Underestimation of complexity* Attention is only given to a simplified description of the problem, without being consciously aware of doing so. The devil lies in the details.
- *Diagnosis problems* Often solutions are based on an incorrect diagnosis of the problem. Such solutions can have a strongly counterproductive reaction, as in the near disaster in the nuclear power station at Harrisburg. There it was believed that the radioactive material that was leaking away was caused by a defect that had existed for some time. The actions which were subsequently taken made that problem greater rather than smaller. Even when the solution has been proven to be wrong there is a tendency not to review the diagnosis.

9   LATENT FAILURES

While psychological precursors provide the conditions under which unsafe acts are committed, it is questionable whether a safety management system should be based upon the identification of such precursors. Psychological preconditions are "mental states" that are not directly accessible to external inspection. While some precursors may be extant for some time, many often come and go almost as rapidly as the unsafe acts they permit or generate. Precursors, such as haste or ignorance, are also notoriously difficult to quantify. The specialised experience of a contractor and the almost inevitable blind spots that go with that experience may be guessed at, but are not to be measured. This is probably the reason why there are no safety systems that, while attempting to go beyond the unsafe act, concentrate upon the immediate precursors. The next stage, that of latent failures, is where attention falls, because they are capable of being made visible and can be defined objectively. The thought behind this is that psychological precursors are, in their turn, created by latent failures and can be best prevented by removing those latent failures.

This thought process mirrors that of the old stimulus-response psychology. To alter behaviour it is necessary to change the stimuli that generate that behaviour; a direct influence from intervening variables is not possible. While the last word has yet to be spoken about the theoretical differences between stimulus-response and more cognitively oriented models in terms of what happens between stimulus and response in the brain, in practice this difference is less important than is often assumed. It is almost always more effective to influence behaviour by altering the context within which it is generated. In the case of unsafe acts within an industrial environment this means removing the latent failures that lie at their root.

Latent failures are weaknesses in the organisation that exist not only at the time of an accident, but are there for some time in advance. Such failures are traceable before any accidents happen and, therefore, form the most important target for preventative action. The trick is to know what sorts of failures lead to accidents and how they can be uncovered. In general these failures are to be looked for at the level of management. Examples of such approaches are MORT analysis (Johnson, 1980) and the ILCI system (ILCI, 1978). The disadvantage attached to these systems is that there is no scientific basis, while at the same time there have been no attempts to validate these systems using data gathered in the field. The only theory, and preventative approach, that is both theoretically based as well as practically validated is the Tripod method developed in co-operation by the universities of Leiden and Manchester with financial support from Shell International Petroleum Ltd (cf. Wagenaar, Hudson, & Reason, 1990).

9.1   Short description of the tripod approach

On the basis of analyses of many hundred accidents, in which the causes of all accidents, in agreement with the model in Figure 4.1, are broken down into unsafe acts, psychological precursors, latent failures and fallible decisions, it has been found that it is possible to describe the latent failures comprehensively using eleven categories of latent failure. These are called "general failure types" (Wagenaar, Hudson, & Reason, 1992). Systematic observation within a company can serve to measure the relative frequency of these underlying problem areas. This can be represented as a Failure State Profile, such as Figure 4.4, that can serve to define priorities for remediation (Hudson, Reason, Wagenaar, Bentley, Primrose, & Visser, 1994). Next one can trace the most threatening categories of latent failures back to the higher level decisions that were taken earlier, or failed to be taken. These decisions can be reviewed and such decisions can, in the future, be taken with greater weight attached to safety issues.

One case can serve as an example (Wagenaar, Souverijn, & Hudson, 1992). The intensive care departments of two hospitals were concerned about a number of small but potentially dangerous failures. The "failure state profile" of one of those wards showed that equipment failures, a hardware problem, contributed a disproportionate number of causes. The reason is that this department was perceived to be ultra-modern ten years previously, but has not been refurbished since then. The recommendation is to assign greater priority, within the financial constraints, to renewal of the equipment. The Tripod method is characterised by a dissociation from the many small errors at the workplace and a concentration of information in the direction of common factors at a managerial level.

9.2 Eleven types of latent failure

The Tripod philosophy recognises the following eleven general failure types (GFTs):

1. *Design (DE)*
Failures in the design of equipment and work areas; the design fails to take any or sufficient notice of the human factor. The probable cause is that feedback between the shop floor and the design departments is lacking, which would have prevented or removed such problems.

2. *Hardware (HW)*
Even with adequate design, the materials and availability of tools and equipment can lead to breakage or *ad hoc* substitution. There is too little attention paid to optimising the relationship between work and apparatus.

3. *Defences (DF)*
Even obvious defences can be found to be missing or inadequate for the hazards; simple alarms, protective clothing, rescue plans, holding of exercises as well as specialised containment measures and automatic shut-down equipment.

4. *Error-enforcing conditions (EC)*
The working conditions can be sub-optimal for those who work in them, such as shift work,

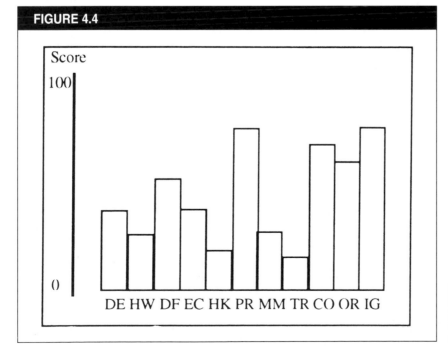

FIGURE 4.4

Score

100

0

DE HW DF EC HK PR MM TR CO OR IG

Failure State Profile of a hypothetical unit, such as an oil production platform or an intensive care ward of a hospital.

working under extreme heat, cold or time pressure or without sufficient knowledge to perform the task. While such conditions may always arise, when these are chronic the chances that errors will be made rise alarmingly.

5. *Housekeeping (HK)*
Often we find situations in conflict with the requirements and good practice. Housekeeping problems signal that management has little grip on affairs, or does not wish to know.

6. *Procedures (PR)*
Here we mean the existence of good procedures, accurate, comprehensible and available as well as actually being followed. Recognising problems in this area leads to the analysis of work practices to reduce the number of situations requiring administrative controls such as procedures, the introduction of procedures that can help reduce risks and extra attention being paid to compliance with the procedures that exist. Often there are too many procedures.

7. *Maintenance management (MM)*
Here we mean not just the failure to perform maintenance, but the pursuance of the appropriate management strategy for the machinery and operation in question. Maintenance is a major source of errors, especially omissions, and allows failures to be introduced where previously there was no problem. The *Piper Alpha* disaster was set off by maintenance activity.

8. *Training (TR)*
This can involve both under- and over-qualified workers performing the work. Training refers to the competence of the workforce rather than just safety training. Training and procedures can be used as substitutes for good design. All too often management does not know or try to assess whether the training has any effect.

9. *Communication (CO)*
Communication systems that break down, or people who fail to understand one another, result in people not knowing what is going on and acting mistakenly. On *Piper Alpha* the satellite platforms mistakenly thought that everything was under control so they continued to pump oil and gas into the burning platform.

10. *Organisation (OR)*
Is the organisational structure fit for the task that needs to be done? Are the managers aware of what goes on or are they believed by the workforce? Bureaucratic organisations may be just right for some critical and long-term operations, while empowerment may be the only way to get things done in other fields. In poor organisations no one knows who to tell, even when they see a danger.

11. *Incompatible goals (IG)*
Trying to do several things at once is always difficult, like juggling. The balance between production and safety has to be maintained and over-eagerness to cut costs may result in increased danger. Making deadlines and furthering one's career are goals that, just this once, may take priority over safety.

The Tripod approach is bottom-up, beginning with the information available on and from the work floor. This is where the reality of the venture is to be assessed and represented as a "failure state profile". This becomes a message sent to the management who need to see if their beliefs and the operational reality are in synchrony. The management's response to this message is the diagnosis they make of why they have the profile they do and, most importantly, what they are going to do about it to make things better. An example of a "failure state profile" is shown in Figure 4.3.

9.3 Validating tripod
The pretension that Tripod makes is that it enables one to predict the causes of an accident *before* an accident takes place. Tripod makes the prediction in terms of the organisational problems that exist before anything has actually gone wrong, proactively, rather than just waiting for an accident and analysing the causes reactively (cf. Figure 4.5). The latter approach is also perfectly possible, and even necessary, but a proactive approach is always to be preferred. The reactive approach is driven by the discovery of what clearly is wrong, because it led to an accident or at least an unsafe act. The proactive approach allows a manager to get ahead of events and solve problems applying cost-benefit analyses rather than being forced by events. In order to justify using such a proactive tool it is, nevertheless, essential that such a tool be

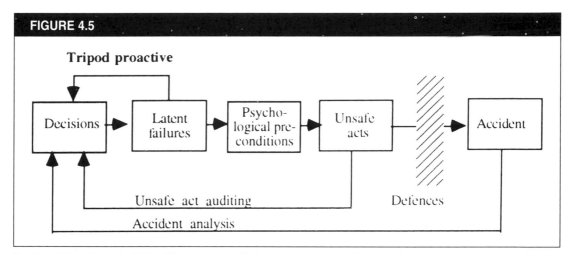

FIGURE 4.5

The General Causal model with the different sources of information that can be delivered to decision makers. The reactive approaches measure what has happened, such as unsafe acts and accidents, the proactive approach measures what can happen, based upon the identification of the latent failures.

validated with existing accidents. The general causal model presented in section 4 allows for both the proactive analysis of existing conditions in terms of latent failures and the reactive analysis of accidents and incidents in terms of the conditions and latent failures that caused them. The Tripod model, then, is consistent for both the proactive and reactive approaches to safety management.

First it is necessary to understand how a failure state profile can be developed without the use of accident data. In order to do this we introduce the notion of an "indicator", a small but objectively observable pointer to success or failure in the area of a specific GFT. For instance, frequent failure of a specific machine despite adequate maintenance can point to design problems, finding too many irrelevant memos in one's in-tray reflects communication problems. For each GFT a database of indicators can be constructed, typically 100 to 150 indicators. This is not to say that the problems phrased as indicators will themselves be anything more than trivial, but if one answered 20 or 30 such indicator questions for training, and found that more than the half were being answered in the "wrong" way, then it is possible to draw the conclusion that the training is a source of serious problems and may need to be looked at in some

detail. Indicators are symptoms of a disease, the latent failures form the disease.

Initially indicators were collected by having a researcher observe the activity in considerable detail. The specificity of the indicators in the Appendix shows how a detailed knowledge of the work involved is necessary to make good indicators. Currently techniques have been developed to allow the workforce to generate their own indicators and construct a database (Hudson et al., 1994). However a list of indicators is not, of itself, enough. The test, as a whole, needs to be calibrated (Hudson, Zieverink, Groeneweg, Akerboom, Wagenaar, & Reason, 1995) in order to be sufficiently accurate and useful in the industrial setting. In order to do this GFTs can be considered as different scales in a psychological test. Indicator items can then be considered as scale items and treated accordingly. Validation becomes the analysis of test–retest reliability, construct validity, content validity and, most important of all, predictive validity.

Construct validity is provided by reference to the theory, especially as it is represented by the fact that the model is based upon the GEMS model of human error and its extension to the reasons why unsafe acts are committed (Reason, 1990) distributed over the eleven GFTs. Content validity is provided by the use of the workforce as the source of the indicator items used in the test. Predictive validity has to be provided by the ability to predict which accidents will happen. The way to assess predictive validity is to measure the correlation between the failure state profiles that can be generated using the proactive test technique and equivalent accident profiles. Accident profiles can be made by analysing a sufficiently large number of incidents into the same format, a profile representing the numbers of latent failures identified as causing the accidents. Finally test–retest reliability, which is a necessary but not a sufficient validity requirement, can be guaranteed by the application of standard scale construction techniques (Cronbach, 1990).

After item analysis and selection in terms of the GFT scales, the test is now capable of achieving a test–retest reliability, without the use of parallel items, in excess of 0.7 (Hudson et al., 1995). Predictive validity had originally been assessed by comparing predicted failure state profiles against the results of analyses of accidents, giving a predictive validity of 0.72 (Hudson, Groeneweg, Reason, Wagenaar, van der Meeren & Visser, 1991) and test–retest reliabilities about 0.80 with many parallel items (Hudson, Wagenaar, Reason, Groeneweg, van der Meeren, & Visser, 1991). Recently a predictive validity in excess of 0.9 has been obtained, using the Spearman–Rank correlation between the indicator-based state profile and a profile based upon reactive analysis of incidents for a shipping operation (A.J. Pearce, personal communication, April 1997).

In its current form, after calibration has been performed, the Tripod proactive approach allows for the accurate prediction of the causes of future accidents in terms of organisational factors. In short it is possible, with considerable accuracy, to predict why an accident will happen. Given a knowledge of the hazards and exposure to those hazards, it is possible to predict where an accident will take place, but with considerably less accuracy. Unfortunately it is not possible to predict when, or to whom, an accident will occur. We have to content ourselves with why and where.

9.4 The ISRS system

The International Standard Rating System (ISRS) of the International Loss Control Institute (ILCI,

1978) is a rating scale, with points assigned to the way in which safety is organised within an organisation. The maximum number of points is 10,800 based upon 20 elements or sub-scales. The sub-scales and the items within them are weighted in accordance to the averaged subjective value of a number of American industries. The most important sub-scale is "leadership" and "administration" (contributing 1170 points); points here are assigned, for instance, with items such as having a good library (175 points), having safety in senior managers' staff reporting system, and by defining a standard by which one wishes to be measured (e.g. LTIs). Items that generate few points are: development of a procedure for refusing work when the conditions are dangerous (35 points) or co-ordination between safety and health workers. Items are similar to the Tripod indicators, but have not been subjected to any more than a test of face validity.

The disadvantage of ILCI's ISRS is that it proposes the same remedy for every disease. The same checklist is applied to very different types of organisation and the resulting remedial proposals are determined by the structure of the test. As the system works with stars (up to five, like restaurants) being handed out for reaching certain overall points levels, the danger is that the stars rather than the safety become the goal. With a limited list of items it is possible to concentrate upon just those that increase the points score rather than to treat the approach as measuring the underlying safety of the organisation. Furthermore the fact that the weights are set by reference to American industry means that locally important factors may be significantly under- or over-weighted. In a Tripod analysis of a North Sea platform a major problem of management of contractor personnel was identified, but within the ILCI system this would have only generated an item worth 35 points.

The ISRS is, nevertheless, very good for organisations at an early stage in their safety evolution. An assessment can be made that tests a great many relevant factors and improvement, no matter how cynically driven, will result in the right things being done. Once, however, the safety levels have reached the point where measurement in terms of crude measures becomes difficult, the Tripod approach is intended to take a location and operation specific approach which is harder to fool.

10 FALLIBLE DECISIONS

Latent failures, weaknesses within an organisation that can lead to unsafe behaviour, themselves also have a cause. For instance, poor quality equipment was selected and purchased and has yet to be replaced. The maintenance schedule may be inappropriate for the equipment but have been determined by cost-cutting exercises or a rigid and mistaken fixation on standardised approaches to work, whether they are the best or not. Error enforcing conditions may be known about and the risk consciously "taken" to operate in ways that will generate unsafe acts.

Most latent failures are not the result of work floor errors, but flow from managerial decisions taken earlier and, often, elsewhere. The exception is maintenance-induced errors such as missing parts that may be hidden from view, waiting to create a failure when it is least wanted. The remaining decisions of managers are not, however, themselves necessarily bad decisions. They are hard decisions that have had both good and bad consequences. The latent failures are the bad consequences; the advantages were what the decision makers saw when the decisions were made, maybe as many as 20 or 30 years previously. Likewise many decisions are taken at a physical distance which precludes anything more than a superficial understanding of what the real problems might be.

Fallible decisions are themselves a form of human error, mistakes that are characterised by the belief or the hope that the good consequences will occur and the bad will not happen. As the life span of many systems is longer than the manager's own career, most people do not see just how their well-intentioned decisions can turn out to be a major source of problems for future generations. Table 4.3 lists the different types of problems that can be encountered.

Fallible decisions need to be identified, if only to see what other negative consequences may be expected. They also need to be handled with care and sensitivity, because the person who made the decision may be the one whose help is needed to

---

TABLE 4.3

The main classes of problems that manifest themselves as fallible decision making.

Habits
- *Bad habits:* people do what they know they should not do, but continue to do nevertheless (tomorrow we'll do better)
- *The organisational culture:* the unfortunate side-effects of the working practices people feel defines their organisation (e.g. can-do cultures)

Resources
- *Time shortages:* failure to allocate sufficient time to perform work
- *People shortages:* failure to allocate sufficient or sufficiently competent people
- *Money shortages:* insufficient funds to cover what needs to be accomplished

Decision making
- *Absence:* not making any decisions at all, decisions are taken by default
- *Inadequate decisions:* making decisions on the basis of incorrect or insufficient information
- *Asynchrony:* making decisions too far removed in time or space from the work floor

Accountability
- *None:* no individuals made specifically accountable for critical tasks
- *Distance:* accountability held too far from the work floor
- *Powerlessness:* people made accountable without the ability to influence events

cure the problem. What is clear is that many decisions that seemed reasonable when they were made have failed to pass the test of time; situations may have changed, new knowledge may have become available, insights may have been won. One of the lessons learned from an intensive study of accidents is that the concept of blame is not merely to be transferred from the immediate actor to the manager. The impossibility of predicting situations with many variables, which explains why the oil workers could not foresee the consequences of their actions, is equally applicable to the managers whose unsafe acts are someone else's fallible decisions.

---

11 CONCLUSION

It is an essential part of any effective safety strategy that the relationship between decisions and possible accidents be brought clearly out into the open. Studying safety statistics is of little help, especially when the frequency is low. As chance factors play an increasingly large role, contributing noise, and the signal becomes increasingly intermittent, it becomes progressively harder for decision makers to filter out the useful information and not be misled by immediate but irrelevant factors. Good accident investigations help, but the level of analysis needs to be reached at which the latent failures and the failures of decision making are exposed. A reactive approach to safety management needs to be served by the provision of information about the problems, the diseases, rather than the symptoms. We often hear that an accident was caused by "human error", without any description of the conditions that led to that error. With fewer accidents there appears to be less to learn about the reasons for those accidents. This is why there has to be a change when the accident frequency drops past the point that the information is reliable. It is more important to take a proactive stance in areas that we know, in advance, are those where accidents will come from if nothing is done.

The proactive stance means that it is better to improve the quality of procedures and ensure that they are followable, and followed, before there is an accident rather than waiting for an accident to

happen before any action is taken. It is better to assess how well information flows within the organisation rather than discover, after the event, that the warning messages from the safety manager were disappearing into the managing director's wastepaper basket and that the management team's intentions were being systematically reinterpreted by middle managers before they reached the shop floor. As all these are in fact nothing more than good practice, and not just restricted to safety, we can now see how our argument has developed from the "in search of misery", based upon accidents as the source of information. Now we propose that the safe way to operate is to operate well and that there need be no incompatibility between production and safety.

What we have learned from studying many different organisations is that those that are safest take safety most seriously. Ideally safety should be considered integrally with all the top-level decisions that are taken and the safety manager should be a full member of the management team. Certainly safety should be a fixed item, ideally first, on the agenda of management and board meetings. Dupont, a company with an exemplary record, has the Chief Executive Officer as the chief safety manager, thereby ensuring that commitment is maintained from the top. The common practice is still, unfortunately, that the safety manager hears of decisions taken, after the event, with the requirement of ensuring that all is safe. In small organisations or divisions of larger ones, there may not be room for the safety manager.

One way of ensuring an adequate understanding of industrial safety is to have "high fliers" spend time in the safety department, preferably carrying real responsibility. In practice safety has all too often been a place where people have been shunted, often because they are too nice to let go. The safety department is, however, an ideal location for a young manager to learn the whole of the business and acquire an overall view that can stand in good stead elsewhere. Furthermore such a young manager can see, often at first hand, just what the consequences of failures in safety policy are. If, added to this, there is a good understanding of the relationship between fallible decisions and accidents, this is knowledge that can serve to prevent accidents when that manager joins the management team and gets to make fallible decisions.

The basic philosophy of this chapter is that safety problems are primarily caused by the working conditions to which people may respond by making errors. When we started our studies of safety, we met people who explained their dangerous working practices by claiming: "These are the conditions under which we work". At first sight it looks as if workers cause their own accidents and, therefore, have all the control over their actions and, therefore, their safety. Managers feel divorced from the actual work and that the people who cause accidents are out of their control. The conditions, however, are set by managers, rather than workers. Workers have a responsibility to look after themselves, but will always work within the conditions, managers allow the conditions to exist. Workers have the responsibility of telling their managers what the conditions are, possibly by using a system such as Tripod, managers bear the responsibility of listening and acting accordingly. In this way safety management is the responsibility of everybody in a company, from top to bottom.

APPENDIX

Provisional checklist for the construction of a failure state profile of intensive care wards.

Hardware failures
1. Is there vital but old equipment of which safer designs are now on the market?
2. Are there cases of breakdown of vital equipment?
3. Do technicians spend more time at incidental repairs than on scheduled maintenance?
4. Are there any incidents based on unnoticed breakdowns?

Design failures
1. Is there sufficient space around each bed?
2. Are there alarms for all malfunctions?
3. Are there cases in which alarms were noticed too late?
4. Has "forgetting to do something" caused any incidents?

5. Are alarms being switched off because of too many false alarms?

Error enforcing conditions
1. Are there fixed protocols for receiving new patients?
2. Are checklists used for the start-up of new equipment?
3. Have incidents been caused by being interrupted during routine tasks?
4. Can stand-by staff be summoned at short notice?
5. Are non-routine tasks discussed in special meetings?

Poor housekeeping
1. Are supplies used and not replenished?
2. Does equipment get lost?
3. Can you tell how many medicine pumps there are, and where they are now?
4. Has anyone asked you in the last week "Where is the . . . ?"
5. Is there a habit of finishing all menial chores before the end of the shift?

Poor operating procedures
1. Has there been any incident in which a violation of procedure was defended as "the thing that is usually done"?
2. Are critical procedures protected by the use of checklists?
3. Are critical procedures checked for routine control at each bed?
4. Is there a checklist for routine control at each bed?
5. Have there been any incidents due to improvisations?

Poor maintenance procedures
1. Is there a regular overhaul schedule?
2. Is the overhaul schedule lagging because of acute repairs?
3. Is maintenance made impossible due to the lack of parts?
4. Is equipment controlled with checklists, after maintenance?
5. Is any technician specially dedicated to the IC ward?

Inadequate training
1. Are all staff assigned exclusively to the IC ward?

2. Are novices supervised systematically?
3. Is there a training programme for novices at all levels, before they start work in the IC ward?
4. Is there a safety training programme for all staff?
5. Are there regular safety meetings in which all incidents are discussed with staff at all levels?

Incompatible goals
1. Is the budget obstructing necessary renewal of equipment?
2. Have tasks been extended without an extension of staff; or staff reduced without a corresponding reduction of tasks?
3. Is there systematic overtime work?
4. Is equipment used while it is known to be inadequate?
5. Are there any differences of opinion between medical and nursing staff on professional matters?

Organisational failures
1. Does the hospital management pay unexpected site visits?
2. Does the hospital management receive reports on accidents and incidents, and act upon them?
3. Is a safety recording system used to compare the ward to other units inside and outside the hospital?
4. Is sticking to written procedures systematically checked?
5. Is there a planning of work in which tasks are allocated on the basis of capacity?

Communication failures
1. Are there regular meetings with related departments in the hospital in which safety issues are discussed?
2. Are there fixed protocols for shift changes?
3. Are there incidents due to services rendered by other departments being too late?
4. Have there been any incidents in which a person who was urgently needed could not be reached?
5. Are there positive checks for the flow of vital information between departments?

REFERENCES

Bignell, V., Peters, G., & Pym, C. (1977). *Catastrophic failures.* Milton Keynes: Open University.

Buchanan, B.G., & Shortliffe, E.H. (1984). *Rule-based expert systems: The MYCIN experiments of the Stanford heuristic programming project.* Reading, MA: Addison-Wesley.

Commissie 'oorzaak Brand Walrus' (COBRAW) (1987). *Rapport oorzaak brand walrus [Report into the cause of the fire on board the submarine Walrus].* Ministerie Van Defensie, 1987.

Cronbach, L.J. (1990). *Essentials of psychological testing.* New York: Harper & Row.

Cullen, the Hon. Lord (1990). *The public inquiry into the Piper Alpha disaster.* London: HMSO.

Evans, J.St.B.T. (1983). *Thinking and reasoning: Psychological approaches.* London: Routledge & Kegan Paul.

Free, R.J. (1995). Unpublished PhD. Thesis. Manchester University.

Hofstee, W.K.B. (1987). Wiens risico's lopen wij? [Whose risks are we running?] *Nederlands Tijdschrift voor de Psychologie, 42,* 47–53.

Hudson, P.T.W., & Verschuur, W.L.G. (1996). *Why people offshore bend the rules.* Report for Shell International Petroleum, The Hague.

Hudson, P.T.W., Reason, J.T., Wagenaar, W.A., Bentley, P.D., Primrose, M., & Visser, J.P. (1994). Tripod Delta: Proactive approach to enhanced safety. *Journal of Petroleum Technology, 46,* 58–62.

Hudson, P.T.W., Groeneweg, J., Reason, J.T., Wagenaar, W.A., Meeren, R.J.W. van der, & Visser, J.P. (1991). Application of Tripod to measure latent errors in North Sea gas platforms: Validity of failure state profiles. In *Proceedings of the First International Conference on Health, Safety and Environment.* Richardson, Texas: Society of Petroleum Engineers, pp. 429–435.

Hudson, P.T.W., Wagenaar, W.A., Reason, J.T., Groeneweg, J., Meeren, R.J.W. van der, & Visser, J.P. (1991). Enhancing safety in drilling: Implementing TRIPOD in a desert drilling operation. In *Proceedings of the First International Conference on Health, Safety and Environment.* Richardson, TX: Society of Petroleum Engineers, pp. 725–730.

Hudson, P.T.W., Zieverink, H.J.A., Groeneweg, J., Akerboom, S.P., Wagenaar, W.A., & Reason, J.T. (1995). *Fixing Tripod-Delta.* Report for Shell International Petroleum, The Hague.

International Loss Control Institute (1978). *International oil and petrochemical safety rating.* Loganville, GA: ILCI.

Johnson, W.G. (1980). *MORT Safety assurance systems.* New York: Dekker.

Jorgensen, N.O. (1988). Risky behaviour at traffic signals: A traffic engineer's view. *Ergonomics, 31*, 657–661.

Nisbett, R., & Ross, L. (1980). *Human inference: Strategies and shortcomings of social judgement.* Englewood Cliffs, NJ: Prentice-Hall.

Norman, D.A. (1981). Categorization of action slips. *Psychological Review, 88*, 1–15.

Östberg, G. (1984). Evaluation of a design for inconceivable event occurrence. *Materials and Designs, 5*, 88–93.

Peters, T.J., & Waterman, R.H. (1982). *In search of excellence.* New York: Harper & Row.

Rasmussen, J. (1982). Human errors: A taxonomy for describing human malfunction in industrial installations. *Journal of Occupational Accidents, 4*, 11–355.

Rasmussen, J. (1983). Skills, rules and knowledge: Signals, signs and symbols, and other distinctions in human performance models. *IEEE Transactions and Systems, Man and Cybernatics, 3*, 257–268.

Reason, J.T. (1990). *Human error.* New York: Cambridge University Press.

Rogovin, M. (1979). *Report of the President's Commission of the accident at Three Mile Island.* Washington, DC: Government Printing Office.

Slovic, P. (1985). Only new laws will spur seat-belt use. *Wall Street Journal*, 30 January.

Swain, A.D., & Guttman, H.E. (1983). *Handbook of human reliability analysis with emphasis on nuclear power plant applications.* NUREG/CR 1278. Albuquerque, NM: Sandia National Laboratories.

USSR State Committee on the Utilization of Atomic Energy (1986). *The accident at the Chernobyl nuclear power plant and its consequences.* Information compiled for the IAEA Experts' Meeting, 25–29 August, 1986. Vienna: IAEA.

Wagenaar, W.A. (1986). *De oorzaak van mogelijke ongelukken* [The causes of impossible accidents]. Duijkerlezing, Deventer: Van Loghum Slaterus.

Wagenaar, W.A. (1987). De constructie van risico. [The construction of risk]. *Nederlands Tijdschrift voor de Psychologie, 42*, 53–54.

Wagenaar, W.A. (1990a). Risk evaluation and the causes of accidents. In K. Borcherding, O.I. Larichev, & D. Messick (Eds.), *Contemporary issues in decision making.* Amsterdam: Elsevier Science Publishers, pp. 245–260.

Wagenaar, W.A. (1990b). Risk taking and accident causation. In J.F. Yates (Ed.), *Risk taking behaviour.* New York: John Wiley & Sons.

Wagenaar, W.A. (1991). *Influencing human behaviour: Toward a practical approach for exploration and production.* Report of Department of Psychology, Leiden University.

Wagenaar, W.A. (1992). Common sense problem solving in conditions of underspecification. In J. Siegfried (Ed.), *The status of common sense in psychology.* New York: Ablex.

Wagenaar, W.A., & Groeneweg, J. (1987). Accidents at sea: Multiple causes and impossible consequences. *Journal of Man-Machine Studies, 27*, 587–598.

Wagenaar, W.A., Hudson, P.T.W., & Reason, J.T. (1990). Cognitive failures and accidents. *Applied Cognitive Psychology, 4*, 273–294.

Wagenaar, W.A., & Keren, G.R. (1986). Does the expert know? In E. Hollnagel, G. Mancini, & D.D. Woods (Eds.), *Proceedings of ASI on intelligent decision support in process environments.* Berlin: Springer, pp. 87–103.

Wagenaar, W.A., Souverijn, A.M., & Hudson, P.T.W. (1992). Safety management in intensive care wards. In B. Wilpert, & Th. Qvale (Eds.), *Reliability and safety in hazardous work systems: Approaches to analysis and design.* Hove: Lawrence Erlbaum Associates Ltd.

5

Work Time and Behaviour at Work

Henk Thierry and Ben Jansen

1 INTRODUCTION

Until the second half of the twentieth century, work time arrangements and operating time arrangements that are applied in work organizations can be characterized by a dichotomy: *daytime work* and *irregular work and shift work*. By far most employees living in the industrialized countries work in the daytime only. This not only means that they do their work from early in the morning until late in the afternoon, but also that they are off at the weekend. To many, a working day amounts to something like eight working hours. Many employed have the impression that this arrangement of work time (four hours in the morning, four hours in the afternoon, off work at the weekend) forms a "natural" or "normal" pattern. One glance at the history of work time arrangements (henceforth WTAs) in Western countries, however, shows that all kinds of variations have existed throughout the centuries and that the number of working hours per day and the number of working days per week have often been (much) larger (see e.g. Ruppert, 1953; Harmsen &

Reinalda, 1975; Levitan & Belous, 1979; Scherrer, 1981). The five-day working week of around eight hours per day was not introduced on a large scale in most countries until the sixties.

It is typical of *shift work* that groups of employees take over each other's work during the 24-hour period. As a result, work is also done in the evenings and possibly also at night. When work is done during the whole 24-hour period, *semi*-continuous working means that no work is done at the weekend; *continuous* working means that work is done in seven 24-hour days. For many shift workers, a "shift"—the number of hours that work is done successively per 24-hour period— has a duration of about eight hours. Many changes have occurred in this field in the course of time (see e.g. Scherrer, 1981; Boissonnade, 1987), for instance with the advent of the guilds, and after the Renaissance, when artificial light was used on a much larger scale. The term *irregular work* is meant to refer to those WTAs in which the work organization may be "operational" throughout (a large part of) the 24-hour period, but in which no "regular" shifts of employees take over work from each other. For example, in the case of public transport, more employees are needed during peak hours only. In hospitals, a large share of the work can be done only during particular parts of the 24-hour period, whereas there is a variety of work time arrangements for employees, etc.

Gradually, however, during the fifties we saw the first signs of change. Initially these changes were WTAs that were applied on an extremely modest scale. For instance, in the fifties, some companies in Germany and Switzerland experimented with "flexitime", probably for the first time (see Robison, 1976; Maric, 1977; Ronen, 1981), allowing employees to choose for each period at what times they started work in the morning and stopped work in the afternoon. Around that time, the "compressed working week" was applied for the first time in one company in the United States (Wheeler, Gurman, & Tarnowieski, 1972; Cohen & Gadon, 1978; Nollen, 1979; Tepas, 1985). The arrangement implied that work was done on fewer days of the week, but during more hours per working day (for example, four 10-hour days instead of five eight-hour days). In addition, "part-time work" started developing: all kinds of arrangements developed in which work time was shorter than in a "full-time" arrangement.

These WTAs have been applied on an increasingly large scale ever since, though fairly gradually. They can be ranged in the "daytime work" category without much difficulty, though the "time limits of the day" (often 7.00am–6.00pm) are exceeded regularly, both in the morning and in the evening. In Europe, however, particularly since the early nineties, there has been an increase of variations of such WTAs that cannot be classed so unambiguously in either of the two categories mentioned at the outset (in the United States that increase had taken place a little earlier). Those WTAs are often referred to by the unfortunately opaque term *flexible* arrangements. These arrangements involve all kinds of variations in the number of working hours per day, in the part of the 24-hour period in which work is done, in the number of working days per week, in the average number of working hours per week, per month or per season, etc. We will mention merely a few examples:

- A standby contract may stipulate that there is

no work in one period, whereas work is done in the daytime, or in the evenings, or at night and/or at the weekend, in another period.
- A "compressed" working week may stipulate that work is done every three or four 24-hour periods in a series consisting of three consecutive 12-hour shifts: in one series from 7.00am–7.00pm, in the other from 7.00pm–7.00am. From time to time it also includes a weekend.
- Groups of employees decide to negotiate with principals over schedules containing both work time and leisure time, for instance in the context of a project. Such a schedule may contain, for instance, six weeks of work (of seven 14-hour working days each), followed by two and a half successive weeks of holidays.
- Certain occupational groups have to "work overtime" for a long time during part of the year—such as chartered accountants who have to audit the annual accounts of companies—after which the overtime hours are allowed to be taken off as days off in a later part of the year.
- Shops are allowed to (or have to) also be open in the evening. "Part timers" and "full timers" who were used to working during the daytime (save for the odd late evening shopping day) are called in for other parts of the 24-hour period, possibly by introducing "minishifts".

Several WTAs mentioned here briefly have been introduced in connection with developments towards a 24-hour economy. This is something that shiftworkers—especially those in semi-continuous shifts—have been dealing with a great deal longer. A characteristic feature of the changes in the last few years is nonetheless that a growing number of companies and institutions expect from their employees (in daytime work) and temps that work is normally also done in the evenings and in parts of the weekend. These changes may also entail that the "weekend" will no longer continue to fall on a Saturday and Sunday for large groups of the employed. As has been noted earlier, the distinction between daytime work and irregular work and/or shift work will consequently become less manageable.

Of course, the introduction of flexible WTAs does not take place in isolation. Instead, it is part of the easing of restrictions for organizations covering many more areas. The "easing of restrictions" is, in essence, present-day "jargon" for organization change (see also Chapter 8, Volume 4 of this Handbook). This means that generally there are radical changes in technology, in markets and in classes of customers, in designing the production process or the process of service, in coordination and management of employees, in job requirements, and in training and retraining employees. Concerning the behaviour of individuals and groups, these changes will lead to consequences in, for example, the "lifespan" of abilities and skills acquired, the role of previous experience in performance, the possibility of no more than one career, the meaning of "commitment" for motivation, etc. This automatically raises the important question as to what extent it is possible for a person's work to have a sufficient amount of routine and "rhythm", aspects that are very important for health.

Most of the topics mentioned just now will be paid special attention to, as independent topics in other chapters of this Handbook. In this chapter, we will specifically concentrate on the meaning and the consequences of various work time arrangements for behaviour at work. The first section contains a discussion of various psychological perspectives that may be important in investigating (and designing) WTAs. This discussion leads to a model to which we will return in the next sections. Next, in section 3, some flexible WTAs are discussed: we limit these to three that have been topics of research at least more than once before. Finally, section 4 contains a presentation of the main features of research into irregular work and shift work. Attention is also paid to various kinds of intervention in this context.

2 PSYCHOLOGICAL PERSPECTIVES

Does someone's work time, however, actually have any effect on his/her behaviour at (and possibly outside) work? And does this imply that different WTAs in turn also have a differentiating meaning? Of course, time does have a certain regulating effect, e.g. at the individual level. This is shown by research into a person's temporal orientation, for example (cf. Nuttin & Lens, 1985; Lens, 1986): it may be focused on one's own past (achievements in the past determine one's self-image), but also on the future which is expected (the person attempts to achieve challenging goals). In addition, references to time in human intercourse reveal the dominant cultural pattern of a society (cf. Durkheim, 1912; Elchardus, 1988; Van den Berg, 1995). An "endogenous" reference is story-like, episodic, "narrative", such as in the phrase: "that summer's day, when we came across her at the corner". Whereas an endogenous use is typical of a rural society with stable social relationships, "exogenous" references are found in a highly differentiated, if not segmented, urban society. An example is: "yesterday at 3.30". This usage of time is general, abstract, "chronological". It is this cultural pattern to which the phrase "I haven't got any time" belongs, with which not only the mutual relations among two or more people can be structured, but in which also time is expressed as a (scarce) resource. But again: does the distinction of *work* time (in relation to other forms or types) really contribute so much importance? The slight scepticism emergent in this question is recognizable in the perspective to be discussed next.

2.1 WTA as an additional factor

In a strict sense, this is not a typically psychological perspective. What is characteristic is precisely the lack of a theory or a model. The train of thought is that any consequences of a WTA can be demonstrated by a description of those features and effects of the WTA that *deviate* from the regular pattern of daytime work (i.e. Monday to Friday, eight-hour working day). And so attention is focused on the effect of "deviations" as frequent evening work, work at very early hours, work during the weekend, working longer than eight hours, etc., on the attitudes and preferences of employees, on their health and possibly their performance, on the productivity of the enterprise, on the coordination of work, etc. It cannot be ruled out that research on the topic of flexible WTAs that has taken place, mostly exploratory and descriptive (see also section 3), is caused to an important extent by taking this point of view.

The view that the arrangement of work time can be seen as an "addition" to the "work" (in normal circumstances) already existent has had repercussions in, for example, specific legislation and regulation, in particular concerning shift work. Both as a result of the International Labour Organization (ILO) and a large number of industrialized countries, more detailed stipulations have been formulated and ratified concerning work conditions, e.g. on the length of a working day, the frequency and the duration of breaks and rest periods, etc. (see also Thierry & Meijman, 1994). Stipulations concerning financial compensation (the shift work bonus), meals at unusual times, commuter traffic, etc., have been included in a collective labour agreement fairly often.

One of the great difficulties associated with the approach of a WTA as an additional factor, at least for scientific research, is the assumption that it is possible to identify "normal" or "usual" circumstances, conditions and consequences. This is expected primarily from the dependent variables in which a researcher is usually interested in the analysis of a WTA, such as motivation, commitment, fatigue, stress, performance, absenteeism, etc. However (as is also apparent from every relevant chapter in this Handbook), there is no such thing as "normal" motivation, usual stress, and the like. Consequently, it is neither possible to locate the "inherent" effects of a specific time arrangement. Researchers have attempted to solve this difficulty by analysing the consequences of (the introduction of) a WTA in longitudinal research, which may or may not be in comparison with the application of another WTA to one or more samples.

Yet this strategy, however useful when considered in isolation, involves the problem that, usually, the *ceteris paribus* assumption cannot be upheld. Various "remaining variables" have generally not remained constant precisely because another time arrangement causes, for example, the job content to change, or its load and the mutual relations (in this respect, and secondly, it is not strictly correct to speak of expected "normal" conditions). The application of continuous work-

ing, for example for nurses in a hospital, demonstrates what may be the case. During the night only a few nurses are present (compared to the daytime situation); various care tasks are carried out during the shifts before and after night-time if possible; only a few doctors can be paged; quiet and hectic periods alternate, etc. In business, much fewer differences occur during the shifts in a 24-hour period, but here it has also been demonstrated that variations arise in work, in supervision, in work climate, etc. The question to what extent the *ceteris paribus* clause is plausible has been hardly ever posed at all in research into flexible WTAs (see also Barling & Gallagher, 1996).

A related problem is caused by the selection effect. Various studies have shown that, in time, a smaller or larger number of shift workers tend to leave of their own accord (see e.g. Aanonsen, 1964; Thiis-Evensen, 1969; Frese & Okonek, 1984; Frese & Semmer, 1986; Jansen, Thierry, & Van Hirtum, 1986). The cause can be found in health complaints, dissatisfaction with the working hours and/or the work, etc. If workers doing shift work are now compared in a study to those in daytime working, for example in terms of aspects of health, level of performance, attitudes and satisfaction, the results will probably be slightly distorted. The possibility of a selection effect cannot be ruled out if flexible WTAs are applied for a longer period, either.

2.2 Adjustment

The second perspective draws attention to the way in which employees—individually or in groups—and the work organization try to adjust to the changes that are necessarily involved in the application of a changed WTA. All kinds of habits, both in work and in private life, have to be changed. As a result, emotions (such as uncertainty), tension and resistance often develop (see for example Bandura, 1986). In many cases, the sequence of work activities has to be arranged differently because of the new schedules, in view of the availability of groups of employees. Also, altered performance standards have to be met regularly.

At the individual level, abandoning shift work as discussed above in connection with the selection effect, can also be interpreted as a "coping" strategy, even if a drastic one. If the new WTA should require that performance is done at night from time to time, the instruction to those involved to prevent variations in the level of performance can have effect under certain conditions (see for example Chiles et al., 1968). The same can also be achieved for some time by greater dedication and effort among staff members; the disadvantage in the long term is, of course, that more fatigue develops. If the new WTA frequently results in a lack of sleep, adjustments to be considered are, for example, work schedules with fewer successive (or shorter) shifts, a noiseless bedroom, having a nap, relaxation techniques, etc. It is also highly important to what extent any members of the family are able and willing to adjust to the new WTA in terms of eating habits, spending leisure time, shopping, etc.

Yet also the company or institution, or important parts thereof will have to adjust. This not only relates to internal changes such as other forms of consultation and coordination, differently organized canteens, altered transport facilities, etc. At least as important is the way in which the work organization regulates its transactions with the environment. In quite some organization theories this topic is approached in terms of "contingency" (see also Chapters 2 and 3, Volume 4). In this approach, the emphasis may be on organic versus mechanical forms of adjustment (cf. Burns & Stalker, 1961), on differentiation and integration of sections of the organization (cf. Lawrence & Lorsch, 1967), on managerial choice (see Child, 1972), or on the environment that has a selective effect on organizations (cf. population ecology; Morgan, 1997). This topic—the mutual adjustment of organization and environment—is also important in the choice that a company makes for a flexible WTA. In terms of extremes: there are companies that translate variations in the demand for workers (depending on the supply of work) as directly as possible into attracting and then, if required, dismissing staff (consider standby workers for zero to forty hours or more). But there are also companies that try meeting such variations by a contingent, flexible organization of activities, combined for example with the application of the compressed working week and flexitime. The type of company—organic or rather mechanical—

therefore plays a major role in introducing a WTA (see Thierry & Tham, 1994; De Lange, Van Eijk, & Tham, 1995; Chapter 8, Volume 4).

2.3 Regulation of non-work time

The third perspective relates to the influence that a WTA has on the time outside work. One of its first aspects is highly obvious: every arrangement of work time marks the amount of time that can be spent in other ways. This observation acquires more meaning when non-work time—sometimes incorrectly termed "leisure" in a broad sense—is classified in categories. There are many ways of doing this. We will follow the classification according to Parker and Smith (1976) who after mentioning work time subsequently distinguish:

- "work-related time": the time for commuter traffic, for preparing or finishing work at home, etc.;
- "existence time": time for meals, sleep, personal care;
- "semi-leisure": time for activities with a somewhat committing nature such as walking the dog, visiting other people, etc.;
- "leisure": time spent entirely at one's own choice.

In the word "leisure", the Latin verb "licēre" can be recognized: "to be permitted to . . .", meaning: to be able to choose, to have options.

This aspect will be brought out in a little more relief when the "location" of the work time during the 24-hour period and during the week is added to the equation. An example will make this point clear: an average weekly work time consisting of 36 hours may produce a WTA of four nine-hour working days in the daytime (for example from 5.00am–2.00pm or from 9.00am–6.00pm), but also an arrangement of four nine-hour nights. Or one with three twelve-hour days (or nights), or even six six-hour days, etc. This should make clear that features of a WTA—apart from the average weekly work time—may affect the spending of non-work time drastically and hence also various facets of individual behaviour at work.

A second regulation aspect concerns the extent to which *meanings of work* and *leisure* interrelate. The "Central Life Interest" scale (CLI) developed

Not much, say Ralston et al. (1985), at least in the period between 1965 and 1985. They evaluated one hundred studies in the field of flexitime using four criteria. In order to qualify, a study was required to have used direct measures for productivity, to contain a pre-test and a post-test, to have an experimental and a control group, and to have applied correct techniques for data analysis. Only two studies met these requirements.

But what characteristics of individual behaviour (and that of groups of employees) would mainly be expected to be affected by a flexitime WTA? And what aspects of the working of an organization are considered in this connection? Moreover, are these expectations based on hypotheses of some kind or on founded assumptions at the very least? Very few authors appear to have gone into this question. Ralston et al. (1985) employ a sociotechnical point of view: in their opinion, the individual's "self control" is enhanced due to flexitime, particularly when he/she is able to determine how long work is done per day. If various departments have to contend with scarce resources (for example: the access to a "mainframe"), then this WTA will also lead to less competition. Employees can also concentrate on their work better in the case of a flexitime WTA. Hence, Ralston et al. expect flexitime to result in higher levels of employees' productivity if they have to contend with scarce resources. Their expectation was confirmed in a field experiment, in which the experimental and the control condition were formed by natural (thus not "randomized") groups. Particularly in the longer term (twelve to eighteen months after introduction of the flexitime arrangement) productivity had increased. Dunham, Pierce & Castaneda (1987) monitored the introduction of flexitime in a section of a utility company, while using a field experimental design. Respondents were randomly assigned to either the experimental or the control condition by department. No significant changes of performance occurred however. What the introduction of this WTA was associated with was a higher degree of commitment, more satisfaction, etc.

Dalton & Mesch (1990) raise the question on the basis of what considerations a relation may be expected between a flexitime WTA and a lower turnover or a lower level of absenteeism, respectively. Three arguments concerning turnover are mentioned:

1. Due to flexitime both the "extrinsic" motivation (for example less travelling time) and the "intrinsic" motivation (for example more autonomy) increase. If the level of motivation is higher, the turnover is lower.
2. In this WTA, mutual adjustment of work time and time for private activities is better, the attitudes (towards work time and leisure) are more positive and commitment to the organization is greater. This increased "work adjustment" leads to a lower level of turnover.
3. A flexitime WTA leads to a new transaction between the organization and the employee: more stability in the individual adjustment between work and non-work is combined with greater commitment to the organization.

Dalton and Mesch also claim that absenteeism can become lower in a flexitime arrangement. There are two types of explanation:

(a) Motivation becomes higher (see 1), hence one is at work more often.
(b) It is possible to organize private circumstances better. Employees ascribe the causes of the resulting higher rate of attendance to the WTA.

Data from previous studies and data from their own study show that turnover is not affected. With regard to absenteeism, the results are not identical, i.e. sometimes they are higher, sometimes they are lower, and regularly no change occurs.

Nearly all the remaining research on flexitime WTAs is basically descriptive. The following results are shown (a more extensive treatment is provided in Orpen, 1981; Lendfers & Nijhuis, 1989; Ralston, 1989, 1990; Krausz & Hermann, 1991; Åberg, Cocke, & Söderberg, 1983) for example by:

- performance/productivity: equal or higher (rather often according to employees' or managers' *impressions*);

- absenteeism: equal, lower or higher;
- satisfaction: higher (regarding work, the time arrangement, respectively), particularly short term);
- commuter traffic: with more ease.

The result of a study conducted by Krausz & Hermann (1991) is interesting: employees with a preference for flexitime have a stronger "growth need". Clearly these people are not concerned with solving existing problems, but with gaining more outcomes, according to the authors.

Now, does the foregoing mean that this WTA is not harmful and possibly not so very important either? We tend towards this view to the extent that it only involves the choice of the moments at which work is started and stopped. Even so, it is an interesting question to what extent flexitime is viewed by employees as an expansion of the possibilities of influencing the work situation, also in the longer term. Remarkably, very few data have been collected on this. Another interesting issue is to what extent the choice of very early starting times is linked to the incidence of (near) accidents.

This WTA is probably much less "harmless" if it also involves a *debit–credit* system. In this case, very long work times may occur per 24-hour period, possibly occurring during a longer period (weeks, months). We will return to this subject more extensively in the following section.

3.2 Compressed working week

In the "compressed", (henceforth COM) working week, work is done in a smaller number of working days and a greater number of hours per day. Given a forty-hour working week, this does not involve five working days of eight hours each, but for example four days of ten hours, or three days of each twelve or thirteen hours (with an extra working day once every period). Precisely as in other time arrangements, its introduction may be combined with a reduction or an extension of the average weekly work time. What is indeed typical of COM is that the operating time of a company is almost always extended to a considerable degree. This is why COM arrangements regularly occur in combination with the application of shift work. They can also apply to part-time workers. In the United Kingdom, COM is sometimes applied in connection with two-shift working: after a shift of, say, ten hours in the daytime, a second shift of ten hours in the night-time follows after an interruption, (so-called "alternating day and night shift system; see e.g. Sloane, 1975; Walker, 1985). In addition, the EOWO schedule has received some fame in Canada and the United States (Northrup, Wilson, & Rose, 1979). In this "every other weekend off" system (which occurs mainly in the chemical and the petrochemical industry) work is done in such an order of twelve-hour shifts that every employee has every other weekend off. There are also combination arrangements in which work is done in eight hours per day during the week and twelve hours in the weekend. Although we shall not make a sharp distinction between "daytime arrangements" and "shift work arrangements", our attention in this section will focus mainly on COM arrangements in the daytime.

With what *objectives* do work organizations introduce this type of WTA? Their objectives are nearly always to improve the service provided to customers and to make better use of the means of production, by way of extending the operating time (see Maric, 1977; Tepas, 1985; Colligan & Tepas, 1986; Loontechnische Dienst, 1991b, 1992). In this sense, the intended flexible character of COM relates mainly to adjusting the composition of the workforce better to fluctuations in the demand for labour in the market. Another cause for the introduction of COM is that employees can make better use of their nonwork time, such as resting more, training and development, hobbies, etc. (for example, Meijman, 1992). Flexibility therefore involves the utility of leisure. A third consideration is that less time needs to be spent on commuter traffic (and waiting in traffic jams).

COM has been recommended as a "managerial" innovation, particularly in the early seventies. According to Maric (1977), it is really a European WTA introduced to (West) Germany and the United Kingdom in the sixties. Tepas (1985) however states that this WTA was applied in the United States in the early forties, although in another name. Around 1990, COM arrangements were found in The Netherlands in about 1 percent of the companies (especially in more operative

Miller, K.E., & Terborg, J.R. (1979). Job attitudes of part time and full time employees. *Journal of Applied Psychology*, 64, 380–386.

Moors, S.H. (1990). Learning from a system of seasonally-determined flexibility: Beginning work earlier increases tiredness as much as working longer days. In G. Costa, G. Cesana, K. Kogi, & A. Wedderburn (Eds.), *Shiftwork: health, sleep and performance.* Frankfurt: Peter Lang.

Morgan, G. (1997). *Images of organizations* (2nd edn). London: Sage.

Nicholson, N., Jackson, P., & Howes, G. (1978). Shift work and absence: An analysis of temporal trends. *Journal of Occupational Psychology*, 51, 127–137.

Nijhuis, F., & Soeters, J. (1983). Ziekteverzuim, arbeidsongeschiktheid en de organisatie van de arbeid. *Tijdschrift voor Sociale Gezondheid*, 61, 686–693.

Nollen, S. (1979). *New patterns of work.* Scarsdale: Work in America Institute.

Northrup, H.R., Wilson, J.T., & Rose, K.M. (1979). The twelve-hour shift in the petroleum and chemical industries. *Labor Relations Review*, 32, 312–316.

Northrup, H.R. (1989). The twelve-hour shift in the petroleum and chemical industries revisited: An assessment by human resource management executives. *Industrial and Labor Relations Review*, 32, 312–326.

Nuttin, J., & Lens, W. (1985). *Future time perspective and motivation: Theory and research method.* Leuven: Leuven University Press.

Orpen, C. (1981). Effects of flexible working hours on employee satisfaction and performance: A field experiment. *Journal of Applied Psychology*, 66, 113–115.

Parker, S.R., & Smith, M.A. (1976). Work and leisure. In R. Dubin (Ed.), *Handbook of work, organization and society.* Chicago, Rand McNally.

Peacock, B., Glube, R., Miller, M., & Clune, P. (1983). Police officers' responses to 8 and 12 hour shift schedules. *Ergonomics*, 26, 479–493.

Perret, D. (1980). *Experiments involving productivity and "work sharing".* Paper presented at the 5th EAPM/EFPS Congress on "Rewarding Work", Amsterdam.

Pocock, S.J., Sergean, R., & Taylor, P.J. (1972). Absence from continuous three-shift workers: A comparison of traditional and rapidly rotating systems. *Occupational Psychology*, 46, 7–13.

Praag, B.M.S. van (1996). Flexibiliteit heeft een prijs. *PW*, 20(4), 16–18.

Ralston, D.A. (1989). The benefits of flexitime: Real or imagined? *Journal of Organizational Behavior*, 10, 369–373.

Ralston, D.A. (1990). How flexitime eases work/family tensions. *Personnel*, 67(8), 45–48.

Ralston, D.A., Anthony, W.P., & Gustafson, D.J. (1985). Employees may lose flexitime, but what does it to the organization's productivity? *Journal of Applied psychology*, 70, 272–279.

Reinberg, A., Vieux, N., & Andlauer, P. (Eds.) (1980). *Night and shiftwork: Biological and social aspects.* Oxford: Pergamon Press.

Robison, D. (1976). *Alternative work schedules.* Scarsdale: Work in America Institute.

Ronen, S. (1981). *Flexible working hours.* New York: McGraw-Hill.

Rosa, R.R. (1995). Extended workshifts and excessive fatigue. *Journal of Sleep Research* (in press).

Rosa, R.R., Wheeler, D.D., Warm, J.S., & Colligan, M.J. (1985). Extended workdays: Effects on performance and ratings of fatigue and alertness. *Behavior Research Methods, Instruments and Computers*, 17, 6–15.

Rosa, R.R., & Colligan, M.J. (1988). Long workdays versus restdays: Assessing fatigue and alertness with a portable performance battery. *Human Factors*, 30, 305–317.

Ruppert, M. (1953). *De Nederlandse vakbeweging. I.* Haarlem: Bohm.

Rutenfranz, J., Knauth, P., & Angersbach, D. (1981). Shiftwork research issues. In L.C. Johnson, D.I. Tepas, W.P. Colquhoun, & M.J. Colligan (Eds.), *The twenty-four hour workday.* Cincinnati: NIOSH.

Schalk, M.J.D. (1989). *Determinanten van veelvuldig kortdurend verzuim.* The Hague: Delwel.

Scherrer, J. (1981). Man's work and circadian rhythm through the ages. In A. Reinberg, N. Vieux, & P. Andlauer (Eds.), *Night and shift work: Biological and social aspects.* Oxford: Pergamon Press.

Schmidt, R.F., & Thews, G. (1983). *Human physiology.* New York: Springer Verlag.

Schoemaker, N., Gageldonk, A. van, Demenint, M., & Vianen, A. van (1981). *Deeltijdarbeid in het bedrijf.* Alphen a/d Rijn: Samsom.

Schuster, M., & Rhodes, S. (1985). The impact of overtime work on industrial accident rates. *Industrial Relations*, 24, 234–245.

Shank, S. (1986). Preferred hours of work and corresponding earnings. *Monthly Labour Review*, 109(11), 40–44.

Sloane, P.J. (1975). *Changing patterns of working hours.* London: Department of Employment, Manpower paper. No. 13, HSMO.

Smulders, P.W.G. (1984). *Balans van 30 jaar ziekteverzuimonderzoek.* Leyden: HIPG/ TNO.

Stafford, E.F., Sherman, J.D., & McCollum, J.K. (1988). Streamlining 12-hour work shifts. *Personnel Administrator*, 51–57.

Steffy, B.D., & Jones, J.W. (1990). Differences between full-time and part-time employees in perceived job strain and work satisfaction. *Journal of Organizational Behavior*, 11, 321–329.

Steinberg, L., & Dornbusch, S.M. (1991). Negative correlates of part-time employment during adolescence: Replication and elaboration. *Developmental psychology*, 27, 304–313.

Taillieu, T.C.B., & Wielen, J.M.M. van der (1995). Waardering van telewerk afhankelijk van funktie. *Telewerken*, *2*(2), 36–38.

Taylor, P.J. (1967). Shift and day work: A comparison of sickness absence, lateness, and other absence behaviour at an oil refinery from 1962 to 1965. *British Journal of Industrial Medicine*, *24*, 93–102.

Taylor, P.J., Pocock, S.J., & Sergean, R. (1972) Shift and day workers' absence: Relationship with some terms and conditions of service. *British Journal of Industrial Medicine*, *29*, 338–340.

Tepas, D.I. (1985). Flexitime, compressed work weeks and other alternative schedules. In S. Folkard & T.H. Monk (Eds.), *Hours of work: Temporal factors in work scheduling*. Chichester: John Wiley.

Thierry, Hk. (1980). Compensation for shiftwork. In W.P. Colquhoun., & J. Rutenfranz (Eds.), *Studies of Shiftwork*. London: Taylor & Francis.

Thierry, Hk., Hoolwerf, G., & Drenth, P.J.D. (1975). Attitudes of permanent day and shift workers towards shiftwork—a field study. In W.P. Colquhoun, S. Folkard, P. Knauth, & J. Rutenfranz (Eds.), *Experimental Studies of Shiftwork*. Opladen: Westdeutscher Verlag.

Thierry, Hk., & Jansen, B. (1982). Social support for night and shiftworkers. In K. Kogi, T. Miura, & H. Saito (Eds.), *Shiftwork: its practice and improvement*. Tokyo: Center for Academic Publications Japan.

Thierry, Hk., Koopman, P.L., & Flier, H. van der (1992). *Wat houdt mensen bezig?* Utrecht: Lemma.

Thierry, Hk., & Ng-A-Tham, J.E.E. (1994). Vrijplaats en verandering. *Gedrag & Organisatie*, *7*, 422–436.

Thierry, Hk., & Meijman, T.F. (1994). Time and behavior at work. In H.C. Triandis, M.D. Dunnette, & L.M. Hough (Eds.), *Handbook of Industrial and Organizational Psychology* (2nd edn., Vol.4). Palo Alto: Consulting Psychologists Press.

Thiis-Evensen, E. (1969). Shift work and health. *Studia Laboris et Salutis*, *4*, 81–83.

Velzen, M. van. (1994). *De vijfde dag*. The Hague: Ministerie van Sociale Zaken en Werkgelegenheid (Ministry of Social Affairs and Employment).

Vidacek, S., Kaliterna, L., & Radoseric-Vidacek, B. (1986) Productivity on a weekly rotating shift system: Circadian adjustment and sleep deprivation effects? *Ergonomics*, *29*, 1583–1590.

Volle, M., Brisson, G.R., Pérusse, M., Tanaka, M., & Doyon, Y. (1979). Compressed workweek: Psychophysiological and physiological repercussions. *Ergonomics*, *22*, 1001–1010.

Walker, J. (1985). *The human aspects of shiftwork*. London: Institute of Personnel Management.

Wedderburn, A.A.I. (1967). Social factors in satisfaction with swiftly rotating shifts. *Journal of Occupational Psychology*, *41*, 85–107.

Wheeler, K.E., Gurman R., & Tarnowieski, D. (1972). *The four-day week*. New York: American Management Association.

Wielen, J.M.M. van der (1995). Onduidelijkheid over telewerken verhindert representatief onderzoek. *Telewerken*, *2*(1), 6–9.

Wilensky, H.L. (1969). Work, careers and social integration. *International Social Science Journal*, *12*, 543–560.

Williamson, A.M., Gower, C.G.I., & Clarke, B.C. (1994). Changing the hours of shiftwork: a comparison of 8- and 12-hour shift rosters in a group of computer operators. *Ergonomics*, *37*, 287–298.

Wippler, R. (1968). *Sociale determinanten van het vrijetijdsgedrag*. Assen: Van Gorcum.

argue that negative emotions constitute a major feature of stress (cf. Gaillard & Wientjes, 1994). For example, Pekrun and Frese (1992) suggested that stressors at work may produce a variety of negative emotions, including anger and disappointment, and that such emotions should be regarded as the crucial dependent variables in the stress process. Warr (1987) conceptualized mental health at work primarily in terms of various affective states, i.e., anxiety, depression, and discontent. There is general agreement that negative emotions are usually elicited by the evaluation that an event is a threat to, or blocks the attainment of important needs and goals (Oatley & Jenkins, 1992). According to Spielberger (1985), stress always involves a situation or stimulus that is perceived as potentially harmful, dangerous or frustrating. Such a perception causes a certain emotional reaction in which either *anxiety* (varying from tension, nervousness and apprehension to fear and panic) or *anger* (varying from irritation to anger and rage) is central. Negative emotions are often accompanied by physiological changes like increased heart rate and blood pressure, increased secretion of certain hormones, and rapid breathing—which are often refered to as stress symptoms. There is evidence that different emotions—in particular anger, fear and depression—involve different neuro-endocrinological responses (Zillmann & Zillmann, 1996).

There are many different kinds of negative emotions that may be experienced in the context of occupational stress (see e.g., Lazarus, 1993). Although a complete typology of these conditions is beyond the scope of this chapter, we mention the most important negative emotional experiences in the occupational context:

1. *Anxiety* and *apprehension* may be evoked by threatening or ambiguous situations. Examples of such situations are ambiguous expectations on the part of others, the threat of a potential dismissal, an impending evaluation, a promotion that is questioned.
2. *Anger*, *irritation*, and *resentment* may result from frustrating situations, like work that has been done in vain, being interfered with, or failure to reach a goal.
3. *Depression*, *disappointment*, and *grief* characterize situations of loss or depri-

vation, such as a promotion that is cancelled, the loss of interesting work or control, or actual dismissal.
4. *Envy* and *jealousy* are found primarily in situations characterized by an unfavourable social comparison, for example observing similar others who have obtained a promotion that one wanted oneself, or who are perceived as being more competent in their work.
5. Feelings of *shame* and *embarrassment* are found in situations in which moral imperatives are violated or goals are not accomplished due to one's own faults or behaviours, for example displaying rudeness to someone due to an inability to control oneself.

Although anxiety is often considered to be the most typical emotion associated with stress (cf. Hamberger & Lohr, 1984), there are indications that other emotions mentioned here may occur at least as frequently in the face of occupational stress (cf. Warr, 1987). For instance, in a study among young engineers, Keenan and Newton (1985) found that respondents seldomly reported anxiety, but much more frequently reported anger and irritation, accompanied by feelings of frustration.

Although a variety of negative emotions that can be distinguished on an experiential and a physiological level, at the same time it is true that emotions can be quite malleable and plastic (Zillmann & Zillmann, 1996). People may not always be able to distinguish emotions from each other, and various emotions may merge into each other. Moreover, there may be a large gap between people's conscious awareness of their emotions, and physiological and behavioural indications of these emotions (Oatley & Jenkins, 1992, Thoits, 1984). Stress is often accompanied by nonspecific tensions and ambiguous physical sensations, which may be labelled in different ways, and such labels may change under the influence of cognitive processes and social influence (Buunk, 1994). Indeed, Schachter and Singer (1962) showed in their classical experiment that subjects who are in a state of unexplained arousal as a result of an epinephrine injection are readily influenced by the angry or euphoric behaviours of a stooge, and assimilate such emotions. In a similar vein, there is evidence that particularly when individuals are under stress, they may copy certain health complaints from others, sometimes even without communication (Hatfield, Cacioppo, & Rapson, 1994; Skelton & Pennebaker, 1982; Sullins, 1991). Moreover, even when the individual is aware of the nature of the emotions he or she experiences, these emotions may transform into one another when a different interpretation of the situation arises. For instance, through communication with colleagues individuals may attribute their stress symptoms to organizational factors and may replace their anxiety by anger (Geurts, Buunk, & Schaufeli, 1994a).

Most individuals experience negative emotions from time to time, and when such emotions are coped with adequately, they often will have no long-term negative consequences for mental and physical health. However, health damage is likely to occur when a person experiences prolonged, intense emotions that he considers undesirable, and when he is unable to remove or avoid the cause of these emotions or to reduce the negative feelings themselves. Indirect support for these assumptions was provided by, for instance, Van Dijkhuizen's (1980) in-depth study, which showed that the relationship between stressors and health were *mediated* by negative emotions. There was no direct effect of stressors at work on psychosomatic complaints and physiological variables, but only an indirect effect through negative feelings. Similarly, Barling and MacIntyre (1993) showed that the effects of role stressors on daily variations in emotional exhaustion among military instructors were largely mediated by negative mood. In the light of these findings it is hardly surprising that many surveys have found only weak associations between the presence of certain psychosocial stressors and health complaints, because stressful situations first lead to negative emotions, and only in the long run, and under certain conditions, to impaired health.

MODELS OF OCCUPATIONAL STRESS

Many different models focusing on occupational stress have been presented in the literature,

especially with respect to occupational burnout (see Schaufeli, Maslach, & Marek, 1993 for an overview). We will confine ourselves here to the most well-known general occupational stress models, i.e., the Social Environment Model (Kahn et al., 1964; Kahn, 1981), the closely related Person-Environment Fit Model (French, 1973; French, Caplan & Harrison, 1982), the Demand-Control-Support Model (Johnson & Hall, 1988; Karasek & Theorell, 1990), and finally the Vitamin Model (Warr, 1987, 1994).

Social Environment Model

The Social Environment Model, which was developed at the Institute for Social Research of the University of Michigan (hence it is sometimes designated as the "ISR Model" or "Michigan Model"), is the best-known occupational stress model. As noted before, this institute has played an important, stimulating role with regard to research on organizational stress (French & Kahn, 1962; Kahn et al., 1964; Kahn, 1981). Since the model was first devised, several different versions of it have been developed (Van Dijkhuizen, 1980; Kahn & Byosiere, 1992). We describe only the most general model here (e.g., Kahn, 1981; Winnubst, De Jong, & Schabracq, 1996). The Social Environment Model is basically a combination of a number of conceptual categories (i.e., types of variables) rather than a coherent theory, although some attempts have been made to define these categories more precisely and to determine their interrelations. The following conceptual categories are identified within this model:

1. *Objective environment.* The objective environment refers to organizational characteristics such as company size, hierarchical structure and job description. This environment is independent of the worker's perceptions of it.
2. *Subjective environment.* The subjective environment, on the other hand, is part of a worker's perceptions, and is also called the "psychological environment" (Lewin, 1951). It contains phenomena such as role conflict, role ambiguity, lack of participation and role overload. These are called "stressors", and may lead to:

3. *Stress reactions or strains.* Strains are affective, physiological, and behavioural responses of the individual, such as job dissatisfaction, high blood pressure or high heart rate, and smoking. Long-term stress reactions may include absenteeism, turnover, and early retirement from the job.

4. *Illness.* Illness refers to both mental and physical illness, including, for example, burnout, depression, cardiovascular disease and gastric ulcers. These illnesses may result from persistent stress reactions.

5. *The person.* The conception of the person includes all more or less enduring genetic, demographic or personality characteristics of the person (like Type A behaviour and rigidity) which serve as conditioning or moderating variables on stressor-strain relationships.

6. *Social support.* Social support refers to interpersonal relationships either at work (supervisor, colleagues) or at home (partner, family). Two kinds of support are particularly important in the model: (1) tangible support, and (2) emotional support. Social support is conceived as a relatively enduring variable that moderates stressor-strain relationships.

Although the Social Environment Model can be adequately operationalized (see Winnubst et al., 1996), and has stimulated a lot of research, several criticisms of the model still remain. First, it is not based on a clear theoretical perspective that leads to specific hypotheses. This means that most studies using this model examine large amounts of potentially relevant variables, which generally leads to some statistically significant, but not necessarily theoretically meaningful, relationships among these variables. This makes it hard to empirically evaluate the model. Second, all kinds of stress reactions are lumped together, whereas some of these reactions may occur immediately in a stressful situation (e.g., anxiety), others may only occur after extensive exposure to stress (e.g., high blood pressure), whereas again others may not necessarily be due to stress (e.g., turnover). Third, the model tells us little about mediating processes between different elements in the model, and it ignores various social psychological

processes that may play a role, such as social comparison of one's situation with that of colleagues (e.g., Buunk & Ybema, 1997), and cognitive interpretations of stressful events and health complaints (e.g., Peeters, Schaufeli, & Buunk, 1995a).

Person-Environment Fit Model

The theory underlying the Person-Environment Fit Model is also an example of a mediational perspective on stress. The model is based on the view that behaviour is a function of both the person and the environment (Lewin, 1935, 1951; Murray, 1938, 1959). Following Lewin, French (1973) suggested that the interaction between environmental variables and relevant characteristics of the person determines whether stress occurs. According to the P-E Fit Model, occupational stress is the result of a discrepancy ("misfit") between what the individual desires, and what the job supplies, or between the abilities of the individual and the demands in the work environment. The P-E Fit Model makes a distinction between subjective and objective misfit. The first type of misfit refers to a discrepancy between the people's view of themselves and their view of the environment (referred to as the subjective person and the subjective environment). For instance, workers may feel that they lack the abilities that they perceive the work situation demands, or they may have desires, for instance for career advancement, that cannot be realized. The second type of misfit concerns the discrepancy between how the person actually is and the objective characteristics of the work environment (referred to as the objective person and the objective environment). For instance, there may be a discrepancy between the required level of typing speed and the actual typing speed of a secretary. The correspondence between the objective person and the subjective person is labelled "accuracy of self-assessment", while the correspondence between the objective and subjective environment is labelled "contact with reality". According to the model, *defence mechanisms* are supposed to reduce the subjective misfit without any changes in objective misfit, for instance by denial. In contrast, *coping* refers in this model to strategies that may reduce objective misfit (cf.

Caplan, 1983; French et al., 1982), for instance, by learning new skills or by securing a lower workload.

An important assumption in the P-E Fit Model is that both a positive misfit (e.g., one has more capabilities than are required, or one wants less than is provided) and a negative misfit (e.g., one has less capabilities than are required, or one wants more than is provided) lead to stress. Thus, a curvilinear, U-shaped relationship between fit and strains is assumed. In a number of studies such relationships as proposed by the model have indeed been found (for a review, see Edwards, 1991). For example, in the pioneering study by Caplan, Cobb, French, Van Harrison, and Pinneau (1975) among over 2,000 workers a U-shaped relationship was found between the discrepancy of actual and desired complexity of work on the one hand and level of depression on the other. Both too little and too much complexity were related to depression. More recently, Edwards and Van Harrison (1993) found additional evidence that a perfect fit between what an employee desires and obtains is related to the lowest level of strains.

In spite of the plausible assumptions underlying the model, several problems must be mentioned. To begin with, various aspects of the model have hardly been tested empirically. In particular, defence and coping mechanisms are seldom measured, and therefore there is little evidence for such mechanisms. In addition, usually only the subjective person and environment, and not the objective person and environment, are assessed (Cox & Ferguson, 1994). Furthermore, the fit between person and environment characteristics often does not have unique effects on strains compared to the effects of person and environment characteristics assessed independently (Caplan, 1983; Semmer, 1996). Finally, the P-E Fit Model does not specify where the standards—i.e. desires and aspirations—come from. Such standards may also be adapted to reality, such that they are made consistent with the opportunities and restrictions that are found in the actual work setting. In that case, the causation may even be the other way round: People who are psychologically healthy have realistic aspirations, which leads to a good P-E Fit, whereas unadapted workers have unreal-

istically high or low standards, leading to a misfit between person and environment.

Demand-Control-Support Model

Karasek and his team originally developed a model known as the Job Demand-Control (JD-C) Model, but extended this model later to the Demand-Control-Support Model. In order to understand the basic ideas of both models, we will first discuss the Job Demand-Control Model. This model, which was first mentioned in a widely cited article by Karasek (1979), can be considered a synthesis of two well-known lines of research, viz. the job redesign tradition (e.g., Hackman & Oldham, 1980) and the Michigan stress tradition which is apparent in the Social Environment Model and the Person-Environment Fit Model (e.g., Caplan, et al., 1975; Kahn, 1981). The aim of the JD-C Model was to provide a theoretical framework for the development of guidelines for the enhancement of the quality of working life. In addition to emphasizing the necessity of reducing work-related strains, the model also emphasizes the importance of promoting work motivation, learning and growth. Therefore, the model includes as outcome variables not only the consequences of stress such as exhaustion, psychosomatic complaints, and cardiovascular disease, but also work motivation, learning and job satisfaction. In this way, the model reconciles the stress tradition with the insights of social learning theory and adult education theory (Landsbergis, 1988).

The JD-C Model postulates that the primary sources of stress lie within two basic characteristics of the job (Baker, 1985). The JD-C Model emphasizes the need to categorize these job characteristics as either *demands* or *control*, and does not simply list all job features as potential stressors (Schnall, Landsbergis, & Baker, 1994). In line with the mediational definition of stress, psychological strains are viewed as a consequence of the joint effects of the demands of a job and the range of job control available to the employee (Karasek, 1979). Accordingly, four different kinds of psychosocial work situations may result from four combinations between high and low levels of psychological job demands and job control. Karasek (1979) uses the following terms for the four kinds of work situations: (1) high strain jobs: (2)

active jobs; (3) low strain jobs; and (4) passive jobs.

The first major prediction of the JD-C Model is that the strongest aversive job-related strain reactions (e.g., exhaustion, anxiety and health complaints) will occur when job demands are high and worker's control is low (i.e., high strain jobs). High job demands produce a state of arousal which is normally accompanied by increased heart rate and adrenalin secretion. If there is also an environmentally based constraint, i.e., low control, the arousal cannot be converted into an effective coping response. Such conditions produce a more extensive reaction for a longer period, a so-called damaging, unused residual strain. The opposite situation is termed "low strain jobs", that is, jobs in which workers' control is high and job demands are low. In this situation the model predicts lower than average levels of residual strain. The second prediction of the model, which is sometimes overlooked, is that motivation, learning and personal growth will occur in situations where both job demands and workers' control are high (i.e., active jobs). The opposite of this situation is formed by passive jobs, in which skills and abilities may atrophy, a situation which resembles the "learned helplessness" phenomenon (cf. Abramson, Seligman, & Teasdale, 1978; Lennerlöf, 1988).

The expansion of the model by including social support came from the realization that job control is not the only resource available for coping with job demands (cf. Johnson & Hall, 1988; Johnson, 1989), but that *workplace social support* may also function as a moderator of job demands (Johnson, 1989). Therefore, Johnson and Hall (1988) redefined the JD-C Model by adding workplace social support. Karasek and Theorell (1990) defined workplace social support as overall levels of helpful social interaction available on the job. In the extended model, called the Demand-Control-Support Model (DCS Model), eight instead of four kinds of work situations were modelled, i.e., the four types of work situations in the JD-C Model in combination with either low or high social support. Thus, the DCS Model describes the joint, interactive, effects of the three basic characteristics of the work organization, viz. job demands, job control and workplace social support.

A large number of studies evaluating the two models failed to provide clear and unambiguous support (Jones & Fletcher, 1996). Most studies did not find the postulated interaction effects (e.g., Carayon, 1993). A number of reasons for this have been presented in the literature. First, a large number of studies was based on secondary analyses of already collected data, in which the variables often were not operationalized adequately. Second, the measures of job control usually included not only items reflecting control about various workplace conditions, but also items reflecting skill utilization and job complexity (Ganster & Fusilier, 1989). Indeed, Wall, Jackson, Mullarkey, and Parker (1996) showed that when job control was measured specifically, the hypothesized interaction was found, whereas the interaction was not found when the much broader definition of job decision latitude, including variables like skill use and task variety, was used. Third, the interaction effects between job control and job demands have been tested in at least four different ways, not all of which were appropriate (cf. Landsbergis, Schnall, Warren, Pickering, & Schwartz, 1994). Fourth, in some studies it is not clear to what extent the variables in the model are confounded with other variables (such as socioeconomic status and health behaviour). Fifth, the models were confirmed by studies using large and heterogeneous samples, while studies based on small and homogeneous samples could not confirm the predicted interaction effects. This might be due to the lack of variance in the latter samples. Finally, many studies have failed to take into account individual differences (such as locus of control, or Type A/B behaviour), emotional responses and coping strategies.

Vitamin Model

This model, that is very similar to the P-E Fit Model, was developed by Warr (1987). The central idea underlying the Vitamin Model (VM) is that mental health is affected by job characteristics in a way that is analogous to the effects that vitamins have on physical health. Generally, vitamin intake initially improves health and physical functioning, but beyond a particular intake level no further improvement is observed. Continued intake of vitamins may have two different kinds of effects. First, a so-called constant effect may occur: health does not improve any further, nor is the individual's physical health impaired. Second, an excessive intake of vitamins may lead to a toxic concentration in the body ("hypervitaminosis"), which causes poor bodily functioning and ill health. In this case, observed associations between vitamin intake and health are expected to be inversely U-shaped.

Because, according to Warr (1987), certain job characteristics may affect mental health in the same way as vitamins affect physical health, De Jonge and Schaufeli (in press) refer to these characteristics as "psychological work vitamins". Generally, the absence of certain job characteristics will impair mental health, and initially the presence of such characteristics will have a beneficial effect on employee mental health. However, beyond a certain required level, a plateau has been reached and the level of mental health remains constant. Further increase of job characteristics may either produce a constant effect or may be harmful and impair mental health. According to Warr (1987, 1994) the type of effect depends upon the particular job characteristic under consideration. After a thorough examination of the literature, Warr identified nine job features that act as "vitamins", i.e., as potential determinants of job-related mental health. Warr assumes that six of these features (i.e., job demands, job autonomy, social support, skill utilization, skill variety, and task feedback) have curvilinear effects. The lack of such features as well as an excess of such features will affect mental health negatively. The remaining three job characteristics (i.e., safety, salary, and task significance) are supposed to follow a linear pattern: the more such a characteristic is present in the work situation, the higher the level of mental health will be.

In the VM, a more specific conceptualization of affective well-being is proposed than in most other models of occupational stress. This model, therefore, comes closest to our earlier presented view of occupational stress as an emotional process. According to Warr (1987), affective well-being as an indicator of *job-related* mental health has three dimensions: (1) discontented-contented; (2) anxious-comfortable; and (3) depressed-actively

pleased. In occupational settings, the first component has usually been operationalized through measures of job satisfaction, but measures of job attachment and organizational commitment have been used as well. The second component is usually tapped through measures of job-related anxiety, job-related tension, and job-related strain. Finally, the third component has been assessed by measures of, for example, occupational burnout, job-related depression, job boredom, and fatigue.

Although the VM focuses on characteristics of the work environment rather than on the experience of the worker, individual characteristics are viewed as possible moderators of the effects of job characteristics on mental health. That is, such effects are supposed to occur more for some than for other people. Warr (1994) mentions three categories of individual characteristics: (1) *abilities*, i.e., all kinds of personal skills that can be viewed as relatively stable characteristics (e.g., intellectual and psychomotor skills); (2) *values*, i.e., all sorts of specific value orientations, such as preferences, motives and attitudes; and (3) *baseline mental health*, i.e., dispositions such as negative affectivity. Moderating effects of such characteristics are expected especially in the case of a so-called "matching" individual characteristic (Warr, 1994). Individual characteristics that match particular job characteristics will cause a stronger moderating effect than those which lack this matching property. Job autonomy may serve as an example: a matching individual characteristic might be "need for autonomy". It is assumed that the need for autonomy is a moderator for the relationship between job autonomy and, for instance, job satisfaction (cf. Warr, 1987).

In a thorough summary of the empirical evidence with respect to several aspects of the VM, Warr (1987, 1994) showed that *in isolation* his nine job characteristics act as predicted by the model. In recent years, however, a number of cross-sectional studies have investigated the patterns proposed by the VM (e.g., Fletcher & Jones, 1993; De Jonge & Schaufeli, in press; Parkes, 1991; Warr, 1990; Xie & Johns, 1995). Taken together, the results of these studies are mixed and inconclusive. Job demands and job autonomy, for instance, seem to be curvilinearly related to some aspects of employee mental health in the way that is predicted by the model, whereas the effect of workplace social support does not follow the model. Most importantly, however, all studies failed to take account of the ways in which possible combinations of the nine job characteristics affect job-related well-being.

METHODOLOGICAL PROBLEMS IN OCCUPATIONAL STRESS RESEARCH

Almost 20 years ago Kasl (1978) wrote a critical review in which he called many occupational stress studies trivial and expressed fundamental criticism of most research in this field. The field seems to have made little progress, considering similar critical comments on occupational stress research that have appeared in more recent articles (Kasl, 1986, 1987, 1989, 1996). In general, the following methodological problems with much research and many models in this field can be noted.

1. The mediational definition of stress often acts as a self-serving methodological trap, in which the measurement of the independent variable (such as perceived role ambiguity) and the dependent variables (such as feelings of insecurity) are sometimes so close that they appear to be two measures of the same construct. Several authors have argued for independent assessment of stressors and strains, using a multi-method approach, in which objective measures, peer ratings, and subjective measures are paired (cf. Cox & Ferguson, 1994; Frese & Zapf, 1988; Kasl, 1986; Semmer, Zapf, & Greif, 1996; Spector, 1992).

2. Strains may in some cases wrongly be attributed to the work situation. The influence of the work situation on strains and illness is often overestimated, not only in comparison to the home situation (Robinson & Inkson, 1994), but also relative to the influence of stable personality characteristics. The assumption in much occupational stress research is that negative emotions and psychosomatic complaints, such as dizzi-

ness, loss of appetite, palpitations, sleeplessness, loneliness and dissatisfaction, are *caused* by stressful working conditions. However, similar reactions are included in personality measures of neuroticism, and may simply reflect a stable personality disposition. Indeed, various authors have argued that many symptoms that are usually considered as strains, basically reflect the negative affectivity characteristic of neurotic individuals, and that neurotic individuals also tend to perceive more stressors in their work environment (e.g., Payne & Jones, 1987; Spector & O'Connell, 1994). This could mean that associations between stressors and strains merely reflect this personality dimension (e.g., Burke, Brief, & George, 1993). Although well-designed research (Semmer, 1996) shows that substantial associations between stressors and strains may remain even when negative affectivity is controlled for, these associations do become weaker. Therefore, it is important to control for neuroticism when examining such associations (Parkes, 1994).

3. Because most studies on occupational stress have cross-sectional designs, the causal direction of the relationships can rarely be established. It is generally assumed that the causal flow is unidirectional from stressors and social support to strains. However, not only do stressors and support affect strains, but strains can also affect people's perceptions of stressors and of social support. For example, in a longitudinal study, Marcelissen, Winnubst, Buunk, and De Wolff (1988) found that the existence of strains had a deteriorating effect on perceived support from co-workers, and a few studies have demonstrated that simultaneous reciprocal causation between stressors and strains does occur (e.g., James & Jones, 1980; James & Tetrick, 1986; De Jonge, 1995; Kohn & Schooler, 1983). Nevertheless, most evidence seems to suggest that strains tend to occur *after* stressor perceptions, rather than vice versa (De Jonge, 1995; Warr, 1987).

4. Related to the previous points, in most stress research, stressors, strains, and moderating variables such as social support are assessed *between* subjects, and these variables are usually measured through global assessments of how the respondents experience their work situation in general. We learn, for example, how many somatic complaints are experienced by people who perceive a high degree of overload in their work situation. Relatively little attention has been paid to the effects of stressful *events* at work on changes in strains on a day-to-day basis. Indeed, it is important to examine such *within* subjects' effects, and to assess events and strains at work in a much more detailed way. Buunk and Verhoeven (1991) developed a method referred to as the Daily Interaction Record in Organizations (DIRO) with which, over the course of a week, daily the number and nature of stressful events, the number and features of all social interactions, and the degree of negative affect at the end of the day are assessed. A number of studies has shown the viability of such an approach (for a review, see Buunk & Peeters, 1994).

5. By analogy to Warr's ideas (1987, 1994) there may be non-linear relationships between stressors and strains. Van Dijkhuizen (1980), for instance, found that only 32% of all causal connections examined in his study were really linear. In addition, De Jonge and Schaufeli (in press) found several curvilinear, U-shaped, relationships between job characteristics and psychological outcomes. For instance, most anxiety was found in people who experienced either low or high job demands. Nevertheless, most studies test only the linear associations between stressors and strains.

6. Differences in stress, mortality or morbidity between occupational groups are not necessarily caused by the nature of the work, but may also be due to, for instance, self-selection in occupations and positions, selection by organizations, the fact that unhealthy workers leave certain occupations earlier ("healthy worker effect"), or differences in living conditions and health behaviour.

7. In general, criterion variables are measured and analysed as if they were continuous variables, while this is not always the case. Brown (1985) points out that correlational analyses with psychological disorders like depression are inadequate. According to Brown this is rather a dichotomous variable; a person either is, or is not clinically depressed. In a similar vein, it may be the case that, for example, individuals are either experiencing burnout as a disorder or not, rather than experiencing burnout to a certain degree.

ASPECTS OF OCCUPATIONAL STRESS

Guided by the models outlined above, and cautioning against the methodological limitations of many occupational stress studies, we will now examine a number of categories of psychological variables and processes that are involved in occupational stress, and how these variables are related to the emotional stress process.

1. *Stressors.* We focus in particular on the psychosocial causes of negative emotions at work, such as role ambiguity and low status.

2. *Coping behaviour.* Coping refers to the way in which individuals try to change, reinterpret or reduce the negative emotions, either directly or through modifying the causes of these emotions, e.g., through instrumental action and cognitive effort.

3. *Moderator variables.* Some characteristics may moderate the effects of stressors on the experience of negative emotions and health. The most notable of these are personality traits and social support.

4. *Long-term stress reactions.* In the long run, occupational stress may have several adverse health consequences, such as burnout, depression, psychosomatic complaints, and impairment of physical health.

Stressors

Hamberger and Lohr (1984) have pointed out that there are many different definitions of stressors: stimuli that are unpleasant, stimuli that lead to a stress reaction, stimuli that result in a strong attempt to adapt, every problem that a person needs to solve, and every situation that requires a major adaptation. In accordance with the view of stress as an emotion, we consider here as a stressor every event, situation or cognition that may evoke a negative emotion in an individual. A first implication of this definition is that every stressor is only a stressor in a *probabilistic* sense, as Lazarus (1985) emphasizes. There are few events or situations that will lead to negative emotions in everybody under all conditions. A second implication is that the nature of stressors may strongly vary: they may be day-to-day worries, major events, but also prolonged problematic work situations (Bailey & Bhagat, 1987). A third implication is that stressors may also be certain ideas, thoughts and perceptions that evoke negative emotions. A typical example of such stressors is formed by mid-career problems, such as the idea that one may not reach the position that one aspires to, or the idea of almost belonging to the older generation in the organization (Buunk & Janssen, 1992).

This reasoning suggests that many occupations have their own characteristic stressors. This may be illustrated by a few examples. Female managers may experience typical stressors such as sexual harassment, sex discrimination, and a denial of access to challenging assignments (Burke, 1996). Keenan and Newton (1985) asked engineers which stressful incidents they had experienced. The most frequent experience was the situation that one's time or efforts were wasted, immediately followed by interpersonal conflicts and qualitative underload (having to do work that is too simple). For nurses stressful incidents are obviously of an entirely different nature. Bailey (1980) developed seven categories of work aspects that function as potential stressors for nurses, including interpersonal relationships, physical work environment and patient care. Bus drivers have been found to experience characteristic stressors as well, including irregular work-schedules, traffic pressures, responsibility for passengers, and stressful contacts with passengers (Kompier, 1996). Among police officers typical stressors include upsetting situations such as traffic incidents and problematic and frustrating interactions with the public (Buunk & Verhoeven, 1991).

It is, of course, impossible to give an overview of all potential stressors within the scope of this chapter. It is also not possible to present a theory-based, all-embracing categorization of stressors. Most categorizations of stressors in the work situation are descriptive and pragmatic (e.g., Burke, 1988; Cooper & Marshall, 1978; Fletcher, 1991; Ivancevich & Matteson, 1980). We will therefore confine ourselves to five groups of common psychosocial stressors without claiming to be exhaustive (cf. Fletcher, 1991; Fletcher & Payne, 1980; Karasek, 1979; Karasek & Theorell, 1990; Payne, 1979).

1. *Task and work characteristics*. This refers to stressful aspects inherent in the task and in the work environment, for example high workload, high physical effort, great responsibility, shift work and time pressure. Various studies have shown that such stressors play a major role as contributors to different job strain outcomes, including dissatisfaction, coronary heart disease, high blood pressure, musculoskeletal problems, psychosomatic symptoms, anxiety, exhaustion and depression (for an overview see Bongers, De Winter, Kompier, & Hildebrandt, 1993; Crandall & Perrewé, 1995; Karasek & Theorell, 1990). It must be noted that, unlike the stressors described below, demanding task and work characteristics do not necessarily involve psychosocial stress in terms of negative emotions. Indeed, a high mental load is not by definition stressful (Gaillard & Wientjes, 1994), but negative emotions may result from an overload as well as from an underload, depending on the discrepancy of mental load and the capabilities and aspirations of the individual worker.

2. *Role problems*. Occupational stress can be due to the particular role the individual worker plays within the organization. In an

organization, there are certain, often unspecified expectations about which behaviours are and which behaviours are not acceptable in a certain position. Especially these role expectations may contain major stressors. As noted above, Kahn et al. (1964) have focused in particular on the effects of role conflict and role ambiguity. *Role conflict* occurs when expectations and demands are difficult to meet or are mutually incompatible. Four basic types of role conflicts can be distinguished: (1) the intrasender conflict (different expectations and demands from the same other person); (2) the intersender conflict (different demands from different persons); (3) the interrole conflict (expectations from different roles that are difficult to combine, such as the role of parent and that of employee); and (4) the person-role conflict (a tension between the needs and values of the person and the demands and expectations from the environment). *Role ambiguity* arises when people do not have sufficient or adequate information to fulfil their role properly. Kahn et al. (1964) point out that employees should know which rights, duties and responsibilities belong to a certain position, how the required activities should be carried out and which behaviours will be rewarded or punished. Important areas of role ambiguity are the scope of one's responsibilities, the question whose expectations should be met, and the question how one is appreciated by others. There is considerable support for the stress-inducing properties of role conflict and ambiguity. In an early review, Van Sell, Brief and Schuler (1981) showed that role conflicts and role ambiguity in different occupations are indeed related to job dissatisfaction and feelings of job-related strain. Recent research has supported this conclusion. For example, in a study among public sector employees, Terry, Neilsen and Perchard (1993) found that, when controlling for neuroticism, role ambiguity and role conflict remain significant predictors of psychological well-being and job satisfaction. Manlove (1994) found that burnout

among child care workers was related to role ambiguity as well as role conflict. In the context of the perspective outlined above, we would expect relationships between particular stressors and particular negative emotions. There is some evidence for this. For instance, Van Dijkhuizen (1980) reported that role conflicts were particularly related to irritation, while role ambiguity showed a stronger relationship with feelings of anxiety. In a similar vein, Keenan and Newton (1984) described that role ambiguity was a better predictor of job dissatisfaction and anxiety than role conflicts were.

3. *Interpersonal conflicts.* Just like other interpersonal relationships, relationships between people at work may also be characterized by all kinds of stressful situations, including open conflict, lack of trust, poor communication, hostility, and competition. According to Van de Vliert (Chapter 15, Volume 3) a situation may be called a conflict when either of the parties feels thwarted or irritated by the other; this is characterized by some kind of subjectively experienced frustration. This means that a conflict need not be acted out openly, but that it is also possible to have a conflict with somebody without the other person being aware of it. Also, a conflict is not necessarily about another person's behaviour. For instance, somebody else's appearance or opinions may lead to interpersonal conflicts. Stokols (1992) argued that *conflict-prone* organizations exist in which the physical arrangements and social conditions predispose the members of the organization towards chronic conflict and health problems. Such organizations are characterized by, among others, an absence of shared goals, rigid ideologies, competitive coalitions, little participation in organizational decision making, an anomalous and turbulent environment, a relatively unstable role structure and membership, an ambiguous allocation of space and territory in the organization, and inadequate environmental resources for meeting organizational goals. Although the stressful consequences of

interpersonal conflicts have not been studied as extensively as those of other stressors, there is evidence that conflicts at work are in general very stressful, and are accompanied by a high level of strains (e.g., Keenan & Newton, 1984; Spector & O'Connell, 1994). For example, in a study among nurses, Tyler and Cushway (1995) found that conflicts with other nurses and medical doctors were negatively related to mental well-being. In two studies, one among police officers and the other among secretaries, Buunk and Peeters (1994) found that, over a period of five days, the number of interpersonal frustrations in the relationship with colleagues and superiors, had a higher correlation with negative affect at the end of the day than any other type of stressful event. Moreover, there is evidence from longitudinal research among bus drivers that conflicts with superiors predict absence frequency as recorded by the company (Geurts, Schaufeli, & Buunk, 1993). Finally, it must be noted that not only conflicts with co-workers and superiors may lead to stress, but also conflicts with the people to whom one's work is directed. For example, in a study among teachers, Sutton (1984) found a high correlation between a lack of job satisfaction and problems in discipline with students, and in a study among correctional officers, Buunk and Peeters (1994) found that disobedience by prisoners was correlated with negative affect.

4. *Status and career problems*. This category includes problems experienced with regard to status, recognition, prospects, and material and symbolic rewards. The low status of a profession may affect employees' well-being negatively, particularly when they feel they are entitled to more. For instance, a study among teachers in Connecticut showed that the low pay and low status of the job were considered to be the main problems (Litt & Turk, 1985). Siegrist and Peter (1994) argued that among blue collar workers, low status control (low expectations of job stability and promotion prospects) impairs self-esteem and the sense of mastery, and subsequently physical health. In line with this reasoning, Siegrist and Peter showed a relatively much higher risk of coronary disease among blue collar workers who experienced, in addition to poor rewards, a low status control. Social comparison plays a central role in matters of status, pay, and promotion, and individuals may experience stress when they perceive that similar others are in such respects better off (Buunk & Ybema, 1997). For example, in a study among blue collar workers, Geurts, Buunk & Schaufeli (1994b) found that the perception that one was in various ways less well off than one's colleagues, was accompanied by feelings of resentment. Especially people who value upward mobility continually evaluate how they are doing compared to others in similar circumstances. In mid-career the experience of career stagnation may be very painful for such people, and *relative deprivation* may occur. This concept is used to refer to the situation that a person has achieved a lot from an objective point of view (e.g., a relatively high income, many possibilities for self-actualization and clean and safe work), but is still dissatisfied because he or she has not attained the status, salary and recognition to which he or she feels entitled, compared to similar others. Research has shown that such perceptions lead in general to feelings of resentment and depression, especially in mid-career when career prospects appear bleak (Buunk & Janssen, 1992).

5. *Lack of control and influence*. As has been noted above, in many theories of stress (e.g., Lazarus, 1995) a lack of control of one's situation is considered to be an important factor that may both cause and aggravate stress. Indeed, a lack of control has been found to be a major dimension of stressful events at work (Peeters, Buunk, & Schaufeli, 1995b). Control has often been studied as a personality characteristic that acts as a moderator, i.e., as a variable that may buffer the negative effects of stressors on strains (e.g., Etzion & Westman, 1994; Fox,

Dwyer, & Ganster, 1993; Theorell & Karasek, 1996). However, a lack of control has also been studied as a stressor in the work environment. Nevertheless, control as a personality characteristic and control as a feature of the work environment are difficult to separate, especially because both types of variables are usually measured through subjective assessments. In general, the term "control" is defined as power or mastery of the environment (Fisher, 1989), and refers more specifically to a sense of having the cognitive or behavioural possibilities to bring about a desired situation, or to end an undesired situation. Early experimental social psychological research showed that the same noise level was experienced as less stressful when it was possible to switch the noise off (even though this possibility was not used!) than when no such possibility existed (Glass, Reim, & Singer, 1971; Reim, Glass, & Singer, 1971). Generally, lack of control initially leads to feelings of anxiety, anger or hostility, and to attempts at restoring control. At a later stage it may lead to depression, if failure to gain control of a situation after repeated attempts is ascribed to general stable personality factors ("I am just not much good at anything") (Abramson & Seligman, 1981; Fisher, 1989).

In the work situation, various types of control can be distinguished. Fisher (1985) made a distinction between three basic forms of control: (1) *personal competence*: the feeling that one is able to achieve and create things; such expectations may occur in work situations when a person makes more or less complete, clearly recognizable products; (2) *interpersonal control*: the idea that one is able to exert power and influence over others, an expectation that may be stimulated by, for example, a participatory leadership style; and (3) *sociopolitical control*: the expectation that one is able to reach one's goals as a group, through, for example, strikes and participation in workers' councils. It must be noted that, although this typology may have high face validity, it does not seem to be supported by psycho-metric studies (Ingledew, Hardy, & Cooper, 1992). Moreover, control in the workplace has been conceptualized most often in a different way, i.e. terms of autonomy or freedom in scheduling one's own work and determining how to perform one's job (e.g., Hackman & Oldham, 1980). Such a lack of autonomy has been recognized as a major stressor at work (cf. Frese, 1989; Ganster & Fusilier, 1989; Sauter, Hurrell, & Cooper, 1989; Jones & Fletcher, 1996). In general, many studies have shown that a lack of control at work operationalized in a variety of ways is associated with adverse health outcomes, including cardiovascular risks, emotional exhaustion, psychosomatic complaints, anxiety and depression (e.g., Ellis & Miller, 1993; Evans & Carrere, 1991; Ganster & Fusilier, 1989; Sauter, et al., 1989; Schaufeli & Buunk, 1996).

Coping behaviour

In the literature on stress it is often assumed that the way in which people cope with stressful events and situations partly determines the eventual consequences of such events and situations for their physical and mental health. Nevertheless, there are many definitions and ways of measuring coping (for overviews, see Latack & Havlovic, 1992; O'Driscoll & Cooper, 1994; Parkes, 1994). In some of these definitions, coping is conceptualized as a stable dispositional characteristic or *coping style*, which is measured by asking individuals how they usually deal with stress, or somewhat more specifically, with stress at work (e.g., Pearlin & Schooler, 1978). However, whereas some coping strategies, such as thinking positively, seem to be more or less stable across situations, other coping responses, such as seeking social support, are not (Lazarus, 1993). Therefore, most perspectives on coping emphasize that an individual's coping responses may *vary* strongly across situations, and that coping responses should not be regarded as a stable personal style. A study by Scheier, Weintraub, and Carver (1986) demonstrated, for instance, that in controllable situations, people high in optimism mainly used problem-focused coping and positive reinterpretation of the situation, whereas in uncontrollable situations, they showed acceptance and resignation. To capture such variation in coping responses, O'Driscoll and Cooper (1994) propose a "critical incident analysis" in which individuals specify a number of stressful situations, specify their coping behaviours in these situations, and specify the consequences of these behaviours. In contrast, Latack and Havlovic (1992) suggest that middle-range specificity in coping measures may be the most fruitful way to study coping. Assessing coping responses to categories of stressful situations (e.g., role conflicts) has more predictive value for actual behaviour than assessing general coping styles, and lead to better generalizability of findings than highly specific measures.

Lazarus (1993) conceptualized coping as a *process*, as a person's "ongoing efforts in thought and action to manage specific demands appraised as taxing or overwhelming" (p. 8). To be a little more specific, we define coping behaviour as all the cognitive and behavioural attempts aimed at changing, reinterpreting or reducing the negative emotions themselves, or the factors in the environment that cause these emotions. An important implication of this definition is that coping behaviour primarily refers to *attempts*, i.e. actions that may or may not be effective, and may in the long run even be harmful, such as drinking and smoking (Folkman, 1984). Many different taxonomies of coping strategies have been developed. One type of taxonomies is based on the *goal* of the behaviour, and a frequently found distinction is the following (cf. Pearlin & Schooler, 1978; Semmer, 1996):

1. Attempts to change, remove or reduce the stressor, which is often labelled *problem-focused* coping (e.g., Lazarus, 1993). Problem-focused coping may include behaviours like seeking help or advice, increasing efforts to encounter the threat, and more cognitive responses such as thinking out a plan of action. According to Lazarus, problem-focused coping will be found especially when an individual appraises the situation as controllable.

2. Attempts to directly change, reduce or remove the negative feelings, which is generally called *emotion-focused* coping (Lazarus, 1993). This may include behavi-

ours like smoking, drinking, and physical exercise, and cognitive strategies like avoidance and relaxation techniques. According to Lazarus, this will occur particularly when people think that nothing can be done about the problem.

3. Attempts to change the perception or appraisal of the stressor, which may be labelled *appraisal-focused* coping (e.g., Billings & Moos, 1984). This may include comparing oneself with others worse off (Pearlin & Schooler, 1978; Taylor, Buunk, & Aspinwall, 1990; Wills, 1981), and engaging in selective evaluation techniques (Buunk & Ybema, 1995; Taylor, Wood, & Lichtman, 1983), such as thinking how things could have been worse, and focusing on the benefits of the stressful event. Some authors regard appraisal-focused coping as a part of emotion-focused coping (e.g., Lazarus & Folkman, 1984).

Various other typologies have been presented, and various studies have tried to develop a classification of coping responses on a more empirical basis (for overviews see Parkes, 1994; Semmer, 1996). For instance, Carver, Scheier, and Weintraub (1989) have identified four dimensions of coping responses through a second order factor analysis, i.e. (1) active coping, (2) denial and disengagement, (3) acceptance, and (4) seeking social support and venting emotions. Additionally, Cohen, Reese, Kaplan, and Riggio (1986) assessed the following coping responses (1) direct actions, (2) inhibition of action, (3) information seeking, (4) intrapsychic processes, and (5) turning to others for support. In a study among case managers, Koeske, Kirk, and Koeske (1993) distinguished only two factors, which involve "control coping" and "avoidance coping". This dichotomy is similar to the coping styles called "monitoring" and "blunting" (e.g., Miller, 1990; Muris, 1994), i.e., the tendency to seek out information about the threat versus the tendency to cognitively distract from and psychologically "blunt" threat-relevant information. However, there is no consensus about the number and kind of coping dimensions that should be employed, and about the precise definition and content of the various dimensions (Semmer, 1996).

Although quite a few studies on occupational stress included coping measures, these studies have not produced very consistent results on the *effectiveness* of coping strategies in reducing stress in work situations. In an early review article, Murphy (1985) pointed out that coping directed at the source of stress may, in fact, even lead to more stress. In a well-known study, Pearlin and Schooler (1978) found that coping strategies were effective in reducing stress in interpersonal relationships, but had little effect on stress that results from problems at work. There is some evidence from the coping literature indicating that problem-focused coping is associated with better mental health when the problem can be remedied, whereas emotion-focused coping may be beneficial when the problem is uncontrollable (Semmer, 1996). For example, Bowman and Stern (1995) found in a study among medical centre nurses that problem-focused coping was effective in reducing stress especially when the stressful episode was deemed controllable. Moreover, they found that appraisal-focused coping generally had positive effects on well-being, whereas avoidance was strongly related to negative affect for both controllable and uncontrollable stressors. This suggests that coping directed at the cognitive appraisal of one's situation may be quite effective in reducing stress in a variety of situations.

In the past decades, it has become increasingly clear that social comparison—comparing one's situation and responses to those of others—is a quite prevalent way of coping with stress (Taylor et al., 1990). Nevertheless, the coping literature has, with the exception of the early work by Pearlin and Schooler (1978), in general paid little attention to the role of social comparison. One would expect that stress would generate social comparison activity particularly in work situations, because individuals are usually surrounded by similar others. Classical social comparison theory maintains that especially when individuals are uncertain about their own emotional responses, they will be interested in comparing these responses with those of others in a similar situation in order to evaluate their own reactions (Schachter, 1959). Buunk, Schaufeli, and Ybema (1994; see also Buunk & Schaufeli, 1993) showed indeed that nurses who experienced a high degree

of uncertainty were relatively more interested in learning about the way in which others in a similar situation responded, and in talking to such others. In addition, these comparison needs were elevated among nurses high in emotional exhaustion. However, these nurses high in burnout at the same time seemed to avoid comparisons with others more experienced and competent, although such comparisons might have provided information relevant for problem-focused coping. To conclude, we like to suggest that a focus on the *social* aspects of coping may be a fruitful approach for studying coping with occupational stress.

Personality characteristics

Personality characteristics play an important role in the process by which demanding work conditions affect mental and physical health (Taylor & Cooper, 1989). As noted by Parkes (1994), personality characteristics affect what kind of jobs people select, and thus to what type of stressors they are exposed. In addition, some persons may find themselves in stressful circumstances more often than others because they, often unwittingly, create their own stressors. Moreover, due to differences in personality, there are considerable differences in the way individuals respond to similar stressors. The pioneering study by Kahn et al. (1964) already showed that, for example, the presence of role conflicts did correlate with the level of experienced tension in flexible persons, but not in rigid persons. For rigid persons a slight degree of role conflict was more stressful than for flexible persons, but a high degree of role conflict evoked more tension in flexible than in rigid persons. Following this pioneering work, many other occupational stress studies have shown that the relationship between a certain stressor and a certain stress reaction mainly, or even exclusively, occurs in persons with certain personality characteristics. We will discuss three of the most studied characteristics in more detail, i.e., locus of control and self-efficacy, Type A behaviour, and hardiness.

Locus of control. The concept of locus of control refers to the extent to which individuals believe that their outcomes are determined primarily by their own efforts and ability rather than by external factors, like fate, chance, the circumstances, or powerful others (Rotter, 1966).

gratitude, in return for the care we provide to others. Within human service professions, such expectations are often not fulfilled, and the interaction with recipients of care typically generates more costs than rewards (cf. Maslach & Jackson, 1982). For example, patients may be worried and anxious, and interactions with such individuals is often not rewarding. Working with difficult groups, such as inmates of psychiatric hospitals, may even be less rewarding in spite of the large investments in terms of time, energy and attention. Buunk and Schaufeli (1993) suggested that in human service professions, burnout may be particularly related to the perception of having imbalanced relationships with the recipients of one's care. Indeed, this has been found in studies among nurses (VanYperen, Buunk, & Schaufeli, 1992), family physicians (Van Dierendonck, Schaufeli, & Sixma, 1994) and therapists working with inmates (Van Dierendonck, Schaufeli, & Buunk, 1996).

STRESS MANAGEMENT: PREVENTION AND INTERVENTION

One of the main objectives of occupational stress research should be to provide several forms of prevention or intervention aimed at reducing occupational stress. Numerous methods for the prevention of and intervention in occupational stress have been described (for reviews see Ivancevich & Matteson, 1988; Murphy, 1988). Many of these methods have not specifically been developed for occupational stress, but were borrowed from clinical psychology. Such individual-oriented methods teach individual employees to improve their stress-coping strategies and to prevent stress. Such programmes almost invariably contain some form of relaxation exercises, including rational emotive therapy, physical exercise, meditation or relaxation techniques, as well as social skills training. In addition, there are general workplace health promotion programmes aimed at smoking cessation, reduction of alcohol use, reducing blood pressure, stimulating physical exercise and reducing body weight.

In addition to these individual-oriented methods there are also work-oriented measures aimed at reducing or preventing employee stress (Burke, 1993). Worksite interventions which could improve the psychosocial, stress-inducing, characteristics of work have become more and more important. However, a common problem of these worksite methods is the difficulty in changing the work or task structure when the embedding organizational structure remains the same (cf. Karasek, 1992; Landsbergis, 1988). Therefore, a more integrated approach to change should not focus on one aspect within the organization, but on long-term change and development throughout the organization. Work redesign methods have long been advocated as improving work motivation and performance. More recently, attention has been paid to the potentially adverse health consequences of work redesign (Karasek & Theorell, 1990). There are a variety of worksite redesign methods that focus on work or task characteristics. Of all these methods, *job enrichment* has been the most crucial for a long time. Job enrichment involves changing a job both horizontally (i.e., adding tasks) and vertically (i.e., adding responsibility and authority). *Autonomous work groups* are another means for implementing change in the nature of work and increasing job control and social support (Gardell, 1982). Despite the enormous amount of studies on the effects of work redesign on the well-being of workers, there still remain few examples of carefully controlled evaluations of worksite interventions (Ganster, 1995). Karasek (1992), for instance, reviewed some basic trends in 19 case studies of stress prevention programmes. He found that work environment restructuring has been equally or even more effective than person-based coping enhancement programmes. From this point of view it may be desirable to redesign the job as well as to alter the worker's needs, values and abilities. Work-oriented and individual-oriented methods are dealt with in (amongst others) Chapters 2 & 6, Volume 2; Chapter 17, Volume 3; and Chapters 4 & 8, Volume 4 of this Handbook.

FINAL REMARKS

In this chapter we have emphasized that stress refers to the occurrence of negative emotions. Considering that work occupies a central place in the lives of many individuals, it is hardly surprising that situations and events at work are capable of evoking strong negative emotions. We have shown that structural characteristics of a job, role problems, interpersonal conflicts, lack of control, and lack of status may lead to occupational stress, and subsequently to all kinds of physical and mental complaints. However, individual differences in the appraisal of the situation play an important role in the stress process. A situation that constitutes a challenge for one person may be a threat for someone else. Moreover, coping strategies and personality factors, such as locus of control and hardiness, may in some situations prevent the occurrence of negative emotions. It should be noted that much occupational stress research is characterized by a lack of theoretical foundation. In this chapter we have broken a lance for more theoretical approaches from a social psychological and work psychological perspectives, with the emphasis on the psychosocial determinants of occupational stress. Although other theoretically oriented approaches to stress in work situations may be quite interesting and useful as well, we do hope we succeeded in presenting a fruitful perspective that will stimulate valuable future research on stress at work.

REFERENCES

Abramson, L.Y., & Seligman, M.E.P. (1981). Depression and the causal inference process. In J.H. Harvey, W. Ickes & R.F. Kidd (Eds.), *New directions in attribution research* (Vol. 3). Hillsdale, NJ: Erlbaum.

Abramson, L.Y., Seligman, M.E.P., & Teasdale, J.D. (1978). Learned helplessness in humans: Critique and reformulation. *Journal of Abnormal Psychology, 87*, 49–74.

Appels, A. (1993). Exhaustion as endpoint of job stress and precursor of disease. In L. Levi & F. LaFerla (Eds.), *A healthier work environment* (pp. 258–265). Copenhagen: WHO.

Argyle, M., & Henderson, M. (1985). *The anatomy of relationships*. Harmondsworth, Middlesex, England: Penguin Books.

Bailey, J.M., & Bhagat, R.S. (1987). Meaning and measurement of stressors in the work environment: An evaluation. In S.V. Kasl & C.L. Cooper (Eds.), *Stress and health: Issues in research methodology*. Chichester: John Wiley & Sons.

Bailey, J.M. (1980). The stress audit: Identifying the stressors of ICU nursing. *Journal of Nursing Education, 19* (6), 15–25.

Baker, D. (1985). The study of stress at work. *Annual Review of Public Health, 6*, 367–381.

Bandura, A. (1986). *Social foundations of thought and action: A social cognitive theory*. NJ: Prentice Hall.

Barling, J., & MacIntyre, A.T. (1993). Daily work role stressors, mood and emotional exhaustion. *Work and Stress, 7*, 315–325.

Barrera, M. (1986). Distinctions between social support concepts, measures and models. *American Journal of Community Psychology, 14* (4), 413–445.

Billings, A.G., & Moos, R.H. (1984). Coping, stress, and social resources among adults with unipolar depression. *Journal of Personality and Social Psychology, 46*, 877–891.

Blanc, P.M. Le, & Schaufeli, W.B. (1995). *Job demands, burnout and medical performance in intensive care units*. Paper presented at the IV ENOP Conference, Munich.

Bongers, P.M., Winter, C.R. de, Kompier, M.A.J., & Hildebrandt, V.H. (1993). Psychosocial factors at work and musculoskeletal disease. *Scandinavian Journal of Work, Environment, and Health, 19*, 297 312.

Booth-Kewley, S., & Friedman, H.S. (1987). Psychological predictors of heart disease: A quantitative review. *Psychological Bulletin, 101* (3), 343–362.

Boumans, N.P.G., & Landeweerd, J.A. (1992). The role of social support and coping behaviour in nursing work: Main of buffering effect? *Work and Stress, 6*, 191–202.

Bowman, G.D., & Stern, M. (1995). Adjustment to occupational stress: The relationship of perceived control to effectiveness of coping strategies. *Journal of Counseling Psychology, 42*, 294–303.

Brown, G.W. (1985). *Some notes on doing research on stress. A scientific debate: How to define and research stress*. National Institute of Mental Health, Center for Prevention Research. Washington, DC: US Department of Health and Human Services, Public Health Service.

Burke, R.J. (1982). Impact of occupational demands on nonwork experiences. *Journal of Psychology, 112*, 195–211.

Burke, R.J. (1988). Sources of managerial and professional stress in large organizations. In C.L. Cooper & R.L. Payne (Eds.), *Causes, coping and consequences of stress at work* (pp. 77–114). Chichester: Wiley.

Burke, R.J. (1993). Organizational-level interventions

Another reason is the variety of views held within companies on supposed links between a person's age and certain output variables such as productivity and creativity. For example, in certain sectors such as research and development and the software industry it is argued that only employees younger than 35 or 40 have the flexibility, inventiveness and élan to keep up with the high rate of successive innovations in knowledge and technology as well as in market requirements. Considerable added value is expected from the efforts of this age group. As regards the performance of innovative, creative work, the over-40s are simply written off. In such sectors one is labelled "too old" for some tasks at a relatively young age. Other sectors reserve the term "older" for those nearing retirement. The vagueness in defining who is termed an "older worker" is reflected in literature on this subject and consequently in this chapter as well.

In the remainder of this chapter the following will be discussed:

- fluctuating interest in the subject of "the older worker" (section 2);
- decline in job opportunities and the position of older workers (section 3);
- dejuvenization, aging and the position of older workers (section 4);
- the functioning of older workers (section 5);
- the mobility and employability of older workers (section 6);
- education, training and development of the over-40s (section 7);
- motivation and well-being of older workers (section 8);
- social networks of older workers (section 9).

The chapter concludes with an epilogue (section 10) summarizing observed necessities for further research.

2   FLUCTUATING INTEREST IN THE SUBJECT OF "THE OLDER WORKER"

Interest in the older worker on the part of the business community and government fluctuates and seems to be connected with the economic climate and the situation in the labour market. In periods of increasing prosperity and full employment, such as the post-war period up to around 1965, the older skilled and unskilled worker was in demand. At that time, themes such as functional age, further training/retraining and task changes were studied against this background (Belbin & Shimmin, 1964; Griew, 1964; Munnichs, 1966; Munnichs, Dirken, Dohmen, & Thierry, 1968). In this period, schemes were even set up to offer older employees work *after* retirement on a voluntary basis (Boerlijst-Bosch, 1962).

Subsequently, with the ebbing of the period of boom, interest in the added value of older, skilled and unskilled employees declined rapidly. They were no longer in great demand or even welcome on the labour market. Increasing international competition, hectic market developments and the need for drastic organizational, economic and technological modifications and innovations forced companies and organizations to face the possibility of rapidly increasing obsolescence of knowledge on the part of management and workers (Dalton & Thompson, 1971; Dubin, 1971; Kaufman, 1974, 1975). In this period the theme of "survival, renewal and rejuvenation" of the organization came to the fore and was then never to disappear from the scene. Personnel play a crucial role in this theme. The human activities and qualities needed for survival and renewal have never been systematically studied, presumably being thought self-evident and trivial. In business and in management literature, the view is held that salvation is to be sought in "creativity", "innovative ability", "élan", "decisiveness", "flexibility" or qualities of similar purport, more often attributed to younger than to older workers. Those lacking in these qualities to any degree are not wanted. Older workers tend to be labelled "less capable", "less efficient", "slower on the uptake" and so on (Boerlijst, Van der Heijden, & Van Assen, 1993; Rosen & Jerdee, 1976a; Stagner, 1985, p. 789f). The question as to whether this is a "valid" attribution in the sense that *under all circumstances* younger people are supposedly more creative etc. than comparable older colleagues is difficult to investigate. Double-blind psychological experiments would have to be conducted to exclude the possibility of *self-*

fulfilling prophecies. However, these are scarcely feasible in everyday business practice.

Prejudices have left their mark on personnel policy for younger and older employees. They foster considerable age discrimination, which starts right from recruitment and selection (Rosen & Jerdee, 1976b, Craft, Doctors, Shkop, & Benecki, 1979). The substantial investments made by organizations in the development of younger personnel are often unforthcoming in the case of older personnel (Boerlijst, 1995). Moreover, organizations are not averse to taking measures to exclude older people from work before their official retirement in order to make room for "more capable" younger people. In certain sectors in The Netherlands there are virtually no workers over 60 and the cohorts of the over-55s are in the process of being significantly depleted. The lack of confidence in the creativeness and renewing value of older people is not the only significant factor here. Declining employment within companies and increasing concern about the relative level of labour costs have also undermined the position of older people. We will return to this in section 3.

Around 1985 a re-evaluation of "being older" and the meaning of "older workers" began. The reason for this lay more in force of circumstance than in doubt as to the prevailing prejudices pertaining to older versus younger people. These circumstances relate to the expected changes in the composition of the (working) population and are generally referred to by the terms "dejuvenization" and "aging". In most prosperous industrial countries, an absolute as well as a relative increase in the number of over-40s both on the labour market and in industry is envisaged over the coming decades. This group will attain a hitherto unparalleled size. The consequences for the afore-mentioned attitude towards older people will be examined in section 4.

3 DECLINE IN JOB OPPORTUNITIES AND THE POSITION OF OLDER WORKERS

In most industrial countries of Western Europe, increased prosperity and a range of other social factors have caused a sharp rise in labour costs since the end of the Second World War. In addition, companies and organizations have been obliged to make increasingly larger financial sacrifices to be able to meet international competition, ever more demanding markets and the necessity for rapid adaptability to abrupt changes in the ratio between supply and demand. In private and public sectors alike, there has been a considerable reduction in the positive margin between the costs and benefits of human labour. In the past 20–30 years, more and more companies have found themselves obliged to reduce their labour costs drastically. For this, three measures are appropriate:

- structurally eliminating work tasks by no longer carrying out certain activities or having them carried out elsewhere;
- replacing human labour by other, cheaper means of production; or
- "exporting" jobs to so-called "low-wage countries" outside Western Europe.

The last two measures in particular have resulted in a considerable growth in structural unemployment. For large numbers of employees, workplaces and work have been lost without any alternative compensatory employment. Many school leavers are no longer offered appropriate work when entering the labour market.

In theory, decisions on shedding jobs may be taken without consideration of individual personnel, in other words without taking account of the status, age and so on of those holding those jobs. This does actually happen in some cases, for example when a company or organizational unit as a whole is closed down and all the employees, young and old and from top to bottom, are made redundant.

If a more favourable cost/benefit ratio is to be achieved not by closure but by downsizing or shrinking the personnel ranks, a "blind" choice of those to be retired from the field is not the most appropriate method. In terms of productivity and expendability, employees cannot be treated as if they were all the same. Seen in the long term the expected benefits to be derived from one employee are greater than those from another and in theory it is possible to make selections on this basis. Often, however, decision makers—employers as well as trade unions—prefer to indicate at a category level rather than at an individual level those first in line to go. The selection of a personnel category has advantages in terms of industrial law. It can be regulated via a collective bargaining process or a "social plan", and requires fewer contestable "judgments of Solomon". Furthermore, it tends to make a more "objective" impression on those concerned as well as on the outside world than the designation of individuals. With the dismissal of entire categories, a process of downsizing can be accomplished quickly and the desired economizations achieved without delay. This is especially important when a company is in financial difficulties and must change course as fast as possible. Obviously, the categories to be laid off are preferably those which will generate relatively large economizations and encounter relatively little internal or external resistance. In practice the first choice often seems to fall on "older personnel". Various reasons can be found for this:

1. Older workers entail higher costs for an organization than younger ones. In our remuneration system, the sum of salary, labour costs and emoluments (extra holidays, gratuities, etc.) of older workers is on average higher than in the case of their younger colleagues (cf. Gelderblom & De Koning, 1992b, p. 15). It is plausible that older workers' productivity is therefore assessed as lower than that of younger colleagues, even when the latter achieve roughly the same productivity or less. It is therefore assumed in the business community and by the government too that if older people were to stop work or be obliged to stop work *en masse*, there would be a considerable rise in average productivity per employee. This hypothesis does not, in fact, have a sufficiently empirical basis (WRR, 1992, p. 112). In this context we refer to countries such as Japan (Boerlijst, 1986; Boerlijst, Van Dijk, & Van Helvoort, 1987) and Australia, where personnel in some companies are given the choice at the age of 55 of whether to retire or to continue at a lower salary than previously. The second alternative avoids loss of returns in terms of economics. Of special interest are cases where employees have been given other jobs to which they, as older people, are eminently suited in view of their experience and expertise. In this way, they do not stand in the way of the careers of the young people.

2. In our present-day labour force, older workers as a group are at a considerable educational disadvantage. The need for restructuring and reorientation of a company generally implies the need for training/retraining and, respectively, changing of employees' functions, the costs of which are higher for older people and with less likelihood of adequate returns. The time remaining for recovery of training costs is, after all, shorter. This is a highly complex issue. Many kinds of technological, informational and market developments have led to the life span of functions in companies being sharply reduced in comparison with 20 or 30 years ago. Those who are entering the labour market today should take into account a number of often radical changes in their functions.

3. Our society finds redundant younger workers harder to accept than older ones. To our knowledge, no systematic research has been carried out into the social motives for this. Furthermore, older workers are accorded less "right to work". It is significant that in most countries, including The Netherlands, companies are allowed to keep their doors closed (and very often do so) to applicants above a certain age (Van Beek & Van Praag, 1992). There is no law in The Netherlands comparable to the "*Age Discrimination in Employment Act*" in the USA, which makes this illegal. Another example is the fact that in the period of high unemployment among young school-leavers round about 1985, there was public support for initiatives calling for older employees to make way for younger ones. The first voluntary early retirement schemes owe their existence to this (Van Koningsveld, 1988).

4. Personnel reorganizations are often necessitated by a sudden deterioration in economic conditions. Prompt, firm decisions are called for. Under great pressure of time, rational choices are superseded by decisions based on prejudices and stereotypes which appear to meet the set target (Bodenhausen, 1990; Gilbert & Hixon, 1991; Kaplan, Wanshula, & Zanna, 1992). Many studies have revealed that a person's age forms one of the principal bases for stereotypical characterizations of people (Brewer & Lui, 1989; Fiske, 1993). The business world is no exception to this attitude. The stereotypes relating to "older" and "younger" workers widely accepted in our culture are, to some extent, opposites. The qualities attributed to "the young" match the image of an energetic, self-renewing, creative, dynamic organization. The qualities attributed to "the old" tend largely to be associated with the reverse (Boerlijst et al., 1993, pp. 44–46; Bromley, 1988, pp. 191–192; Wiggers, Baerts, Van Rooy, 1990, p. 18). As the object of personnel cuts in general is to breathe new life into a company, it is understandable that the "new shoots" should be saved and the "dead wood" pruned (Sheppard & Rix, 1977). Incidentally, before things get to the "pruning" stage, numerous discriminatory actions take place, felt as such by older personnel (McAuley, 1977). Stagner (1985) points out that stereotyping of the young versus the old is also encouraged by some researchers, Levinson (1978), for example. They make suggestive generalizations about observed significant differences, even when these are very slight and the groups overlap to a great extent. What is more, their conclusions often cannot hide the fact that they do not doubt the correctness of such stereotypes. Stagner suggests using other methods of reporting which ensure that managers and personnel officers do not forget that older employees simply cannot be treated as if they were all in the same category. In a survey, Craft et al. (1979) and Rosen and Jerdee (1976a) have revealed the stereotypical reactions of employers on the subject of the young versus the old. Employers were presented with curricula vitae of applicants identical in every respect. The only difference was the age stated. The employers were asked to give their opinion on a number of qualities possessed by these applicants. Their negative stereotypical opinions on the older among them were only too clear. Furthermore, they defended their unwillingness to employ the over-50s on the same basis.

An additional factor is that the young and old themselves often believe in such stereotyping and match their behaviour to the qualities attributed to their age group (Kogan & Wallach, 1961).

5. Compensating loss of earnings to an acceptable level on becoming redundant is easier for older people than for younger people. The same applies to filling gaps in pension build-up. After all, for older employees, the time still remaining before retirement is comparatively short. A host of financial provisions and schemes have been put into effect by the government and the business community to make it possible and even attractive to stop work before normal retirement age. In addition, large-scale use has been made of schemes which were actually intended for other purposes. In The Netherlands the main case in point is the statutory financial incapacity benefit. Older employees have often been assessed as qualifying for this benefit by the medical boards concerned without exhibiting any obvious signs of dysfunctioning (Van't Hullenaar & Van Koningsveld, 1986). Utilization of this provision is advantageous to companies because the costs involved are met out of general government funds. Nowadays, its abuse is widely acknowledged.

This summary is not complete. Additional examples are given by Kamstra and Van der Craats (1991, p. 23).

In combination with the structural developments in the economy referred to earlier, the above-mentioned factors have contributed to a serious undermining of the position of older employees on the labour market, especially that of older men. Up to 1960 approximately 90% of the male population between 50 and 65 participated in the labour process. By 1988 this level had dropped to a mere 60%. In contrast, the participation of older women has shown an upward tendency since 1960, from 13.5% to 19.3% in 1988. Following the trends, the proportion of older women in the working population has increased, like that of younger women, though continuing to be much smaller than for men. If we consider the composition of the working population as a whole, the proportion of the younger age cohorts between 25 and 50 has shown a substantial rise (from 50.9% in 1971 to 66.2% in 1988), at the expense of the older generations (CBS, 1989, pp. 77–78).

It is striking that redundancies in "older" people are generally found acceptable by the people concerned. An important factor is undoubtedly that many redundancy and retirement schemes are financially attractive. In some companies, other factors may be that the persons in question feel freed from the stress brought about by physical discomforts (such as wear and tear in the back or knees), as well as by impending reorganizations and increasing work pressure (Durinck, 1993). In the second place it is notable that the "exodus" of older employees is not confined to the lower echelons with a relatively low educational level. Economic conditions necessitate an increase in effectiveness. Organization experts have put forward a number of methods for this, including so-called "delayering" of the organization. By this is meant the reduction of the number of hierarchical layers in an organization, both at top and middle levels (Keuning, Maas, & Ophey, 1993). In view of the fact that management levels in the organization are invariably achieved via seniority, implementation of a delayering process results mainly in the departure of older employees. Other forms of "downsizing" do not spare top and middle management either (*vide* Philips and IBM). Again it is the older rather than the younger worker who is put forward for redundancy, whether voluntary or otherwise. Financial compensation at these levels is often so attractive that it tempts many who the organization can actually ill afford to do without. This undesirable effect of a collective approach to age groups has meant that the business community and government have

begun to give consideration to possible "flexible" early retirement schemes or to "flexibility" in the official retirement age as well as to other forms of individualization of terms of employment (WRR, 1992, p. 210; Loen & Van Schilfgaarde, 1990).

What then is the psychological implication of the worsening position of older employees in the labour market and of the dismissive attitude recently adopted by the business community *vis-à-vis* older employees? We will mention two aspects:

1. With the disappearance of so many older people from the labour process, management's *interest* in the pros and cons of the over-50s in the organization has been virtually reduced to nil. Employers' and employees' organizations have not, until recently, seriously concerned themselves with potential problems of the over-50s *in employment*. This has only become a subject for policy consideration since it became apparent that the working population is starting to age and that the costs of continuing premature redundancies of older employees cannot be met in the long term. This problem was first observed—and dealt with!—in the still very young-looking but rapidly aging Japan (Boerlijst, 1986; Boerlijst et al., 1987; POA, 1983).

2. Older employees in an organization discover that the organization as well as their own immediate circle more or less expect them to leave before official retirement age. Many experience moral pressure in this direction. This gives older employees the feeling of being socially isolated within their own working environment or, as Dresens (1989) terms it: "no longer being needed by the others". Stress and frustration are the all too frequent consequences. Departure from the organization is then experienced almost as a liberation. This is probably one explanation of why so many take up the offer of a so-called "voluntary" redundancy scheme, despite the appreciable loss of income that this may entail.

4 DEJUVENIZATION, AGING AND THE POSITION OF OLDER EMPLOYEES

The labour market is in the process of aging. This is the consequence of a number of demographic factors which, for The Netherlands, have been excellently summarized and clarified in a publication by the Advisory Council on Government Policy (WRR, 1992, p. 35f). A brief summary follows:

- a substantial decrease in "fertility" (the number of children per woman) (Van Hoorn, 1989): the average number of children dropped from 3.04 to 1.51 between 1965 and 1985 (and in fact rose again to 1.62 between 1985 and 1990 (WRR, 1992, p. 38)).
- a high, and still rising, life expectancy between 1965 and 1990: this rose for men from 71 to 74 and for women from 76 to 80 (WRR, 1992, p. 38).
- a rise in the age at which people get married and a fall in the number of marriages, as well as a weaker link between marriage or other forms of cohabitation on the one hand and procreation on the other hand (WRR, 1992, p. 45).
- a substantial increase in the number of divorces (a fivefold increase percentage-wise since 1960, CBS, 1985).

Economic and demographic analyses indicate the existence of a close link between these demographic factors and economic, medical and institutional developments (Clark, 1988). Examples are the improvement of the food supply, hygiene and living conditions and the improvement and accessibility of the health care system.

The process of aging and the fall in the number of births is not unique to The Netherlands but is manifested in all OECD countries, albeit with varying duration, rate and intensity (De Jouvenel, 1989; Van de Kaa, 1987; Warr, 1994). In this development, The Netherlands lags behind compared with most other European countries. It has had a comparatively young population for a relatively long period of time, but the drastic decline in fertility means that in 2040 it will probably be one of the oldest populations in the world, along with Switzerland, Germany and Denmark (OECD, 1988). The rate at which the population of The Netherlands is aging is only surpassed by Japan and Canada (UN, 1991; Feeney, 1990). The increasing immigration of foreigners into The Netherlands may well cause this picture to change, but up to now its effects appear to be relatively slight (De Beer & Noordam, 1988).

As the great majority of those entering the labour market for the first time were born and registered 15 to 25 years earlier, the consequences of demographic developments for the composition of the working population in a particular calendar year have been more or less firmly established for a very long time. The qualification "more or less" has to be made because substantial changes in the participation in the labour process by 15 to 64-year-olds—population migrations, natural disasters and so on—may, of course, undermine such a prognosis.[1] It would now appear that with participation in the labour process assumed to be at a constant level (reference year 1990), the proportion of younger people in the working population (the 15 to 29-year-olds) will drop from 36 to 27% in the period up to 2005. This phenomenon is referred to by the term "dejuvenization of the working population". After that, it will rise again, but up to 2050 the proportion will remain smaller than it was in 1990. In the same period, the proportion of older people in the working population (the 45 to 64-year-olds) will be permanently higher than in 1990, when it was approximately 24%. In 2005 it will have risen to 31% and in 2020 it will have reached a maximum of 35%. Up to 2050 it will remain a few per cent under this maximum (WRR, 1992, p. 105). This development is an illustration of "aging".

It is highly likely that the less than rosy outlook for the position of older employees in the labour market (NFB, 1984) will undergo a change as a consequence of the change in structure of the working population. Whether this will also mean an improvement remains to be seen.

There is an increase in the pressure caused by the large proportion of the over-65s compared with the total number of 15 to 64-year-olds in the population. It is from the latter group that the active working population is recruited which will have to realize a large proportion of the costs of the older non-working population (income provisions, costs of sickness and incapacity). In view of the fact that the group of over-65s will become larger in an absolute sense as well, these costs will become greater. The present situation is that every 100 Dutch people between the ages of 15 and 65, working or not working, provide financially for roughly 19 over-65s, fully or partially. By 2030 this number will have risen to somewhere between 33 and 43, depending on the actual developments in fertility, life expectancy and migration (WRR, 1992, p. 69). The rise in costs for the working population is disproportionately large because, within the group of older people, the proportion of the elderly in need of care will also increase as a result of a higher life expectancy. At present, the costs expended on the health care of the average over-85-year-old are nine times as high as those of the 30 to 50-year-old. The average over-65-year-old necessitates significantly fewer health care costs, though this figure is still twice as high (Koopmanschap, Van Royen, Bonneux, Bonsel, Rutten, & Van der Maas, 1994). This means that the working population, diminishing in proportion, will have to produce disproportionate efforts in the next 50 years to go some way towards financing the costs of the increasing numbers of the retired and the senior citizens.

At the same time, the costs of children and young people are also borne almost entirely by the working population. Every 100 Dutch persons from the group of 15 to 64-year-olds bear the costs of 26 to 27 people from this group. As births are now going up again, the pressure caused by the large proportion of younger people is expected to increase rather than decrease both in the long and the short term (WRR, 1992, p. 67f). It is very much the question as to whether productivity per working person is still capable of being stepped up enough to be able to keep the costs of the pressure caused by both these large groups permanently at the current level. It is more likely that a structural enlargement of the base to support this burden is needed, in other words the *number* of people productively participating in economic life.

A consequence of the "dejuvenization" of the working population is that in the somewhat longer term this base must be broadened by increasing the proportion of over-40s in employment.[2] Suitable, that is adequately trained, younger people are not available in sufficient numbers. Older people not or no longer in employment are in abundance. Enlarging the base by deploying older people will not, however, be easy to accomplish (Kamstra & Van der Craats, 1991). Companies have more faith in the contribution of the young than the old. It is therefore expected that discussions on the necessity for enlarging the base will be frozen and that preference will be given to "siphoning off" younger people from the labour market for as long as possible. Besides this, many organizations are experiencing "internal aging" as a result of the fact that their expansion and growth has stagnated while the "real" older employees (over 60 or 55) have already stepped down via an early retirement scheme or on incapacity grounds. Every year the personnel ages and the number of over-40s increases both in an absolute and a relative sense. It is therefore only too obvious that in such circumstances vacancies are not going to go to jobseeking older people. In any case, companies in general have little idea of their "internal" long-term demographic development. They rarely have access to usable prognosis models or valid initial data (Boerlijst et al., 1993).

Nonetheless, it is realistic to assume that the increase in dependent older non-working people is becoming so great that the deployment or re-entry of older people can no longer be avoided. Bearing this in mind, it is important to consider what problems *older working people* do or do not cause, and how particular problems might be prevented or solved (cf. Hale, 1990; Kerkhoff & Kruidenier, 1991). In the following sections we will discuss a few aspects of these problems. We will concentrate as far as possible on findings derived from work and organization psychological research. A selection will have to be made from the multitude of subjects and results available. Anyone wishing for a broader perspective may consult the compilations of Stagner (1985) and Warr (1994), from whom some of our information has been derived.

5 THE FUNCTIONING OF OLDER WORKERS

Can any criticism be made about the *functioning* of older employees? If the answer to this question is in the affirmative, the potential for a more positive influence on this should be looked into.

One then comes up against a problem which is difficult to overcome. Normally speaking, results from present-day research cannot simply be generalized to apply to situations in the more distant future. When we compare various age cohorts with each other—a cohort comprises all those originating from the same, usually short, birth period—we are not only concerned with age differences but with generation differences as well. The over-20s, over-40s and over-60s of the year 1995 are in a different position from the corresponding age groups of 25 years ago. Neither can they simply be compared with those of the

year 2020 (Rhodes, 1983; Doering, Rhodes, & Schuster, 1983). The greater the difference in the historic contexts in which they lived or will live, the more difficult a generalization of one generation of over-40s to the next becomes. A much used example is the fact that owing to the influence of many kinds of cultural and socio-economic factors, the educational level of the young is much higher these days than 20 or 30 years ago. Education often influences functioning in a positive sense. If the older people of this day and age do not on average function as well as is desirable, this may well be attributable to their poor educational base. With this in mind, it is dangerous to draw conclusions about the older people of the future merely from research on the functioning of the older people of today. The risk of misrepresentation could be reduced by involving in the research older people (and possibly younger people) who are assumed to have the same level of education as their corresponding peers in the future.

A further problem is that employers and managers tend to approach the functioning of individuals from a business economics-related rather than a human point of view. They look for "hard" facts, for example in the matter of the productivity or

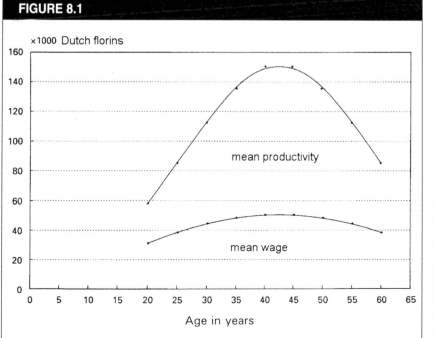

FIGURE 8.1

×1000 Dutch florins

mean productivity

mean wage

Age in years

Source: A. Gelderblom & J. de Koning. (1992c) *Meerjarig, minder-waardig? een onderzoek nar de invloid van leeftijd op produktiviteit en beloning.* [More years, less value? Investigation into the influence of age on productivity and wages.] OSA-pilot study V39, April 1992.

thought by their managers capable of undertaking completely new activities in their work and are also assumed to have little inclination to undergo drastic changes (Boerlijst et al., 1993). However, the dejuvenization and aging of the available potential labour force mean that one should not automatically reject the possibility of "poly-employability" of older workers as unfeasible (WRR, 1992, p. 124f). Research must be carried out into whether older employees are capable of activities and achievements of an interdisciplinary nature, meaning lying beyond their own, familiar functioning territory. If this should prove to be the case, management must be persuaded to change its attitude.

Section 5 mentioned the fact that the cognitive abilities of older employees generally continue to be adequate up to retirement age as far as "day-to-day work" goes. But would these abilities also be adequate for a switch to other areas of knowledge, skills and expertise? The aforementioned studies by Pelz and Andrews (1966) and Van Assen and Keijsers (1993) provide an answer that is relevant to this question. Their results point to the importance of a carefully planned variation in task/working environment factors for the field of expertise to be broadened, which is a necessary condition for successful switching to new areas of function and experience. Warr (1993, p. 537f) observes that up to now the business community and researchers alike have concentrated on the question as to the influence of age on behaviour and attitude in the workplace. The question concerning the influence of the work itself, the influence of the working environment and work experience on "mobility" and "employability" of older employees has hardly been addressed. Warr emphasizes the importance of research into the long-term effects of environmental components on the development of personnel (cf. Hall & Parker, 1993).

Discussion of and research into the possible growth of cognitive abilities and the part played in this by experience accumulation during adulthood are an important theme in so-called "life-span psychology" (Avolio & Waldman, 1987; Avolio, Waldman & McDaniel, 1990; Brouwer, 1990; Butler & Gleason, 1985; Cavanaugh, 1993; Green, 1972; McEvoy & Cascio, 1989; Schaie & Willis,

1986, 1991; Schmidt, Hunter, & Outerbridge, 1986; Schooler & Schaie, 1987; Sparrow & Davies, 1988). There is certain evidence that "life experience" may also be a stimulus for the development of higher forms of "transcendent reasoning"—labelled "wisdom" by some people (including Birren, 1985; Dittmann-Kohli & Baltes, 1985) and "intuition" by others—and "plasticity" in adults and older people (Baltes & Willis, 1982; Munnichs, Mussen, Olbrich, & Coleman, 1985). These higher forms can enable them to continue to sustain their position in the broad and dynamic social everyday context (for more details and references to relevant literature, see Chapter 12, Volume 3 of this Handbook). It is advisable to investigate whether, and in what way, these findings from developmental psychology may be helpful in the context of "growing older in the working environment" (Boerlijst & Van der Heijden, 1997).

Deployment of personnel in what is for them a new area requires them to be able to command sufficient relevant skills, knowledge, routine and expertise within a relatively short period of time to be able to meet the required standard. In the business world, development of new expertise or skills in older employees has hardly been addressed up to now. A great deal is known about the *dynamics* of expertise development in a wide variety of areas (cf. Anderson, 1982; Ceci, 1990; Charness, 1989; Charness & Bosman, 1990; Chi, Glaser, & Farr, 1988; Ericsson & Smith, 1991 and Salthouse, 1990). It is worth investigating to what extent general conditions for the development of new expertise are present or lacking in the work situation of (older) personnel and to what extent they could be "built in". Whether or not older people will be able to meet certain conditions of expertise development in what is for them a new area is still an open question. The fact that the possession of expertise helps older people to compensate for particular handicaps not experienced by younger people—for example reduced reaction time—has been demonstrated by Salthouse (1984) amongst others.

Our use of the term "expertise" may possibly create the misunderstanding that we consider the possibility of broadening of skills to be confined to an elite amongst older personnel. In our view, almost every employee, from top to bottom, from well-educated to less well-educated, from old to young, should either be or be able to become an "expert", at least in a number of aspects of his own work.

In terms of mobility enhancement, it is debatable what would be wiser: acquiring *more than one area of expertise* within adjacent or radically different fields, or acquiring a *strategy* to be able to master a new area of expertise in another territory as quickly as possible. The latter option would seem to offer more advantages. It is, after all, exceptionally difficult, if not impossible, to predict the progress of every individual career. Many changes and transitions (cf. Barton, 1982) take place suddenly and unpredictably. It is therefore equally difficult to divine what "subject of expertise" will be needed at a later stage. However, it should be borne in mind that actual *experience in acquiring more than one area of expertise* is also a basic condition for the efficient acquisition of and ability to master a *strategy* for developing *new areas of expertise*. It is not likely that such a strategy can be "picked up from a book". It must also be remembered that the mastery of more skills, routines and expertise in different areas is also accompanied by an increase in the opportunities for transfer to other areas.

There is a widespread assumption in the business community that the ability to acquire new competencies and skills is reduced in older people and that in some it is more a case of loss of competency and inability to continue functioning at the same level. To keep this group in the labour process, downward mobility (Hall & Isabella, 1985), usually termed "demotion" or, more euphemistically, "career shift" (Koningswijk, 1989; Dresens, 1989, p. 141) is considered. By transferring these older workers to functions categorized at a lower level and thus providing an adaptation to proved shortcomings or failings, things will become easier for them. Koningswijk (1989) summarizes a number of conditions which he considers necessary for a successful "career shift", such as a culture change, exemplary behaviour on the part of management, better terms of employment, new functions that are better suited to the employee, application of objective criteria to be satisfied by candidates, remuneration of the

employee's own initiatives and avoidance of constraint. Koningswijk's view is that the culture shift is necessary in order to prevent the career shift from automatically resulting in loss of status. We, however, believe that with labour relations as they are, loss of status on demotion cannot be avoided. For this reason, such a "career shift" will never be an attractive option for all those whose original function and income reflect and guarantee status (West, Nicholson, & Rees, 1990). The management of large and medium-sized companies views demotion as a scarcely realizable option for older personnel at middle and higher levels. We find exceptions to this in cases in which demotion appears to be the only means of avoiding the redundancy of too expensive older workers during a projected reorganization (Boerlijst et al., 1993, p. 135).

As well as cognitive abilities, motivation—and more particularly the willingness of older personnel to change—are factors in their mobility and employability. We will return to this in section 8. We will first go more deeply into a major determinant of their development, namely the combination of education, training and human resource development.

7 EDUCATION, TRAINING AND DEVELOPMENT OF THE OVER-40s

The development of various new kinds of technologies goes hand-in-hand with a growing need for a poly-employable labour force. These people must be enabled to adapt quickly to new circumstances and, without much trouble, to continue the process of qualifying themselves for different/ changing kinds of work during the course of their career. As stated before, it is traditionally assumed that only young people can meet these requirements. It is a fact that older people are at a disadvantage. Their professional qualifications are generally no longer equal to the rapidly changing function requirements of modern dynamic organizations. One of the consequences is that older personnel are often only too readily inclined to make use of any opportunity handed to them to bid a premature farewell to the labour process

Munnichs, J.M.A., Mussen, P., Olbrich, E., & Coleman, P. (Eds.), (1985). *Lifespan and change in a gerontological perspective.* New York: Academic Press.

Nagy, S. (1985). Burnout and selected variables as components of occupational stress. *Psychological Reports, 56,* 195–200.

NFB (Nederlandse Federatie voor Bejaardenbeleid) [Dutch Federation of Organizations for the Elderly] (1984). *De arbeidsmarktpositie van ouderen* [The position of the elderly on the labour market]. The Hague: NFB.

OECD (1988). *Ageing populations. The social policy implications.* Paris: OECD.

Osipow, S.H., Doty, R.E., & Spokane, A.R. (1985). Occupational stress, strain, and coping across the life span. *Journal of Vocational Behaviour, 27,* 98–108.

Palmore, E., & Luikart, C. (1972). Health and social factors related to life satisfaction. *Journal of Health and Social Behavior, 13*(1), 68–80.

Pelz, D.C., & Andrews, F.M. (1966). *Scientists in organizations.* New York: Wiley.

POA (Policy Office for the Aged) (1983). *Aging in Japan.* Tokyo: Prime Minister's Secretariat.

Pond, S.B., & Geyer, P.D. (1987). Employee age as a moderator of the relation between perceived work alternatives and job satisfaction. *Journal of Applied Psychology, 72,* 552–557.

Prevoo, E., & Thijssen, J.G.L. (1992). Bedrijfskundige setting en scholingsdeelname van 35+ personeelsleden [Setting in a managerial perspective and participation in education by personnel over the age of 35]. Utrecht: Rabobank, The Netherlands (internal report).

Price, R.L., Thompson, P.H., & Dalton, G.W. (1975). A longitudinal study of technological obsolescence. *Research Management,* 22–28.

Prins, R. (1990). *Sickness absence in Belgium (FR), Germany and The Netherlands: A comparative study.* Doctoral thesis. Limburg State University, Maastricht.

Reichelt, P.A. (1974). Moderators in expectancy theory: Influence on the relationships of motivation with effort and job performance. Unpublished doctoral dissertation, Wayne State University.

Rhodes, S.R. (1983). Age-related differences in work attitudes and behavior: A review and conceptual analysis. *Psychological Bulletin, 93*(2), 328–367.

Rosen, B., & Jerdee, T.H. (1976a). The nature of job-related stereotypes. *Journal of Applied Psychology, 61,* 180–183.

Rosen, B., & Jerdee, T.H. (1976b). The influence of age stereotypes on managerial decisions. *Journal of Applied Psychology, 61,* 428–432.

Salthouse, T.A. (1984). Effects of age and skill in typing. *Journal of Experimental Psychology: General, 113,* 345–371.

Salthouse, T.A. (1990). Cognitive competence and expertise in aging. In J.E. Birren, & K.W. Schaie (Eds.), *Handbook of the psychology of aging* (3rd ed., pp. 310–319). San Diego: Academic Press.

Schabracq, M.J., & Winnubst, J.A.M. (Eds.) (1993). *Handboek arbeid en gezondheid psychologie, Vol. 2 (Toepassingen)* [Handbook of labour and health psychology, Vol. 2 (Applications)]. Utrecht: Lemma.

Schaie, K.W. (Ed.) (1983). *Longitudinal studies of adult psychological development.* New York: The Guilford Press.

Schaie, K.W., & Willis, S.L. (1986). Can adult intellectual decline be reversed? *Developmental Psychology, 22,* 223–232.

Schaie, K.W., & Willis, S.L. (1991). *Adult development and aging* (3rd ed.). New York: Harper Collins.

Schein, E.H. (1978). *Career dynamics: Matching individual and organizational needs.* Addison-Wesley Publishing Co.

Schmidt, F.L., Hunter, J.E., & Outerbridge, A.N. (1986). Impact of job experience and ability on job knowledge, worksample performance, and supervisory ratings of performance. *Journal of Applied Psychology, 71,* 432–439.

Schooler, C. & Schaie, K.W. (Eds.) (1987). *Cognitive functioning and social structure over the life course.* Norwood, New Jersey: Ablex Publishing Corporation.

Schwab, D.P., & Heneman, H.G. (1977a). Effects of age and experience on productivity. *Industrial Gerontology, 4,* 113–117.

Schwab, D.P., & Heneman, H.G., (1977b). Age and satisfaction with dimensions of work. *Journal of Vocational Behavior, 10,* 212–222.

Sheppard, H.L., & Rix, S.E. (1977). *The graying of working America: The coming crisis of retirement age policy.* New York: The Free Press.

Sinnott, J.D. (Ed.) (1994). *Interdisciplinary handbook of adult lifespan learning.* Westport, Conn.: Greenwood Press.

Snyder, R.A., & Mayo, F. (1991). Single versus multiple causes of the age/job satisfaction relationship. *Psychological Reports, 68,* 1255–1262.

Sparrow, P.R., & Davies, D.R. (1988). Effects of age, tenure, training, and job complexity on technical performance. *Psychology and Aging Journal, 3,* 307–314.

Stagner, R. (1985). Aging in industry. In J.E. Birren, & K.W. Schaie (Eds.), *Handbook of the psychology of aging* (2nd ed.), pp. 798–817.

Sterns, H.L., & Alexander, R.A. (1987). Industrial gerontology: The aging individual and work. In C. Eisendorfer (Ed.), *Annual Review of Gerontology and Geriatrics, 7,* 243–264.

Super, D.E. (1957). *The psychology of careers.* New York: Harper & Row.

Super, D.E. (1984). Career and life development. In D. Brown, L. Brooks, and associates (Eds.), *Career choice and development.* San Francisco: Jossey-Bass.

Taris, T.W. (1994). Analysis of career data from a life-course perspective. Unpublished PhD thesis, Free University, Amsterdam.

Taub, H.A. (1967). Paired associates learning as a function of age, rate, and instruction. *The Journal of Genetic Psychology, 111,* 41–46.

Thierry, H., Koopman, A., & Flier, H. van der (1992). *Wat houdt mensen bezig? Recente ontwikkelingen rond motivatie en arbeid* [What keeps people busy? Recent developments to do with motivation and labour]. Utrecht: Lemma.

Thijssen, J.G.L. (1993). Ervaringsconcentratie: Drempel voor kwalificatievernieuwing in de tweede loopbaanhelft [Concentration of experience: Threshold for renewal of qualifications in the second half of the career]. In J.G. Boerlijst, H. van der Flier, & A.E.M. van Vianen (Eds.), *Werk maken van loopbanen: Ontwikkeling en begeleiding* [Making careers your business: Development and guidance], 121–141. Utrecht: Lemma.

Troyer, W.G., Eisdorfer, C., Bogdonoff, M.D., & Wilkie, F. (1967). Experimental stress and learning in the aged. *Journal of Abnormal Psychology, 72,* 65–70.

UN (1991). *World population prospects.* New York: United Nations.

Vroom, V.H. (1964). *Work and motivation.* New York: Wiley.

Warmerdam, J. & Berg, J. van den (1992). *Scholing van werknemers in veranderende organisaties* [Training of workers in changing organizations]. The Hague: Ministerie van Sociale Zaken en Werkgelegenheid [Ministry for Social Affairs and Employment].

Warr, P. (1994). Age and employment. In M. Dunnette, L. Hough, & H. Triandis (Eds.), *Handbook of industrial and organizational psychology* Vol. 4, pp.

485–550). Palo Alto, CA: Consulting Psychologists Press.

Welford, A.T. (1976). Motivation, capacity, learning and age. *International Journal of Aging and Human Development, 7*(3), 189–199.

West, M., Nicholson, N., & Rees, A. (1990). The outcomes of downward managerial mobility. *Journal of Organizational Behavior, 11,* 119–134.

West, R.L., & Sinnott, J.D. (Eds.) (1992). *Everyday memory and aging: Current research and methodology.* New York: Springer.

Wiggers, J.A., Baerts, J.E., & Rooy, M.J.C.C. van (1990). *Ouderen en arbeidsmarkt: Een onderzoek naar de arbeidsmarkt-participatie van ouderen* [The older employee and the labour market: A study of participation of older people in the labour market]. The Hague: Ministry of Welfare, Health and Cultural Affairs.

Winnubst, J.A.M., Buunk, B.P., & Marcelissen, F.H.G. (1988). Social support and stress: Perspectives and processes. In S. Fisher, & J. Reason (Eds.), *Handbook of life stress, cognition and health.* New York: Wiley.

Winnubst, J.A.M., & Schabracq, M.J. (Eds.) (1992). *Handboek arbeid en gezondheid psychologie, Vol. 1 (Hoofdthema's)* [Handbook of labour and health psychology, Vol. 1 (Main themes)]. Utrecht: Lemma.

WRR (Wetenschappelijke Raad voor het Regeringsbeleid [Advisory Council on Government Policy]) (1992). *Ouderen voor ouderen: Demografische ontwikkelingen en beleid* [Older people on behalf of older people: Demographic developments and policy]. The Hague: Sdu [Government Printing Office].

Zwart, B. de, & Meijman, T.F. (1995). The ageing shift-worker: Selection or adaptation. In J. Cremer, & J. Snel (Eds.), *Work and aging: A European prospective.* London: Taylor & Francis.

9

Labour Market Disadvantage, Deprivation and Mental Health

David Fryer

In this chapter I intend to pay tribute to the massive contribution to psychology of C.S. Myers but also to draw attention to a puzzling omission from his research agenda.[1] I will then attempt to present and integrate evidence relating to mental health consequences of unemployment and other adverse labour market experiences. Finally, I intend to consider the role of deprivation in these mental health consequences, emphasising the role of restrictions upon the personal agency of people experiencing adverse labour market conditions.

C.S. Myers was fascinated early on with experimental psychology, particularly psycho-physics, taught experimental psychology at both Cambridge and London and wrote two influential textbooks of experimental psychology.

However, World War I was an intellectual watershed for him. His work on, what he was amongst the first to recognise as, shell shock and on personnel selection led to Myers choosing to give his Royal Institution lectures in London in 1918 on "Present Day Applications of Psychology with Special Reference to Industry, Education and Nervous Breakdown". In that same year Myers also began a 10-year involvement with the Industrial Fatigue (later Health) Research Board and

wrote what he described as his first book on Industrial Psychology. This was entitled *Mind and Work* and was published in 1921 (Myers, 1921), the year C.S. Myers also founded the National Institute of Industrial Psychology (NIIP), of which he became Director and later Principal. C.S. Myers and the staff of his Institute published literally hundreds of other papers and books in occupational psychology (Chin & Grainger, 1971; Raphael 1971). In addition to many papers and reports Myers himself published: *Industrial Psychology in Great Britain* (Myers, 1926, republished once); *Industrial Psychology* (Myers, 1929, republished seven times over four decades); and *Ten Years of Industrial Psychology* (Welch & Myers, 1932). C.S. Myers founded the *Journal of the National Institute of Industrial Psychology* in 1921. This became subsequently retitled *Human Factor* (1932–1937) and in 1938 was again retitled *Occupational Psychology*.

Amongst nearly 300 publications of the NIIP from 1922 until 1971 (Chin & Grainger, 1971) are many publications on ability, IQ and vocational testing and on education and career guidance, on interviewing and selection and training, on movement study, job analysis and job design, on work efficiency, job satisfaction, fatigue, accidents, absence, accidents, labour turnover and many market research and industrial case studies.

However, it is what is missing from the work of C.S. Myers and the London based NIIP, in particular from 1921–1939, which is in retrospect so striking: unemployment and other labour market experiences with psychologically adverse consequences. It is true that C.S. Myers occasionally referred to unemployment but every example I have found is in passing in the context of attacks on crude scientific management which Myers detested; restriction of output; resistance to occupational psychological interventions; or industrial unrest. I have found no trace of C.S. Myers engaging directly with the relationship between recession, unemployment and mental health and only one NIIP paper addressing it.

This is surely remarkable for several reasons. Firstly, C.S. Myers and colleagues were carrying out occupational psychological research in a very wide range of industries during a major international economic slump during which unemployment peaked at record levels in 1931 and 1932.

Secondly, as a well-read scholar, C.S. Myers can hardly have been unaware of the considerable international applied psychological interest in unemployment. He might reasonably have been expected to have come across Bakke's (1933) unemployment research in London, Beales and Lambert's (1934) unemployment research for the BBC, Zawadski and Lazarsfeld's (1935) unemployment research in Poland, Marie Jahoda's unemployment research carried out in Wales in 1937 and partly published in *Occupational Psychology* in 1942 (Jahoda, 1938/1987; Jahoda, 1942), the Pilgrim Trust's (1938) research on unemployment in the north of England and Eisenberg and Lazarsfeld's (1938) seminal Psychological Bulletin review paper, which reviewed 112 international publications and concluded that the psychological consequences of unemployment were severe, widespread and negative.

Thirdly, Oakley, Director of the Scottish Division of the NIIP which was formed in January 1930, focused specifically on "psychological problems of a depressed area" in a British Association paper which was subsequently published in Myers' own *Human Factor* (Oakley, 1936). In addition to his own experience in Scotland in 1935, Oakley referred specifically to the work of Lazarsfeld-Jahoda and Zeisel (1933) in Austria, of Gatti in Italy (1935) and of the Americans Beckman (1933), Hall (1934) and Israeli (1935).

Oakley summarised his understanding, derived from close personal contact, surveys and preparation of publications, of psychological problems arising out of unemployment as including fear, frustration, irritability, declining self-respect, a sense of time losing its meaning, isolation, apparent apathy, resignation and experienced futility of activity, combined with persistently high levels of employment commitment ("I have never met an unemployed man who did not really want to work. Those persons who say otherwise have, in my opinion, failed to understand the behaviour of the unemployed men to whom they have spoken" (Oakley, 1936: 393).

After nearly 60 years of apparent massive social and cultural change, contemporary researchers have come to very much the same conclusions regarding the mental health consequences of unemployment conceptualised in terms of suboptimal mental health by Warr (1987), drawing on Jahoda (1958) and others, i.e. as concerning affective well-being, aspiration, competence, inter-related independence and integrated functioning—although more generally encountered in the unemployment literature in their negative modes as psychological distress, resigned apathy, helplessness and powerlessness, social isolation and disintegration.

This research is well confirmed across different countries including England, Wales, Scotland, Northern Ireland, the Republic of Ireland, Germany, Austria, Italy, Spain, Australia and the United States by researchers working from very different ideological assumptions, in a variety of institutional settings, on the basis of quite different funding arrangements (see Fryer, 1992).

To illustrate this point, the findings of the Austro-Marxist research group in Vienna in the 1930s associated with Jahoda and Lazarsfeld, recent findings of Research Council funded academics and of psychologists working for Government Departments are in extraordinarily close agreement.

Every respectable, and indeed some not so

respectable, social scientific method has been used by researchers in this field: depth-; semi-structured; and structured interviews; document analysis; sociography; action research; psychiatric assessment; medical/physiological and epidemiological techniques. These studies spanning time, cultures, research groups and research methods converge in their conclusions that unemployment is associated with poor mental health.

For many, however, the most impressive contemporary input has been made by researchers using quantitative psychological methods. Anxiety, depression, dissatisfaction with one's present life, experienced strain, negative self-esteem, hopelessness regarding the future and other negative emotional states, all operationalised in the form of acceptably reliable validated measures, have each been demonstrated by cross-sectional studies to be higher in groups of unemployed people than in matched groups of employed people. Compared with employed people, unemployed people are also disproportionately likely to report social isolation and relatively low levels of daily activity. There is also an emerging consensus that the physical, as well as mental, health of unemployed people is also generally poorer than that of employed people.

It is one of the major achievements of recent research to have demonstrated beyond reasonable doubt that unemployment causes, rather than merely results from, poor psychological health. Well designed, longitudinal studies have tracked large, carefully selected, samples of people in and out of paid jobs, from school or employment to unemployment, from unemployment to employment etc., using valid and reliable measures. Groups which become unemployed during the course of such studies exhibit deterioration in mean mental health compared with continuously employed groups.

Most of these studies deal with the average mental health of large groups of people. Within those groups there are wide variations in experience and health costs. Some people are affected very badly, some hardly at all and there are even some whose psychological health improves when they become unemployed. For many, probably most, the experience of unemployment is multi-faceted, composed of negative aspects, positive aspects and aspects about which they are ambivalent—at one and the same time.

For all these reasons, whilst if a large group of people becomes unemployed one can confidently predict that the mean scores indicating mental health will decrease, one cannot infer from that fact that any particular individual has been made unemployed that that individual's mental health will actually suffer or that those whose mental health do suffer will suffer in every respect. A more useful way to think about it is that the risk of that individual's mental health deteriorating in at least some ways has increased compared with an otherwise similar person who did not become unemployed.

Many of these points can be well illustrated by research by Dooley and colleagues (Dooley, Catalano, & Hough, 1992) who interviewed over 10,000 people in three areas of the United States using a highly structured diagnostic symptom check list developed for use by trained interviewers to reliably assign respondents to specific categories of the American Psychiatric Association diagnostic system. People were categorised as suffering from an alcohol disorder if they were either using alcohol excessively with resulting impairment in work or social functioning as indicated by specified behavioural patterns or if they were physically dependent upon alcohol as indicated by specified behavioural patterns indicating tolerance or withdrawal.

Seventy nine per cent of the original sample (over 8,000 people) were reinterviewed one year later. Those people, with no prior history of alcohol disorder, who had gone from employment at first interview to unemployment a year later were nine times more likely to have become alcohol disordered in the intervening period than the consistently employed.

Interestingly, Dooley and colleagues also reanalysed data on "intemperance" which was available from Rowntree's study of York in 1910 (Rowntree & Lasker, 1910) and again found evidence for a causal link between unemployment and alcohol disorder, as well as some evidence for selection. This research, then, provides persuasive evidence for a causal relationship between unemployment and a specific serious mental health disorder over 80 years of massive social change, two continents and vastly increasing research method sophistication. Many other studies have done the same in relation to other aspects of mental health.

In January 1994 the official, unadjusted, Department of Employment figure for the number of people unemployed in the UK was 2,889,300. However, the Independent Unemployment Unit calculates the number of unemployed people on the basis used by the UK Government in 1982, i.e. ignoring the 30 or so changes made since then for administrative and/or political convenience. Calculated in that way the figure for January 1994 was 4,001,500 (14.3 per cent of the workforce in employment). By comparison, in January 1994 alongside those 4 million unemployed people were a mere 117,100 officially notified job vacancies (Unemployment Unit, 1994: 13–14).

The scale of unemployment combined with the risk to mental health of unemployment is sobering. However, I now want to go on to suggest that the psychological costs of involuntary unemployment are only a tiny fraction of the psychological costs of adverse labour market experience more generally.

Unemployment puts at risk the mental health not only of unemployed people but also their families. Oakley (1936: 400) reported that the German psychologists, Buseman and Harder (1932) had "showed in their investigation that unemployment among German parents brings about a drop in the school marks of two-thirds of their children". Where unemployment was very long term, three or four years, they reported a further decline in school work. Recent Dutch work has again found poorer school performance in children with unemployed fathers (Baarda, 1988; Te Grotenhuis & Dronkers, 1989).

More generally, Oakley (1936) reported that children with unemployed fathers were disproportionately likely to see their fathers as failures, and home discipline to weaken. McLoyd recently likewise concluded, after an extensive literature review, that children with unemployed fathers are at risk of "socio-emotional problems, deviant behaviour, and reduced aspirations and expectations. The child also may model the somatic complaints of the father" (McLoyd, 1989). McLoyd cites specific evidence regarding: mental

health problems, withdrawal from peers, depression, loneliness, emotional sensitivity, distrustfulness, decreased sociability and low self-esteem.

The effects of unemployment on younger children and babies is harder to gauge but babies' growth might be considered one suggestive indication of whether and how well they are thriving. Cross-sectionally, however, the mean birth weight of 655 babies born to unemployed fathers in Glasgow was found by researchers to be significantly less (150 grams on average) than that of babies born to employed fathers, even after controlling for sex, social class, mothers' height etc. Longitudinally, babies with unemployed fathers grew significantly less in length (1.3 per cent) during their first year than babies with employed fathers (Cole, Donnet, & Stanfield, 1983).

Research has also demonstrated that unemployment puts the mental health of spouses of unemployed people at risk. Even in the 1930s the Pilgrim Trust (1938) demonstrated that wives bore the burden of want in most unemployed families and Oakley (1936) reported unemployed fathers' status to be lowered in their families with mothers likely to take over as head of household, with family relationships likely to be disturbed and increasing friction at home as results.

Modern research broadly confirms these claims. McKee and Bell (1986) pointed to the difficulties spouses, generally female partners of unemployed men, face in trying to manage on reduced income, to cope with the spouses' intrusive presence in the household, to support distressed partners and deal with intra-family conflict. Fletcher and colleagues (e.g. Jones & Fletcher, 1993) have demonstrated in recent years that occupational stress can be transmitted to partners and it seems that unemployment distress can also be transmitted. There have also been suggestions in the literature that members of extended families may be affected by unemployment (Binns & Mars, 1984).

So far I have suggested that unemployment puts at risk the mental health not only of unemployed people but also their families. But what about unemployed people who cease to be unemployed?

Some of these people go onto some form of Government quasi-employment/ training scheme—employment training, youth training, community programme etc.

Back in 1936, Oakley reported that "many investigators consider the worst aspect of unemployment ... unemployment of youths and girls ... after they leave school. Not only does inactivity and the absence of an occupational goal sometimes render them permanently unemployable, but ... they may become undesirable members of the community" (Oakley, 1936: 401).

Such fears, amongst other considerations, have prompted British Governments over the last half century periodically to set up training schemes for both young people and adults. Back in 1936, Oakley described Ministry of Labour "Instructional centres" in Scotland where "unemployed men take a three months' course of heavy outdoor work. The aim is to build up physical fitness and confidence, by work, by social life, by order and routine". For women there were centres in Scotland "where women and girls are trained for private domestic service", the service sector of the economy! He added that "these centres should not be confused with the labour camps of some other countries" (Oakley, 1936: 399).

Some research has suggested that participation in modern schemes can be psychologically benevolent in at least some respects. Stafford, for example, found that trainees in a precursor of Youth Training, the Youth Opportunities Programme (YOP), had significantly better mental health scores than members of an unemployed comparison group and their mental health (assessed by GHQ-12) was not significantly worse than an employed comparison group. Longitudinally, it was shown that this could not be accounted for by differences in their scores at school. However, the protection was temporary—when YOP trainees became unemployed, their psychological health deteriorated (Stafford, 1982).

However, other research into Youth Opportunities Programme (YOP) participation has found that YOP trainees were not, on average, significantly less depressed (as assessed by the Beck Depression Inventory) than members of an unemployed comparison group and were significantly more depressed than an employed comparison group. Interviews suggested that the trainees

perceived YOP as low status ("cheap labour"), as providing inadequate training, as lacking in meaningful purpose, as actually hindering search for a "proper" job and as unlikely to lead to adequate, secure employment (Branthwaite & Garcia, 1985). Davies (1992) more recently investigated experience of Community Programme, reporting generally positive participant evaluation of the work but generally negative perception of the context of the scheme and its temporary nature—with frequently experienced anxieties about the future. The psychological well-being of Community Programme participants was on a par with that of comparable employed people but their felt control was as low as comparable unemployed people (Davies, 1992).

So the mental health of unemployed people, their families and those in quasi-employment schemes appears to be at risk. But what about those very many unemployed people who leave the unemployment figures for employment?

The conventional wisdom is that re-employment makes everything better again and indeed a number of quantitative psychological studies have, for example, found that psychological well-being (assessed by GHQ-12) improves after re-employment (e.g. Payne & Jones, 1987).

Others suggest a more complicated picture, however. For example Shamir (1985: 77) states "the implicit assumption that the transition from unemployment to re-employment is symmetrical to the transition from employment to unemployment ... is not fully warranted since it is known that some of the effects of unemployment may persist into the period of re-employment". Kaufman (1982) found that one fifth of his sample of re-employed professionals were under-employed i.e. had to accept jobs which were inferior in terms of salary, type of work and use of skills. Only 47 per cent reported their lives had returned to normal following re-employment (Kaufman, 1982). Daniel (1974, 1990) has shown that re-employment is likely to be at a lower level and that re-employed people are more vulnerable to future redundancy due to last in, first out practices.

Detailed qualitative studies are still more informative on this point. Fineman followed up a previously unemployed sample and found "those re-employed in jobs which they felt to be inadequate were experiencing more stress, and even poorer self esteem, than they had during their period of unemployment" (Fineman, 1987a: 269). Half of Fineman's re-employed informants had what Fineman described as legacy effects, whatever the quality of the new job. This legacy took the form of feeling there was a lasting blemish or stigma on their work record, of continuing doubts about their abilities, of feelings of personal failure. Organisationally they were prepared to give less of themselves to their new jobs.

Incidentally, if the number of people unemployed at any one time is shockingly large, the number who sample unemployment and then move into jobs or schemes is vast. On average about 350,000 people cease to be unemployed each month (Unemployment Unit, 1994, p. 13)—i.e. 4,000,000 per year departures from the unemployment count, although some people no doubt feature more than once.

Mental health risks of unemployment extend, then, beyond unemployed people to their families, to those on schemes and to those unemployed who have become re-employed. However, what about those people who are left in organisations after others have been made redundant—so-called survivors. Can they breathe a sigh of relief?

Longitudinal research has found that anticipation of redundancy is at least as distressing as the experience of unemployment itself (Cobb & Kasl, 1977; Fryer & McKenna, 1987, 1988). During recession and economically unsettled times, many more people, of course, anticipate and worry about unemployment than actually become unemployed.

Powerful evidence comes from studies of job insecurity. Seasonal workers, fixed term contract employees (a growing group), new "probationary" employees are all liable to job insecurity but the largest number of job insecure employees are probably employees who make the "fundamental and involuntary change from a belief that one's position in the employing organisation is safe, to a belief that it is not" (Hartley, Jacobson, Klandermans, & Van Vuuren, with Greenhalgh & Sutton, 1991: viii).

Studies carried out in Israel, The Netherlands and the UK reported by Hartley et al. (1991) have demonstrated job insecurity to be associated with severe uncertainty, experienced powerlessness and impaired mental health, operationalised in terms of reported psychosomatic symptoms and depression, reduced job satisfaction, reduced organisational commitment, reduced trust in management, resistance to change and deteriorating industrial relations. See also Burchell (1994).

So far, I have suggested, unemployed people, their families, those on schemes, those re-employed, those anticipating unemployment or left in insecure employment after others have been made redundant, all have elevated risk of consequent mental health problems. But what about the many people who become or remain employed in economically secure organisations?

Some of the most persuasive longitudinal quantitative studies, have been done with young people. Typically these studies measure the mental health of large groups in school and follow them into the labour market over a number of years measuring the mental health of those who get jobs and those who do not and comparing group mean scores cross-sectionally and longitudinally. In study after study, groups of unemployed youngsters are demonstrated to have poorer mental health than their employed peers but if one looks at the scores of the same groups when at school there is no statistically significant difference, i.e. poor mental health is the consequence rather than the cause of the labour market transition.

Winefield and colleagues followed approximately 3,000 youngsters over eight years in South Australia in just such a design. However they also asked the employed youngsters about their job satisfaction using a widely used and well validated scale. They found that those employed youngsters who were dissatisfied with their jobs were indistinguishable in terms of mental health scores from the unemployed youngsters (Winefield, Tiggemann, & Winefield, 1993), i.e. it was as bad for mental health to make the transition into a job with which one was dissatisfied as into unemployment. Feather (e.g. 1992) has reported similar findings from his research programme.

There is also a massive literature on occupational stress, increasingly referred to as strain. Cooper has spelled this out (Cooper, 1986). A traditional way of coping with such strain has been to change jobs. However, in recessionary labour market conditions, people are increasingly likely to become trapped in psychologically distressing jobs.

Moreover, many in jobs not conventionally associated with psychological strain work with casualties of adverse labour market conditions. General practitioners have reported via their professional journals that they have been inundated with such work (Smith, 1987).

For example, following a statistical analysis of his practice records before and after the closure of the principal local employer, a physician in the west country of England reported an approximately 20 per cent increase in consultation rates and an approximately 60 per cent increase in hospital outpatient visits for job losers and their dependants as a result of the closure. This is a massive increase not only in costs to the UK National Health Service but in workload for medical and health personnel (Beale & Nethercott, 1985).

Fineman has studied the implications of unemployment not only for physicians, but also for clergy, probation officers, and police officers. He has documented not only the quantitative and qualitative work load but also role conflict and other stressors which are producing for these professionals, according to Fineman (1990), a sense of crisis in the face of unemployment.

The British Psychological Society organised a media briefing especially to highlight the negative implications of unemployment for clinical psychologists. Whilst useful this was still only to highlight the demands placed by unemployment upon high profile "High Street" helpers. We should also consider workers in myriad other formal and indeed informal, back street, organisations who are affected directly or indirectly by unemployment.

In addition to all the above, Sinfield has drawn attention to the wider impact of recession. Mass unemployment and its sequelae affect many more people even than those so far discussed: trade union influence is reduced, wages are depressed for those in jobs (minimum wages and wages councils have recently become things of the past), improvements to the working environment

regarding health and safety and the "humanisation of work" are slowed down or put into reverse, employment as rehabilitation after physical injury, illness, mental breakdown and prison becomes decreasingly available and minorities may become increasingly vulnerable to exclusion from the labour market with consequent further marginalisation and impoverishment. All of these factors impinge on mental health via the labour market (Sinfield, 1992).

Finally, mass unemployment is a major factor in inequitable income distribution, i.e. relative impoverishment and there is persuasive evidence that the latter is related to mortality in populations of whole countries. Wilkinson (1990), for example, analysed data from nine Western countries on the relationship between life expectancy and income distribution (the percentage of total post tax income and benefit received by the least well off 70 per cent of families). Income distribution correlated 0.86 with life expectancy at birth. By comparison, across 23 Organisation for Economic Cooperation and Development (OECD) countries, gross national product per capita was not itself significantly associated with life expectancy. There was no relationship whatsoever (0.02) between changes in gross national product per capita and life expectancy over the 20 years from 1970 to 1990, for example (Wilkinson, 1990).

To summarise so far, I have suggested that unemployment puts the mental health of the following groups at risk: unemployed people, their families, those on employment training schemes, those re-employed, those left in insecure employment after others have been made redundant, those trapped in psychologically stressful jobs, those who work formally or informally with people suffering adverse labour market experience and those who are subject to the wider impact of recession, mediated by experience of the labour market.

I have spoken so far as if these are discrete groups of people but this is not necessarily so. Many people have careers of labour market disadvantage consisting of moving from school or insecure, psychologically dissatisfying and stressful jobs within the secondary labour market via training schemes into further unemployment or

of a smaller validity coefficient r_{xy}, or a combination of both. If the bias is caused by a smaller r_{xy} and if σ_y is equal in both groups, then, following formula (2), the standard deviation of the predictor scores σ_x must be smaller in the group with the smaller r_{xy} (because the slope of the regression line is equal in both groups). Furthermore, the smaller σ_x may result in the smaller r_{xy}. It may be worth while looking into the causes of this lower variability of test scores and into other possible determinants for the greater error of prediction in one of the groups, in order to improve prediction in that group. Another reason for investigating differences in standard error of estimate could be that these differences are to the disadvantage of qualified members in the best predicted group, since some of their positions will be taken by false positives in the other group.

In the section above a description is given of three examples of differential prediction and of one situation where no differential prediction exists. These three have been selected because they were considered as important and interesting cases. For a more extensive overview the reader is referred to Bartlett and O'Leary (1969).

Research on differential prediction, according to the model described above, should also indicate whether differences in standard error of estimate, slope and intercept between the distinct groups are significant. A short description of the test procedure is given in Jensen (1980, pp. 456 et seq.). The differences in the three parameters should be tested with a hurdle approach: First of all differences in standard error of estimate are tested, then differences in slope and finally differences in intercept. If, at a prior stage, predictor bias is found as demonstrated by significant differences, it is useless to perform further statistical tests. So, if there are differences in the amount of error in prediction, one does not need to do any further tests for differences in slope; if there are differences in slope there is no need to test for differences in intercept. The statistical reasoning behind this sequential testing can be found in Gulliksen and Wilks (1950).

A practical problem with the testing method described above is that it is rather laborious. A more fundamental drawback was pointed to by Lautenschlager and Mendoza (1986). The step-by-step procedure of Jensen can be compared with a step-up hierarchical multiple regression procedure. Typical for these procedures is that at each step all higher order effects not included in the model are pooled into the sum of squared error term, potentially decreasing the power of the sequential testing procedure. Lautenschlager and Mendoza propose a step-down procedure which begins by testing the hypothesis that a common regression line alone is sufficient to account for the relation of the predictor with the criterion. This is the so-called test of the omnibus hypothesis of prediction bias. If this hypothesis is rejected, subsequent tests for slope and for intercept differences must be performed. This method is more powerful because it deals with the error terms more adequately. Besides, it is more practical because it can be easily done with a standard statistical package. The only disadvantage is that it does not test for differences in standard error of measurement between the groups.

Overviews of research into differential prediction amongst various ethnic groups (mostly African-American and Caucasian in the USA) are given by Jensen (1980, chapter 10) and Arvey and Faley (1988, chapter 5). These studies show great variation in test purposes and in nature of the predictor and criterion measures used. Studies both in educational as well as in working situations are described, where predictors vary from traditional intelligence tests to job samples and criterion measures from school grades to ratings by supervisors. Despite this variation, the general conclusion is that most studies do *not* reveal differential prediction. In the few instances where there is differential prediction, we are mostly dealing with differences in intercept, whereby nearly always the regression line of the majority groups is found to be *above* that of the minority group. Thus, one might say that in most cases the tests proved to be unbiased predictors and that in the cases that bias was found, it was not to the disadvantage of the minority group (when using the common regression line, performance of group members with the lower intercept is *over* predicted).

A study on differential prediction of ethnic minorities in an educational situation in The Netherlands (Evers & Lucassen, 1991) can be taken as an illustration of the results typically found in bias research. In this study, school performance was predicted from the scores on the Dutch adaptation of the Differential Aptitude Tests. Twenty predictor criterion combinations were tested for differences in standard error of measurement, slope, and intercept. No differences in standard error of estimate were found, three differences in slope were found, and of the remaining 17 combinations 10 showed a significant difference in intercept. In these 10 cases the regression line in the ethnic minority group was *below* the one of the majority group. Even for two of the three cases where difference in slope was found, the intersection of the regression lines was at such a point that the regression line of the minority group was below that of the majority group in the whole effective range of the test scores. These results are consistent with the results as summarized by Jensen (1980) and Arvey and Faley (1988), and again, this study shows that if bias is found, it is hardly ever to the disadvantage of the minority group.

2.2.3   Philosophies of fair selection

For several reasons it appears to be impossible to design a foolproof selection procedure, as has been pointed out above. As long as there is a need to select people there will be people who will be treated unfairly. Irrespective of the care that is taken to develop an optimal procedure and the effort that is put into minimizing errors as much as possible, there will always be applicants rejected or accepted by mistake. In general, this is not considered discrimination, as long as it affects random individuals and not a specific group of applicants. But what about the situation when the number of selection errors differs for various subgroups in the population of applicants? According to the differential prediction model described before this is an irrelevant fact and it need not reflect discrimination. Yet it is clear that when (i) the predictor is unbiased, (ii) the cut-off point for members of both groups is the same, and (iii) the groups differ in mean predictor score, there will be differences in the number of false positives and false negatives in both groups. With this fact taken into account there will be less agreement on the non-discriminatory nature of

this predictor. Apart from the correctness of the selection decisions, and to make things a little more complex, it was stated earlier in this chapter that decisions or tools can have a discriminatory effect, although they may be fair decisions (at least from a selection point of view). Moreover, in a selection procedure indirect discrimination may occur. All in all this situation is fairly complex, and both in professional practice and in science there is no consensus on how to deal with selection errors, discriminatory effects, and indirect discrimination. All the different opinions were categorized by Hunter and Schmidt (1976) into three general philosophies of fair selection.

The first philosophy of fair selection is called *qualified individualism*. The basic idea is that only task-relevant variables, such as capacities and skills, may be part of the selection procedure and that variables such as group membership should be left out. Supporters of this philosophy argue that we are to treat everybody alike, one should disregard ethnicity, religion, gender, etc. Furthermore they believe unequal treatment to be the same as discrimination. At first sight, such a point of view is anti-discriminating. However, this policy is only correct if the predictor is unbiased. The regression lines of the subgroups will correspond and moreover this line will be the same as for the whole group. In case of a biased predictor one should use different regression lines for the subgroups to minimize prediction errors e.g. to maximize validity. Disregarding group membership means using one regression line only, even if the predictor is biased. This reduces the predictive value, and introduces indirect discrimination: the criterion performance is underpredicted for one group and overpredicted for the other (or for parts of both groups when regression lines cross each other). A solution of this problem could be to add variables to the regression formula to repair for this loss in predictive value. These should be variables that correlate both with group membership and criterion. Usually these are biographical data such as place of birth, educational background, place of residence, etc. With the addition of these variables the predictive value can be improved without considering group membership. However these variables may not be relevant for job performance either. Moreover, by way of the correlation with group membership, group membership is introduced into the prediction formula, be it indirectly. According to the philosophy of qualified individualism a biased test will result either in indirect discrimination or at best in the introduction of group membership into the prediction, which is not in agreement with the philosophy itself.

The philosophy of *unqualified individualism* like that of qualified individualism aims at maximum predictive validity, yet it justifies the use of any possible predictor, including group membership. Whenever a variable significantly contributes to the predictive validity, it should be included into the prediction formula. This not only means that different regression formulas may be used for different subgroups (introducing group membership), but even different predictors may be used in the different subgroups if prediction is improved by this. The results of both philosophies will be the same, namely one single regression line for the whole group, with an unbiased predictor. In case of a biased predictor the unqualified individualism philosophy scores better. Selection according to this philosophy will result in the highest mean criterion performance of the group of accepted applicants, it will lead to less selection errors and it will prevent indirect discrimination. Both strategies may have a discriminatory effect as its occurrence primarily depends on the relation between the predictors and group membership.

The third philosophy uses *quotas* to secure equal treatment of subgroups. The idea is that each of the demographic groups to be differentiated should be fairly represented in the working population. This implies a deviation from the selection strategies used in the two other philosophies described above. Applicants from different subgroups are deliberately treated unequally. Less capable candidates from one group can be accepted at the expense of better candidates from the other group. Ethic, social or economic arguments may justify this strategy, the goal of which is to counteract disadvantages in the labour-market situation of a specific group which may be the result of any other disadvantages (for instance less admittance to education) they have had in the past. Selection by means of tests is compatible with the quota philosophy, even when identical tests are used in both groups. Selection will either take place within each individual group until a specific quotum is reached, or it will take place within the whole group, using some kind of compensation for the minority group.

In practice many different quotum arrangements are used. Most of them are rather straightforward and use target figures. This means that the ultimate goal of the arrangement is that a specific percentage of all jobs (or of a specific job or group of jobs) should be allocated to members of the minority group. Generally, the target figure is based on the ratio of the minority group to the whole population within a certain geographical region. When for example 30% of the population of the city of Amsterdam belongs to ethnic minorities, then ultimately 30% of the jobs in this region should be taken by ethnic minorities. The use of target figures implies a temporary increase (a higher percentage than the target figure) of people selected from minority groups, in order to eventually reach the target figure. There are several ways to implement this policy. A straightforward and popular way is to stipulate that the selection ratio in both groups should be the same, in other words the percentage of accepted people in the majority group and the minority group should be the same. At first sight this may not look like a quotum arrangement, but like a basic principle of fair selection.[1] However, it is a quotum arrangement if differences in capability between the subgroups are by no means accounted for. Figure 10.1a for example shows that with an unbiased predictor and a difference in mean test performance between two groups, one single cut-off score would just result in different selection ratios for the two groups (and for equal selection ratios one would need different cut-off scores). Apart from that, any quotum arrangement will only have the intended effect when the percentage of members of the minority group in the whole group at least equals the target figure. In order to reach the target figures, it may be useful to formulate intermediate quantitative goals, as in the Dutch so-called EMO plan (Ministerie van Binnenlandse Zaken, 1990). The EMO plan is a policy for affirmative action to employ people from ethnic minorities for governmental services. It requires that from 1987–1990 the percentage of members of ethnic minority groups in governmental services rises from 2% to 3%.

In the types of affirmative action that are mentioned before, no reference is made to the capability of the applicants. An illustration of a mild type of affirmative action is when preference will be given to an applicant of a minority group, when there are two or more applicants of equal capability. However, the effect of such an arrangement appears to be small. The city of Tilburg in The Netherlands uses a stricter method. Of the people that meet the job requirements, they do not simply select the best of the whole group, but only the best of the target group (Krosse, 1991). These target groups for example include ethnic minorities. The purpose of this policy is to fill 100% of the vacancies with applicants from target groups. This should guarantee that in the shortest possible period the target figure will be reached. There are a number of other, more complicated, models for preferential treatment, that include the capabilities of the applicants in defining the quota, and of which the effects are somewhere in between the soft and the extreme model. One of the oldest models is that of Thorndike (1971). This model holds that in a fair selection procedure the ratio of accepted and potential successful applicants in both groups should be equal. Other, partly comparable, models were proposed amongst others by Cole (1973), Linn (1973) and Bereiter (1975). The basic idea of all these models is that it is legitimate to achieve that a higher percentage of people from minority groups will get a job at the expense of a lower profit of the selection procedure in terms of a lower mean criterion performance of the total group of accepted applicants. These models may justify the selection procedure pursued or to be pursued for all parties concerned, i.e. employers (accept a lower mean criterion performance), majority group (the rejection of a higher percentage of capable candidates) and minority group (the time it takes to catch up with the majority group).

If one decides to use the quotum approach, one should justify this. Subsequently, the choice for a specific model, quotum or speed for catching up the disadvantage is a matter to be decided upon as well. Although both choices are rather a matter for politicians (or of employers) than for personnel psychologists, the latter group may contribute to

the discussion by giving so-called utility models. In these models every single decision is evaluated. A predecessor of utility models is the *culture-modified criterion model* (Darlington, 1971). In this model one explicitly states the amount of criterion performance that is sacrificed in favour of affirmative action. When there is agreement on this value K, it will be subtracted from the expected criterion performance of members of the majority group, or the equivalent will be subtracted from the test scores of the majority group, which will have the same effect. Subsequently, in the whole group those candidates with the highest expected criterion performance will be accepted. By means of manipulation of K each desired quotum may be determined in advance. The use of different norm-tables for the minority and the majority group is in accordance with this. This procedure is frequently used. However, often the effects (on criterion performance and selection ratios) are not quantified and therefore remain obscure.

The *expected utility model* (Gross & Su, 1975; Petersen & Novick, 1976) is a complete utility model in that each outcome of the selection procedure is being evaluated. There are four possible outcomes:

(a) acceptance of a potentially successful applicant;
(b) rejection of a potentially successful applicant;
(c) rejection of a potentially unsuccessful applicant;
(d) acceptance of a potentially unsuccessful applicant.

In general the outcomes (a) and (c) will be given positive values and (b) and (d) negative values. There are several ways to determine these values or utilities. Roe (1983) distinguishes objective, subjective and objectified methods. In objective methods some kind of objective appraisal criterion is used to assess the values of all four outcomes (for instance a cost-benefit analysis). In subjective methods the utilities are determined by means of subjective ratings either on management level or

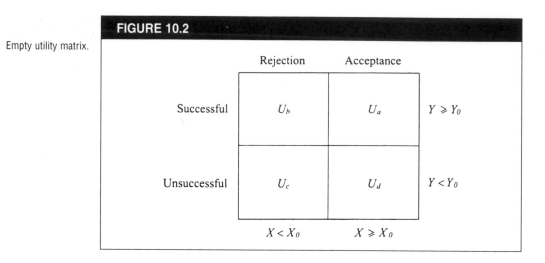

Empty utility matrix.

FIGURE 10.2

	Rejection	Acceptance	
Successful	U_b	U_a	$Y \geqslant Y_0$
Unsuccessful	U_c	U_d	$Y < Y_0$
	$X < X_0$	$X \geqslant X_0$	

by the people who are directly involved in selection. The use of a utility function is characteristic for objectified methods. It quantifies the relation between criterion Y and utility U. With either one of these methods the values in the empty utility matrix can be filled. These are called the *actual utilities*. Hence, the expected utilities of the alternative decisions "accept" or "reject" for each predictor score can be computed with the aid of an expectancy table. In an expectancy table the probabilities of attaining specified criterion scores are given for each predictor score. In general, the higher the test score the higher the probability that an applicant will perform well at a particular level. When the minimum satisfactory criterion level is specified, the expectancy table gives the probability of a success or failure for each predictor score. The *expected utility* is the sum of the products of these probabilities and the actual utilities that belong to the selection outcome concerned.

The importance of this approach is that different values may be attributed to the actual utilities of the minority and the majority group. It illustrates the efforts an organization puts into a policy of affirmative action. Figure 10.3 gives an example of different actual utilities for two groups.

This example shows that the rejection of an unsuccessful candidate has a positive value (U_c) and that accepting an unsuccessful candidate gets a negative value (U_d). The absolute value of U_d is greater than that of U_c: after all, an unsuccessful employee may cost the company a lot of money. In

the example given above, the values for U_c and U_d are equal for the minority and the majority group. This is not the case however for U_a and U_b. Although accepting a successful candidate (U_a) has a positive value for both groups, an affirmative action policy is reflected in a higher value for the minority group. It is obvious that rejecting successful candidates should be avoided as much as possible. Therefore, a negative utility (U_b) is assigned to this outcome. The difference between these utility values of the minority and the majority group shows that rejecting a potentially successful employee from the minority group is considered an even greater loss.

The model described above is a so-called *threshold utility model*. A disadvantage of such a model is that the degree of capability is not taken into account (Petersen, 1976). Candidates with scores just above the success–failure cut-off point on the criterion are given the same utility as those who would be extremely successful. This is compensated for in a *linear utility model*, where the utility value is a monotonically increasing or decreasing function of the criterion score (Mellenbergh & Van der Linden, 1981), and different values for the minority and the majority group can be used.

In summary, caution against the use of qualified individualism is called for. In the case of a biased predictor the effect of this strategy turns out to be a quota strategy, and it stays unclear which group is favoured, which group is disfavoured, and to what extent. Unqualified individualism will give the

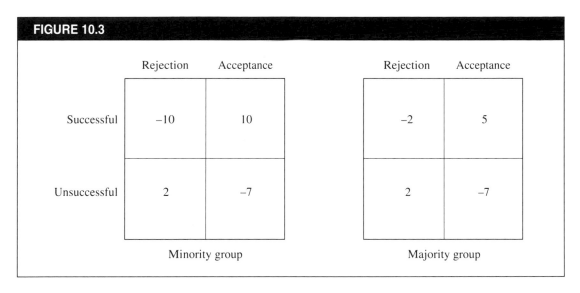

FIGURE 10.3

Example of utility matrices for the same job for minority and majority group in the case of affirmative action.

best selection results. In the case of a biased predictor it provides the opportunity to use different regression formulas for different subgroups avoiding indirect discrimination. Because of the lowest error rate, this model is fairest for all candidates. It is the most profitable strategy, since the predicted mean work performance score is the highest. However, this is all technical reasoning, and from a social or ethical point of view one may argue in favour of a quotum model, which may be the only way to compensate for the lower employability rate of minority groups and to counteract the discriminating effect of selection (even when an unbiased predictor is used). This is why Drenth (1989, p. 79) concludes: "Ultimately it is a political decision which equilibrium in a given situation is preferred between 'fair chances' and 'efficiency' given the economical and political limiting conditions". However, before any decision is made, the basic assumptions and the actual choice for a strategy should be openly and explicitly discussed with all parties concerned.

2.2.4 Criterion bias

Research into prediction bias and its models all assume that criterion measures are unbiased. However, if the criterion contains some kind of bias that runs parallel to the bias in the predictor (that is to say that it equally disfavours one of the groups), then the predictor is wrongly considered

unbiased. Criterion bias is defined as the discrepancy between measures for work performance (the actual criteria) and the employee's real value for the organization (the ultimate criterion) (Schmitt, 1989). It means that in a systematic or consistent way something else other than the ultimate criterion is being measured. Again, as with predictor measures, different scores on criterion measures between groups in itself arc not evidence for bias, since they may reflect real differences in the ultimate criterion. However, a practical problem is that one can never have the scores on the ultimate criterion. One can work with estimates at best, which in turn need not be unbiased.

The way to solve this problem is to collect data on different criterion measures, to investigate the relations with a number of predictors and check if differences in these relations between groups are related to criterion type. Studies dealing with this issue tend to differentiate between *objective* and *subjective* criteria. Examples of objective types of criteria are turnover and absenteeism rates, measures for quantity of output (number of errors, number of units produced, etc.) and cognitive measures (training tests, job knowledge tests), etc. Subjective criteria are ratings by supervisors or colleagues. These may either be ratings of one's overall performance or judgements about specific aspects of one's performance. The idea of differentiating between objective and subjective criteria

called for, in order to prevent this kind of bias as much as possible. This can be done for example by using behaviour-oriented scales and the formation of multi-ethnic rating teams. With respect to objective criteria American research on African-Americans and Caucasians rather consistently shows higher scores for the majority group. The degree of differences varies according to the type of criterion measure used. So these measures are by no means interchangeable and each individual measure by itself cannot be considered a proper indicator for the ultimate criterion. In sum, it appears that additional research into the validity of criterion measures determining the criterion construct is needed.

2.3   Internal test bias

This approach to the problem of test bias does not primarily focus on the degree to which a test over- or underpredicts with respect to a specific external criterion, but on the characteristics of the test itself and the interpretation of the test scores. The central issue here is whether the test refers to a theoretical concept or construct in the same way in different cultural groups.

The importance of this approach, which can be seen as being complementary to the study of prediction bias, lies in its explanatory character. Finding that the meaning of a test changes in a certain direction when it is administered to individuals and groups with different cultural backgrounds will more readily lead to hypotheses about biasing factors and to recommendations for adapting the instrument or the administration procedure.

Analysis of internal bias can take place at the level of the total test or at the item level. In the first case the composition of the test is not a point of discussion and bias analysis is based on the total test scores. It can be determined for instance, whether the total scores are related to other indicators of the construct and whether they differentiate from indicators of other constructs in the same way in the various groups. In addition, the (differences in) relationships of test scores with relevant background variables such as social class and educational level, and the sensitivity of test scores to experimental variations in administration conditions such as the amount of instruc-

tion and training, may also provide information about the degree to which test scores can be interpreted in the same way in the groups distinguished.

In the case of bias analysis at the item level, the individual items are seen as operationalizations of the construct represented by the test as a whole. It is investigated whether the relationships between the items or the relationships between the items and the total test satisfy the requirements of the measurement model in the same way in the various groups. Items that do not satisfy the requirements or which show deviating results are considered to be biased and may be removed from the test.

On the basis of this distinction between bias at the level of test scores and item bias, the main issues in this field of research will be discussed in the next sections.

2.3.1   Bias in measuring the construct

Test bias is not primarily a characteristic of the test as such but is linked to the test interpretation. If person 1 with cultural background x answers more test items correctly than person 2 with cultural background y, this could simply be seen as an empirical fact which (apart from possible discussions about the scoring rule) did not require any consideration about the possibility of test bias. However, a problem is created when, on the basis of this difference, one concluded that person 1 ranked higher than person 2 with respect to some general personality characteristic. A problem certainly arises if this characteristic is held to be stable and/or genetically based.

In the past, researchers have expended considerable efforts constructing so-called "culture free tests" (Cattell, 1940). It was thought to be possible to eliminate the influence of environmental factors on test performance and to draw conclusions about differences in inborn potential irrespective of the cultural background of the persons taking the test. However, for cognitive ability tests at least, these attempts have never been very successful. Cross-cultural test research has provided us with many examples of cultural groups not possessing the specific skills presupposed by standard ability tests to a sufficient degree (Hudson, 1960, 1967; Deregowski, 1979).

Of course, some tests are more widely applicable than others and less dependent on specific learning experiences. A good example of such a test is Raven's Progressive Matrices (Raven, 1960). The Raven test has been used very often in cross-cultural research and is considered to be one of the least culturally dependent cognitive ability tests. However, even for this instrument, construct validity has been shown to be partly determined by cultural factors (Irvine, 1969a; Chan, 1976). A summary of factors that may influence the meaning of test scores is presented in Table 10.2. When comparing persons with different backgrounds, factors such as these may produce unintended variation in test performances and lead to biased interpretations. The influence of these factors can be reduced in different ways. In the first place, one may think of expanding the instructions and adding more practice items for candidates who lack the necessary test-taking skills. A number of studies have shown that additional test training leads to a substantial improvement in test performance, especially for groups lacking these skills (Dyer, 1970; Feuerstein, 1972, 1979; Kroeger, 1980).

In the second place, adaptation of test items and testing procedures may also reduce the influence of culturally determined skills on the test scores. Ord's (1970) adaptation of Koh's Blocks provides an interesting example. For other examples and an overview of procedures to improve the cross-cultural equivalence of test instructions and stimulus materials, the reader is referred to Warwick and Osherson (1973), Brislin, Lonner, and Thorndike (1973), Triandis and Berry (1980) and Lonner and Berry (1988).

Finally, it is also possible to restrict the interpretation of test scores to selected parts of the population that have shown, or can be assumed to possess, the required skills and knowledge to a sufficient degree. Proposals to let a testability or acculturation test precede the administration of the real test are in line with this thought. Others (Hofstee et al., 1990) have pointed out that this means it might be an advantage to a test candidate to get a low score on the pre-test. This problem will also arise if the score on the pre-test is used as a correction factor.

From the foregoing it will be clear that in comparing the test performances of persons with varying cultural backgrounds it will generally not be possible on a priori grounds to exclude the possibility that the differences have to be ascribed to differences in test-taking skills or other unintended factors. In answering the question of whether the test has the same meaning for the various candidates (refers to the same construct in the same way), psychometric criteria will also have to be taken into account.

This question, however, is preceded by the more fundamental question of the validity of the construct or attribute for the cultural groups concerned. Does it make sense, for instance, to apply concepts like spatial ability or arithmetic reasoning outside the Western cultural system in which they originated? Inspired by ideas from cultural anthropology, a number of investigators have argued that cognitive functioning is conceived as an adaptation to specific cultural and ecological requirements and should be defined in terms of these requirements. Cross-cultural comparisons of test performances, in this view, become practically impossible. For an overview of the discussion about this topic we refer to publications by Berry (1972), Jahoda (1977, 1983) and Poortinga and Malpass (1988). We will confine

---

TABLE 10.2

- Understanding the test instructions
- Familiarity with the testing material (pictures, words, grammatical structures, letters, figures, objects), relevant concepts, problem-solving strategies and answering possibilities
- Experience with the testing task or comparable tasks
- Experience with working under time pressure
- Test attitude, motivation, concentration, fear of failure, social desirability

Sources of Unintended Variance in Test Scores.

ourselves here to a pragmatic approach in which an attempt is made to formulate psychometric criteria for the comparability of test scores, taking the "psychic unity of mankind" and the universality of constructs as a point of departure.

A good example of this last approach is the work carried out by Poortinga (1971, 1975), which draws a distinction between different levels of comparability. For total test scores the distinction is drawn between functional equivalence and score equivalence. Functional equivalence relates to the requirement that the test qualitatively measures the same attribute in the different groups. When dealing with more than one test to which this requirement applies, the testable condition follows that the relationships between the tests are the same in the groups concerned. Score equivalence implies that the test should measure the attribute on a quantitatively similar scale in the distinguished groups; when there is more than one test, the requirement of similar regression coefficients follows.

The functional equivalence of measurement instruments across different cultural groups has been studied relatively often. Comparison of factor structures is one of the most appropriate methods. An advantage to the comparison of separate correlation coefficients or correlation matrices is the possibility of starting from an appropriate theoretical framework, which makes the assumption of equal relationships between theoretical concepts a less arbitrary one and creates the possibility of interpreting changes in meaning. Among the intelligence theories based on factor analytic research, both the hierarchical model by Vernon (1950) and Cattell's (1963) theory of fluid and crystallized ability have shown their cross-cultural applicability (Irvine, 1969b; Vernon, 1969; Hakstian & Vandenberg, 1979; Vandenberg & Hakstian, 1978), while most of Thurstone's (1938) "primary mental abilities" have also been recovered in divergent cultural groups (Vandenberg & Hakstian, 1978; Irvine, 1979).

A number of methods have been applied to compare factor structures. The most simple and widely used method is one in which the factors found in the different groups are separately rotated to simple structure. Factor structures or factor patterns can then be compared by inspection (see for instance Irvine, 1969b). A formal test of the differences does not take place. There are also a number of methods in which a factor matrix is transformed in a linear way to a matrix resembling another matrix (the goal matrix) as much as possible. This is called a Procrustian transformation (Niemöller & Sprenger, 1977), though the term "Procrustes rotation" is usually used. The goal matrix may be an a priori determined hypothetical matrix or, in the instance of a comparison between different samples, one of the subgroup matrices or an overall matrix for the combined samples (see for an example Van der Flier, 1980).

Another method for the combined factor analysis of correlation matrices from different populations, developed by Jöreskog (1971) provides an indirect test of the equality of the factor matrices. This method makes no attempt to rotate independent factor structures to a common solution, but the model to be tested is specified on an a priori basis. The LISREL program (Jöreskog & Sörbom, 1984) can be used to carry out this confirmatory factor analysis.

According to Ten Berge (1986) many investigators do not find the statistically advanced LISREL program very practical. Among the reasons are technical problems such as lack of convergence, the fact that the method is particularly suited to showing that a model does *not* fit, and the problem that LISREL provides little information about the question of what has happened to the factors not found in another population. It is also often found to be difficult to specify the elements to be fixed on an a priori basis. As to the more descriptive approaches, where (on the basis of a limited number of components) rotation takes place to maximum congruence, the problem is that a number of arbitrary choices have to be made, such as the number of components to be retained and the type of rotation (orthogonal or oblique) to be used.

A new method proposed by Ten Berge is Pekon (Perfekte Kongruentie: Camstra, 1985) which implies that a second group's factor structure is rotated to perfect congruence with a first (reference) group's factor structure. This is done by applying the weight matrix of the first group to the correlation matrix of the second group. In this way the second group's factor structure has, by definition, the same meaning as the original group's factor structure. The question is then whether the same factors explain as much variance in the second group as in the first. This approach resembles the Multiple Group Method developed by Gorsuch (1983).

2.3.2 Item bias

As for the test as a whole, individual items may contain elements which create additional problems for certain subgroups. This may concern the specific knowledge or specific skills required to produce the correct answer, formal characteristics of the item to which the groups react differently, or differences in the degree to which certain response alternatives are found attractive or socially desirable. If, because of this, the items reflect differences between groups that the test does not intend to measure one may speak of item bias or, more neutrally, about differential item functioning (DIF).

In the field of statistical item bias research many methods have been developed over the last 30 years (Angoff & Ford, 1972; Van der Flier, Mellenbergh, Adèr, & Wijn, 1984b; Holland & Thayer, 1988; Lord, 1980; Mellenbergh, 1982; Scheuneman, 1980; Stricker, 1982; Wright, Mead, & Draba, 1976; see also Holland & Wainer, 1993 and Millsap & Everson, 1993). A distinction can be drawn between unconditional and conditional methods. In unconditional methods an item is considered to be biased when, in comparison with the other items of the test, it is relatively easier or more difficult for one of the groups or in other words, when there is a significant item × group interaction. One of the most widely known unconditional methods is the delta method (Angoff & Ford, 1973; see also Angoff, 1982) in which the transformed difficulty indices (*p*-values) of the items in the different groups are plotted against each other.

Strong deviations from the line indicating the relationship between the difficulty indices in the different groups are interpreted as an indication of item bias. Other unconditional methods based on analysis of variance, such as the one by Plake and Hoover (1979) in which item responses are analysed within an item × group factorial design and a significant interaction between the factors is taken as an indication of item bias, have also been frequently applied.

These unconditional methods lead to a number of practical and theoretical problems (Mellenbergh, 1982). In the first place, the methods are not independent of the score distributions in the various groups and are therefore sensitive to the real differences in trait level between the groups. A second objection is that the bias of the item is defined in relation to the other items in the test and is therefore dependent on the specific collection of items.

Conditional methods for the detection of item bias, however, do compare item responses at the same trait level. Items are being called unbiased if the probability of a correct answer is the same for the distinguished groups. Within the group of conditional methods a distinction can be drawn between methods based on latent trait models, and methods in which the total score on the test is used as an estimate of the trait level. Methods based on latent trait models are preferable in principle, but make higher demands with respect to the characteristics of the items and/or numbers of testees.

Latent traits are hypothetical dimensions which provide an explanation for the relationships between the test items. The complete latent space is made up of all the dimensions needed to explain these relationships. Within this space, the conditional distributions of item scores, given the latent trait positions, are by definition the same for all relevant populations (Lord & Novick, 1968). When a test consists of homogeneous items one may assume that the relationships between the items can be explained by one latent trait. The regressions of the item scores on this trait are called item characteristic curves or item ogives. If the complete latent space is indeed one-dimensional, these item characteristic curves are invariant for the various groups. When item characteristic curves in two culturally different groups appear to be different, there is obviously a second dimension, related to group membership, implying that the items involved have to be considered as being non-equivalent. Deviations between item characteristic curves can be quantified by comparing difficulty and discrimination parameters or by taking the surface between the two curves (see for instance Kok, 1988). Well-known examples are methods based on the three-parameter logistic model (Lord, 1980) and the one-parameter (Rasch) model described by Wright, Mead, and Draba (1976); see also Mellenbergh (1972).

Item bias methods in which total test scores are used as ability estimates are generally easier to apply than methods based on latent trait models. A well-known example is a procedure proposed by Scheuneman (1979, 1981) in which, on the basis of the total test scores, the groups which are to be compared are divided into a number of subgroups, each defined by a certain score range. Per item, it is checked then whether the numbers of correct answers in these subgroups deviate from the numbers that would be expected on the basis of the distribution of the groups over the score categories and the proportions of correct answers within these categories. The differences between the observed and the expected numbers are tested with a chi-square test.

Mellenbergh (1982) has proposed an improved version of this method in which the data are analysed by fitting log linear or logit methods (Fienberg, 1980). An example is given in Table 10.3 below. Respondents from two cultural groups ($j = 1,2$) are divided into five score categories on the basis of the total scores on the test ($i = 1, 2, 3, 4, 5$). For the 10 cells the proportions of correct answers (p_{ij}) are calculated. The item is taken to be unbiased if the proportions of correct answers within the same score category are the same in the two groups ($P_{i1} = P_{i2}$).

For the sake of clarity it should be noted that this condition does not imply that the proportions of correct answers in the groups as a whole have to be the same. This is only the case if the distributions over the score categories are the same in the different groups. Logit models take the natural logarithm of the ratio of (proportions of) correct and incorrect responses as a point of departure for the analysis. The logit model corresponding to an unbiased item is:

$$\ln [p_{ij}/(1 - p_{ij})] = C + S_i,$$

in which C is a parameter for the overall item difficulty and S_i stands for the main score category effect (see also Mellenbergh, 1985). The fit of the

model is indicated with a G^2 value which is asymptotically chi-square distributed.

As to item bias, a difference can be made between uniform bias and nonuniform bias. Uniform bias means that the p_{i1}-values are higher or lower than the p_{i2}-values in all score categories or, in terms of the logit model, that for a good fit an additional parameter (G_j) is needed, indicating the main effect of the group membership. If the model with this additional parameter does not fit the data either, the bias is called nonuniform, meaning that the difference between p_{i1} and p_{i2} varies per score category. In this case a good fit is only achieved by adding a parameter ($SG)_{ij}$ to the model, indicating the score category × group membership interaction effect.

A serious weakness of conditional item bias models is that if the test contains a large number of biased items, the measure of the ability level used in classifying subjects into score categories will also be biased. This can mean that some biased items are not classified as such, and that some unbiased items are erroneously classified as biased. Van der Flier, Mellenbergh, Adèr, and Wijn (1984b) therefore developed an iterative logit procedure. Briefly, this method involves removing biased items from the test (or, more accurately, not counting them in determining the total score) so that the number of items removed increases by one with each successive iteration. At the end of the first iteration the most biased item is removed from the test, at the end of the second iteration the *two* most biased items, etc. Items eliminated at an early stage may be included again

TABLE 10.3

Proportions of Correct Answers per Score Category in Two Cultural Groups. Example of a Biased Item (the Item is Biased against Group 2).

Score category		Group membership	
		($j = 1$)	($j = 2$)
0–11	($i = 1$)	.34	.27
12–15	($i = 2$)	.51	.31
16–19	($i = 3$)	.71	.52
20–23	($i = 4$)	.79	.56
24–29	($i = 5$)	.94	.49

at a later stage. The algorithm is terminated if, at the end of the iteration, one of the following conditions arises: the prescribed number of iterations has been performed or the maximum chi-square of the set of unbiased items is below the critical value.

The iterative logit procedure appears to be very efficient in detecting biased items. The results of simulation studies (Van der Flier, Mellenbergh, & Adèr, 1984a) and studies in which item bias was induced experimentally (Kok, 1982; Kok, Mellenbergh, & Van der Flier, 1985) suggest that the iterative procedure is a substantial improvement on the non-iterative one and that the method is relatively insensitive to real differences in trait level between groups. The iterative logit method has been applied in cross-cultural research (Van der Flier, 1983; Poortinga & Van der Flier, 1988) and more specifically for the analysis of test data of various immigrant groups in The Netherlands (Kok, 1988; Te Nijenhuis & Van der Flier, 1994; Pieters & Zaal, 1991). Kok (1988), especially, has given attention to the problems surrounding the explanation of statistical bias. Three research strategies are distinguished:

1. *post hoc* inspection of statistically biased items, looking for striking features that can be related to well-known differences between the groups;
2. defining specific item qualities and investigating the association between bias and these qualities over the items; and
3. experimental studies in which item characteristics are varied and the consequences for the degree of bias of these items are studied.

While this combination of strategies has certainly led to a clearer picture of the causes of item bias, the conclusion has to be that it is generally not possible to indicate beforehand, on the basis of item characteristics, which items will turn out to be biased against specific groups. Kok's study on item bias in the CITO achievement test at the end of primary education with respect to Turkish and Moroccan pupils in The Netherlands provides a good illustration of this point. Kok formulated three general hypotheses to explain statistical item bias in this test. These hypotheses concerned a

lower level of proficiency in the Dutch language, a lower personal working speed, and a lack of test-taking skills. Based on these hypotheses, expectations were formulated with respect to the critical features of biased items. The hypothesized critical features were: complexity of the question, numbers of difficult words and sentences in the question itself and in the response alternatives (in connection with the lower proficiency in Dutch), rank number in the order of administration (personal working speed) and deviance of chosen (wrong) alternatives (test wiseness). Next, 2×2 tables were set up of numbers of biased and unbiased items with and without a specific feature. For features chosen on the basis of the language proficiency hypothesis, the expected relationship was found in one-third of the cases. The hypothesis about differences in working speed was not supported at all. The hypothesis about differences in test wiseness was only supported for the Turkish pupils.

Another contingency table method for the detection of biased items that has been the focus of much recent research is the Mantel–Haenszel (MH) method (Mantel & Haenszel, 1959), extended by Holland and Thayer (1988). This method is used at the Educational Testing Service (ETS) as the primary DIF detection device. The basic data used in this method are in the form of s (score level) $\times$ 2 (group) $\times$ 2 (item score) contingency tables, and the null DIF hypothesis tested is that the odds of getting an item right at a given score level is the same in both groups across all score levels. The MH statistic provides a χ^2 test of significance. The MH statistic is efficient, conceptually simple and relatively easy to use. A disadvantage, as compared with the logit method just discussed, is that it is less suitable for detecting non-uniform bias. For a description of the MH method and the way it is used at ETS we refer the reader to Dorans and Holland (1993).

Opinions differ about the importance of item bias research. According to some investigators (Humphreys, 1986; Schmitt, 1989) the possible contribution of this kind of research to the solution of the problem of the weak position of minority groups on the labour market is relatively small and is detracting attention from the real problem, which is the cause of the differences in criterion termination because of unfitness. It would seem that older Turkish and Moroccan workers suffer from the consequences of years of physical labour under less favourable work conditions (Reubsaet, 1990). Physical problems are often coupled with psychosocial problems for which Dutch physicians, pychologists and social workers do not have an adequate remedy (Meijs, 1989). Moreover, placement in other jobs is usually difficult because of the low level of schooling.

4   MEASURES

The foregoing has given an overview of the position of minorities on the labour market and within work organizations. The overall picture for minorities is not a rosy one; a relatively high number of unemployed, overrepresentation in lower level jobs, heavy physical labour and a high percentage of dismissals. Much attention has been given to the possibility of discrimination in selection, especially through the use of psychological tests. In this connection, various methods to detect test and item bias have been discussed. Of course, this kind of research is only one of the possible actions that might be taken to reduce the possibility of discriminatory practices.

In The Netherlands there is no general agreement about the question of which (combinations of) measures are required to improve the opportunities for minorities on the labour market and within organizations (Reubsaet, 1990). Points of discussion are the role of government, the responsibilities of employers and unions, and the need for further legislation in this field. Opinions also differ about the role that (organizations of) minorities should play in this discussion, at least implicitly. These different points of view have led to a large variety of recommendations for action and policy.

The diversity of positions often reflects a difference in view on the causes of the disadvantaged position of minorities. Categorization of these views may therefore lead to some order in the actions and measures recommended and provide a suitable starting point for an evaluation. Bovenkerk (1990) draws a distinction between five types of explanations, attributing the lag in socio-economic development to (i) insufficient adaptation to Dutch society, (ii) discrimination within Dutch society, (iii) a world order founded on racism, (iv) inadequate development of the ethnic groups' own cultural potential and (v) the development of a system of ethnic stratification in which ethnic minorities constitute a "subclass". For a detailed discussion of these five theoretical perspectives we refer the reader to the publication by Bovenkerk. The distinction will be used here to structure the discussion of the various actions and policy measures.

1. Based on the idea of insufficient adaptation, it might be expected that additional training and schooling are seen as part of the solution. Both language and general knowledge courses (Bolle et al., 1988; De Haan, 1988; LCT, 1989; see also Perdue, 1987) and training in specific skills matching the requirements of the Dutch labour market can be brought to mind. Training directed at application and selection procedures (see for instance Reynaert, 1988), and programmes to create traineeships and special jobs to acquire work experience also belong to this category.

    An example of a successful project focusing on additional training is the project "Promotion and integration through re-education in The Netherlands" (PION), which aimed at the placement of minority group members in staff and middle management jobs in commercial and non-profit organizations by means of a special training course in the field of informatics (Van Leest & Bleichrodt, 1989). The course was directed at unemployed, but relatively highly educated, minority group members (preferably at college or university level). In addition to the course in informatics, the programme included training sessions in social skills, preparing the candidates for application and selection procedures and the real-life work situation. Finding traineeships and jobs for the candidates was also part of the project. One year after the completion of the project it could be concluded that 90% of the candidates had found paid work, virtually always in jobs where automation was a major element.

2. Measures intended to reduce the possibility of discrimination of minorities on the labour market and within work organizations may focus on selection and promotion decisions or on dismissals. The distinction made between direct and indirect discrimination has relevance within this context.

   Direct discrimination can be reduced by (securing compliance with) fair application of rules for selection, promotion and dismissal. Formalizing the selection procedure reduces the possibility of arbitrariness in connection with the treatment of job applicants. Apart from the advantage that the validity of the selection interview is raised by this, the structuring of the interview is a good example. Training and coaching of those entrusted with the selection of job applicants may also be an effective way to prevent discrimination. Unfortunately, it appears that any change of attitude following such courses and training sessions often has a temporary character. Refresher courses seem to be needed to bring about a permanent change in attitude; in practice it will often not be possible to organize this. From a somewhat different angle, the training of selectors does not focus primarily on reducing discriminatory tendencies, but on informing those involved in the selection procedure about the cultural background of applicants from minority groups and about behavioural patterns following from this. In contrast with the approach described under (1), which tries to further the adaptation and integration of minority groups into majority culture, this kind of training tries to guarantee some degree of understanding of the minority group's culture on the part of the selector. These types of training courses do appear to be effective (Abell, 1988). In connection with this, a study carried out for the Ministry of Social Affairs and Employment in The Netherlands should be mentioned (Hooghiemstra et al., 1990). This study argues forcefully for a better tuning of the recruitment channels of employers to the search channels of minority group members looking for jobs.

   Indirect discrimination can be reduced by a careful analysis of selection procedures, selection instruments and appraisal systems, to check whether equal suitability goes with equal opportunities. The evaluation procedures that can be followed by psychologists have received ample attention in the foregoing.

   A legal framework to prevent discrimination has only partly been effected in The Netherlands. The first article of Chapter 1 of the Constitution (Revision, February 1983) says that "All persons in The Netherlands must be treated equally in equal cases. Discrimination on the grounds of religion, philosophy of life, political views, ethnic background, sex or on any other grounds is not allowed". The elaboration of this in a "General Law on Equal Treatment" has not been effectuated as far as ethnic minorities are concerned.

   A clear rejection of both direct and indirect discrimination has been laid down in the professional code of psychologists (NIP, 1976) and is an official part of the personnel policy employed by the government, municipal organizations and large industries in the Netherlands.

3. Racism stands for the theory of inferiority or superiority of people on the basis of their (supposed) ethnic background (Bovenkerk, 1990). Assumptions based on racism find expression in many ways, for instance in the way employees react to colleagues from minority groups (see earlier in this chapter). This chapter has given scant attention to the boundaries of, and theory around, concepts such as prejudice, stereotyping and racism. This self-imposed restriction does not only follow from its focus on the psychology of work, but also from the fact that it is not possible to treat all aspects of discrimination in a single chapter. For a more theoretical overview the reader is referred, for instance, to Dovidio and Gaertner (1986).

   Information about and the exposition of racist views and behaviour are seen as ways approaches definitely improved the validity of research.

In addition, some structural market changes emerged that did affect the nature and extent of consumer information processing and decision making. Here we will make a very brief review of the most apparent changes.

For many products and services one of the major developments is the reduction of (perceived) inter-brand quality differences, which are due to technological progress and increasing marketing sophistication. Within a particular product category a variety of different brands tends to be located at the high end of the (perceived) quality continuum, where they are perceived to differ only marginally, if at all. To this we should add that their product knowledge is often insufficient, making it difficult for consumers to correctly identify and judge technical product attributes. Communication on these attributes might be functional but is frequently not fully understood. The combination of these developments increasingly reduce the perceived risk involved in purchase decisions, and reduce the consumer's willingness to carefully and elaborately compare different brands prior to purchase. The resulting consumer behavior seems to be in conflict with the more or less rational view traditionally held (see, e.g. Olshavsky & Granbois, 1979; Poiesz, 1993; Poiesz & Robben, 1993).

This general development may have strong implications for the conceptualization of the consumer decision process. The pre-purchase deliberation and information processing may be much more limited than considered possible thus far; shopping behavior may be more related to its hedonic aspects (shopping for fun) than to risk-prevention, the evaluation of the product after purchase and during consumption may not take place to the extent that actual brand loyalty may develop, and consumers may develop tactics to avoid the unpleasant aspects of decision making (e.g. by implicitly or explicitly delegating the decision to the retailer, to an intermediary agent, or to persons with product experience). More superficial brand images may become more important than brand attitudes based upon factual information on the brand's intrinsic qualities, and

the choice of a service may depend more on the person offering the service than on the actual quality of that service. Product knowledge (true or false) stored in memory may turn out to strongly dominate new incoming information from commercial sources, such as advertising.

In summary, it is argued that consumer behavior and consumer behavior theory will increasingly reflect the changes that can be observed in the market place. It is expected that the difference with the traditional rational point of view will even become larger.

3.4.3 Relationship with organizational psychology

Because this is a chapter in a book on organizational behavior, the latter expectation prompts the question to what extent buyer behavior is more rational in an organizational context. This question seems adequate as organizations tend to put a stronger emphasis on the justification of decisions, and where formalized control reduces the dependency upon psychological idiosyncrasies of individual decision makers. Let us finish this chapter, therefore, by addressing the question of the rationality of organizational economic decisions.

In market economies, organizations, as purposefully structured social entities, are usually referred to as "firms" or "enterprises" of which the most general goal is to provide benefits for its owners and members or employees on a continuous basis. Firms can be viewed as being engaged in economic behavior: they allocate scarce resources in order to obtain the desired outcomes. At a somewhat less general level the outcome often translates into profit as the difference between financial outcomes and costs. Profit expresses the organization's quality of performance, it serves as a return on investment, and it guarantees continuity. In organizations, money may be used to compensate suppliers and investors, to compensate workers, or to invest. Time must be allocated to different activities within the organization and, partly independent of time, energy or effort is divided over the various organizational tasks.

In short, like individuals in other settings, individuals in organizational contexts have to deal with scarcity of instruments and scarcity of resources. For the organization's performance and continuity, the quality of economic behavior is an important matter. Erroneous or inappropriate decisions may imply inadequate, that is, ineffective or inefficient, allocations and might even endanger the organization. Therefore, it is important to understand how allocations are made.

For the description and explanation of economic behavior different types of general theories or models may be employed. The nature of these theories or models is determined, to a large extent, by the disciplinary background from which it emerges. Here a crude distinction can be made between economic and psychological bases of existing theories and models of economic organizational behavior. It is important to briefly discuss the differences between these general disciplinary approaches. As we have described earlier, traditional economic theories have a tendency to focus on rational aspects of behavior. They adopt a rational model of the human race which involves the assumption that decision makers strive for utility maximization, have complete information on behavior alternatives, have clear and stable goals and preferences, and have perfect foresight with regard to decision consequences. An (incidental) deviation from rational behavior is assumed to be a temporary phenomenon by self-correcting tendencies based on performance feedback.

In an organizational context the rational approach would amount to the assumption of profit maximization, perfect knowledge of goal alternatives and alternative routes to these goals, and the absence of intra-organizational conflicts.

In daily life and in empirical studies, the rational model of the human race has proven to be too optimistic with regard to the human race's motivation, capacity, and opportunity to maximize utility.

The same observation can be made with regard to economic behavior in firms. March and Sévon (1988) summarized the criticism on the economic approach to the behavior in firms in two points. The first is that rational decision making is unlikely as it would imply extraordinary (= unrealistic) demands for time and information in organizations; the second point is that while rationality assumes absence of inter-individual preference differences, intra-organizational conflicts do in fact occur—and even occur quite frequently.

Simon (1979) reports on empirical observations that do not support the strict rational approach to organizational behavior. Earlier, the same author (Simon, 1957) introduced the notion of *bounded rationality*, thereby pointing at limitations in human decision making capabilities which prevent or hamper profit or utility maximization. Cyert and March (1963) elaborate upon the notion of bounded rationality by introducing four organizational concepts suggesting a departure from strict rationality: *quasi-resolution of conflict* (e.g. the adoption of merely acceptable rather than optimal solutions, or the solution of conflict by separating the concerning organizational units with their own "local rationalities"), *uncertainty avoidance* (rather than facing actual uncertainties, the context is restructured or selected so as to guarantee perceived certainty), *problemistic search* (information search is dominated by the occurrence of problems instead of by the functionality of the information *per se*), and *organizational learning* (expressed in, for example, the adapation of organizational goals to actual performance).

Obviously, these tendencies are not limited to business organizations. However, for business organizations they imply that profit maximization or optimization may not be achieved, and that organizations and individuals within organizations do not behave in accordance with rationality principles. In short, the assumption of rationality should not be taken as the basis for a theory of organizational or individual economic behavior.

4 CONCLUSION

In this chapter, economic psychology as a relatively new branch of psychology was briefly introduced by discussing some of the major issues that have been presented in the economic psychological literature. A number of issues could not be dealt with due to space limitations, and some relevant issues could not be dealt with for the simple reason that no sufficient scientific knowledge has been accumulated.

There are a number of areas that are in need of economic psychological research, not only for academic reasons but for practical reasons as well. Economic psychology as an applied field focuses upon a domain of life that is important for many persons in different roles, to which and in which they allocate a considerable part of their resources. Economic aspects of life are strongly associated with economic well-being, both in a positive and negative sense. On the one hand, consumption experiences add to the quality of life; on the other hand, economic limitations affect well-being in more than only one respect. Economic behavior is often a positively oriented type of behavior that contributes to personal and social well-being. Sometimes, economic behavior appears in a more negative form, such as consumer debt, economic fraud, free riding (e.g. unwarranted use of social benefits), shoplifting, and compulsive buying behavior. These different areas are important and should receive more attention.

Too little is known of the economic behavior associated with some particular decision making roles. For example, there is very limited evidence only on the economic decisions made by entrepreneurs and economic political decision makers. Yet, the consequences of decisions made by persons in these roles may be very important. Organizational psychologists and economic psychologists have, to some extent, different interests. But at this point their interests seem to coincide.

REFERENCES

Albou, P. (1984). *La psychologie economique.* Paris: Presses Universitaires de France.

Andreasen, A.R. (1965). Attitudes and consumer behavior: A decision model. In L.E. Preston (Ed.), *New research in marketing.* Berkeley, CA: University of California, Institute of Business and Economic Research, 1–16.

Antonides, G. (1991). *Psychology in economics and business.* Dordrecht, The Netherlands: Kluwer Academic Publishers.

Atkinson, J.W. (1958). Towards experimental analysis of human motivation in terms of motives, expectancies, and incentives. In J.W. Atkinson (Ed.), *Motives in fantasy, action, and society.* Princeton, NJ: Van Nostrand.

Baldry, J.C. (1986). Tax evasion is not a gamble. *Economics Letters, 22,* 333–335.

Bartels, R., Murray, J., & Weiss, A.A. (1988). The role of consumer and business sentiment in forecasting telecommunications traffic. *Journal of Economic Psychology, 9,* 215–232.

Becker, W., Büchner, H-J., & Sleeking, S. (1987). The impact of public expenditures on tax evasions: An experimental approach. *Journal of Public Economics, 34,* 243–252.

Belk, R.W., & Wallendorf, M. (1990). The sacred meanings of money. *Journal of Economic Psychology, 11*(1), 35–69.

Bettman, J.R. (1979). *An information processing theory of consumer choice.* Reading, MA: Addison-Wesley.

Boulding, K. (1985). *Human betterment.* Beverly Hills, CA: Sage.

Braun, O.L., & Wicklund, R.A. (1989). Psychological antecedents of conspicuous consumption. *Journal of Economic Psychology, 10,* 161–189.

Bruner, J.S., & Goodman, C.C. (1947). Value and needs as organizing factors in perception. *Journal of Abnormal and Social Psychology, 42,* 33–44.

Burgoyne, C.B., Lewis, A., Routh, D.A., & Webley, P. (1992). Customer reactions to automated teller machines (ATMs): A field study in a UK building society. In S.E.G. Lea, P. Webley, & B.M. Young (Eds.), *New directions in economic psychology* (pp. 177–195). Brookfield, Vermont: Edward Elgar.

Cameron, S. (1989). The unacceptability of money as a gift and its status as a medium of exchange. *Journal of Economic Psychology, 10*(2), 253–257.

Campbell, A. (1981). *The sense of well-being in America.* New York: McGraw-Hill.

Cowell, F.A. (1992). Tax evasion and inequity. *Journal of Economic Psychology, 13,* 521–543.

Cyert, R.M., & March, J.G. (1963). *A behavioral theory of the firm.* Englewood Cliffs, NJ: Prentice-Hall.

Dittmar, H. (1992). *The social psychology of material possessions: To have is to be.* New York: Harvester Wheatsheaf.

Easterlin, R.A. (1974). Does economic growth improve the human lot? Some empirical evidence. In P.A. David & M. Reder (Eds.), *Nations and households in economic growth.* New York: Academic Press.

Elffers, H., Robben, H.S.J., & Hessing, D.J. (1992). On measuring tax evasion. *Journal of Economic Psychology, 13*(4), 545–569.

Elffers, H., Weigel, R.H., & Hessing, D.J. (1987). The consequences of different strategies for measuring tax evasion behavior. *Journal of Economic Psychology, 8,* 311–337.

Engel, J.F., Kollat, D.T., & Blackwell, R.D. (1973). *Consumer behavior* (2nd Edn). New York: Holt, Rinehart and Winston.

Engel, J.F., Kollat, D.T., & Miniard, P.W. (1986). *Consumer behavior* (5th Edn). Chicago, IL: The Dryden Press.

Feinberg, R.A. (1986). Credit cards as spending facilitating stimuli: A conditioning interpretation. *Journal of Consumer Research, 13,* 348–356.

Ferber, R. (1973). Family decision making and economic behavior. A review. In E.D. Sheldon (Ed.). *Family economic behavior: Problems and prospects* (pp. 29–61). Philadelphia, PA: Lippincott.

Foa, E.B., & Foa, U.G. (1980). Resource theory: Interpersonal behavior as exchange. In K.J. Gergen, M.S. Greenberg, & R.H. Willis (Eds.), *Social Exchange: Advances in theory and research.* New York: Plenum.

Friedman, M. (1957). *A theory of the consumption function.* Princeton, NJ: Princeton University Press.

Furnham, A.F. (1988). Unemployment. In W.F. van Raaij, G.M. van Veldhoven, & K.-E. Wärneryd (Eds.), *Handbook of economic psychology.* London: Kluwer Academic Publishers.

Furnham, A. (1990). The Protestant work ethic: The psychology of work-related beliefs and behaviours. London: Routledge.

Gasparski, P. (1990). Saving motives: Characteristics of saver groups. In S. Lea, P. Webley, & B. Young (Eds.), *Applied economic psychology in the 1990s* (Vol. 1), Exeter: Washington Singer Press, 476–486.

Gilleard, C.J. (1989). The achieving society revisited: A further analysis of the relation between national economic growth and need achievement. *Journal of Economic Psychology, 10,* 21–34.

Goedhart, T., Halberstadt, V., Kapteyn, A., & Praag, B.M.S. van (1977). The poverty line: Concept and measurement. *Journal of Human Resources, 12,* 503–520.

Goldberg, H., & Lewis, L. (1978). *Money madness: The psychology of saving, spending, loving and having money.* London: Springwood.

Groenland, E.A.G. (1989). *Socio-economic well-being and behavioral reactions: A panel study of people drawing benefits from the Dutch National Social Security System.* Doctoral dissertation, Tilburg University: Tilburg University Press, The Netherlands.

Groenland, E.A.G. (1990). Structural elements of material well-being: An empirical test among people on social security. *Social Indicators Research, 22,* 367–384.

Groenland, E.A.G., & Veldhoven, G.M. van (1983). Tax evasion behavior—a psychological framework. *Journal of Economic Psychology, 3,* 129–144.

Hanley, A., & Wilhelm, M.S. (1992). Compulsive buying: An exploration into self-esteem and money attitudes. *Journal of Economic Psychology, 13* (1), 5–19.

Harrah, J., & Friedman, M. (1990). Economic socialization in children in a midwestern American community. *Journal of Economic Psychology, 11* (4), 495–515.

Howard, J.A. (1989). *Consumer behavior in marketing strategy.* Englewood Cliffs, NJ: Prentice-Hall.

Howard, J.A., & Sheth, J.N. (1969). *The theory of buyer behavior.* New York: John Wiley.

Jahoda, G. (1979). The construction of economic reality by some Glaswegian children. *European Journal of Social Psychology, 9,* 115–127.

Kahneman, D., & Tversky, A. (1979). Prospect theory: An analysis of decision under risk. *Econometrica, 47,* 118–140.

Kapteyn, A., & Wansbeek, T. (1985). The individual welfare function. *Journal of Economic Psychology, 6,* 333–363.

Katona, G. (1974). Psychology and consumer economics. *Journal of Consumer Research, 1,* 1–8.

Katona, G, (1975). *Psychological economics.* New York: Elsevier.

Katona, G., & Mueller, E. (1968). *Consumer response to income increases.* Washington DC: Brookings Institution.

Keynes, J.M. (1936). *The general theory of employment, interest and money.* London: MacMillan.

Kirchler, E. (1988). Household economic decision making. In W.F. van Raaij, G.M. van Veldhoven, & K.-E. Wärneryd (Eds.), *Handbook of Economic Psychology* (pp. 258–294). London: Kluwer Academic Publishers.

Kirchler, E., & Praher, D. (1990). Austrian childrens' economic socialization: Age differences, *Journal of Economic Psychology, 11,* 483–495.

Krugman, H.E. (1965). The impact of television advertising: Learning without involvement. *Public Opinion Quarterly, 29,* 349–356.

Lea, S.E.G., Tarpy, R., & Webley, P. (1987). *The individual in the economy.* Cambridge: Cambridge University Press.

Lea, S.E.G., Webley, P., & Levine, R. (1993). The economic psychology of consumer debt. *Journal of Economic Psychology, 14,* 85–119.

Leiser, D., & Izak, G. (1987). The money size illusion as a barometer of confidence? The case of high inflation in Israel. *Journal of Economic Psychology, 8*(3), 347–357.

Leiser, D., Sévon, G., & Levy, D. (1990). Children's economic socialization: Summarizing the cross-cultural comparison of ten countries. *Journal of Economic Psychology, 11,* 591–614.

Lindqvist, A. (1981). *The saving behavior of households.* Doctoral dissertation, The Stockholm School of Economics.

Maital, S. (1982). *Minds, markets, and money: Psychological foundations of economic behavior.* New York: Basic Books.

March, J.G., & Sévon, G. (1988). Behavioral perspectives on theories of the firm. In W.F. van Raaij, G.M. van Veldhoven, & K.-E. Wärneryd (Eds.), *Handbook*